NOTTING HILL
IN BYGONE DAYS

THE OWNERS AND HOLDERS OF THE MANOR OF NOTTEN BARNS.
Drawing by Miss Woolmer.

NOTTING HILL IN BYGONE DAYS

By FLORENCE M. GLADSTONE

Author of "AUBREY HOUSE, KENSINGTON, FROM 1698–1920"

*A new edition with a
commentary and further
material by*

ASHLEY BARKER

F.S.A., F.R.I.B.A.

ANNE BINGLEY

LONDON

ORIGINALLY PUBLISHED 1924 BY T. FISHER UNWIN LTD

THIS NEW EDITION WITH FURTHER MATERIAL PUBLISHED 1969 BY ANNE
BINGLEY, PUBLISHER, A REGISTERED IMPRINT OF CLIVE BINGLEY LIMITED,
16 PEMBRIDGE ROAD LONDON W I I

PRINTED IN GREAT BRITAIN BY UNWIN BROTHERS LTD.

85157 088 7

THE PUBLISHERS' ACKNOWLEDGEMENTS AND THANKS ARE DUE TO MEMBERS
OF THE LATE MISS GLADSTONE'S FAMILY FOR PERMISSION TO REPRINT THIS
BOOK, AND TO THE LIBRARIAN OF THE ROYAL BOROUGH OF KENSINGTON,
AND HIS STAFF, FOR MUCH ASSISTANCE AND ADVICE OVER THE PRODUCTION.

INTRODUCTION

THE Royal Borough of Kensington in the Administrative County of London covers an area of about 2,290 acres. It is divided by the Uxbridge Road into two parts known respectively as South and North Kensington. The northern portion is somewhat smaller than the southern, but the population is more numerous and it now contains over 90,000 souls.

North Kensington is an irregularly shaped triangle. The base, or south boundary line from Ossington Street to Norland Road is over a mile in length, and the apex in Harrow Road, at the north-west corner of Kensal Green Cemetery, is nearly two miles from Uxbridge Road. When local administration passed into the hands of Borough Councillors, in the year 1900, many slight changes were made. If the boundary cut across houses and gardens it was usually shifted so as to run along the centre of the nearest road. In this process some buildings necessarily changed their parish ; these alterations being marked by inscribed stones let into the pavement. It was suggested that the line of the West London Junction Railway should be made the dividing line between

the parishes of Kensington and Hammersmith. This
proposal fell through, and Latimer Road practically
remains the western limit of North Kensington for
municipal purposes, though a certain amount of
overlapping exists between Kensington and Hammersmith in connection with charitable and Poor Law
administration. The course of the present boundary
can be followed in the modern map facing this page.
The chief difference from earlier days is the inclusion
of almost the whole of Kensal New Town : the
southern part of that curious outlying portion of the
parish of St. Luke's, Chelsea, which is now shared
by the boroughs of Paddington and Kensington.

North Kensington sends one member to Parliament and two members to the London County Council.
But its official name only came into use at the beginning
of the present century, and local inhabitants prefer
to give their address as Bayswater, Notting Hill Gate,
Holland Park, Kensington Park, Notting Hill or
St. Quintin's Park rather than North Kensington,
which represents to them the relatively poor neighbourhood to the north of the Hammersmith and City
Railway.

Modern nomenclature, however, has little to do
with Chronicles of Bygone Days. In the following
pages the Story of North Kensington or Notting Hill
is not carried on much beyond the year 1880, and it
will be found that the strict limits of the borough
are not adhered to, as conditions just over the

border have influenced the development of each district.

In the time of Bowack, Lysons and Faulkner North Kensington was entirely rural, and recent historians of Kensington, such as W. J. Loftie, E. Walford and G. E. Mitton naturally deal with the older and more notable parts. Strangely little is to be found in their writings about the northern half of the parish, and they have taken for granted that there is very little of interest to record in a district which has largely come into existence since 1850.

Those who have grown up in the locality will refuse to accept this verdict. The very fact that much of Notting Hill dates from the later half of the Nineteenth century makes it possible that persons still alive should be able to recall the stages of its growth. And it seems worth while to gather together some of these reminiscences before they have entirely faded from memory. Another reason is that the district contains much more of antiquarian value than is generally supposed, and, in piecing together the history of the past, light is thrown on many of the actual conditions of life. At present "there are thousands of dwellers in South Kensington to whom the North is an unknown land," a land for which they feel no responsibility, and in which they take no interest. It is hoped that a further knowledge of the varied districts will arouse a deeper concern for the welfare of the inhabitants.

The subject has been treated partly chronologically, partly topographically. A certain amount of repetition was inevitable. It has not been possible to mention noteworthy inhabitants except in a very few instances, and the names of persons still living have generally been avoided unless they have supplied information Many friends of all classes who have helped in this way have already passed to the world beyond. Amongst these are Dr. S. D. Clippingdale, and Messrs. Lionel A. Clark and John Lydall. Special thanks are due to Miss E. Woolmer for the care bestowed on her illustrations, to Mr. T. Butler Cato, Mr. Herbert Friend, the Misses Alexander, Miss Thompson of Kensal Town and Mr. F. L. Emanuel for pictures and information, to the late Mrs. St. John of Dinmore for lending Dr. Stukeley's manuscript notes, to Mr. Herbert Jones and the staff of the Public Library, and to Miss Carthew and Mrs. Ashley Carus Wilson for the loan of maps and books. Without such encouragement the task would have been impossible.

FLORENCE M. GLADSTONE.

46, LADBROKE GROVE, W. 11.
May, 1924.

CONTENTS

NOTTING HILL
IN BYGONE DAYS

CHAPTER I

CHENESITUN AND KNOTTING BARNS

On the north side of the Thames as it crosses London there is a range of low hills. Beginning with Tower Hill close to the river, the range ends with Campden Hill, three-quarters of a mile from its bank. Each hill is divided from the next by a stream. These streams rise on the northern edge of the Thames Valley and fall into the left bank of the winding river.

Campden Hill, Bayswater Hill and the " Knoll " surmounted by St. John's Church form one group which practically constitutes Notting Hill. This high land is bounded on the east by the Westbourne or Bays Water, and on the west by a "rivulet" known as Bridge Creek or Counter's Creek. Both the Westbourne and Counter's Creek are now carried underground.

The map facing page 2 shows this formation of hill and stream. It also shows two important Roman roads which approached the town of Londinium from the north and west : Watling Street, now Edgware Road, and that portion of the Great West Road at present represented by High Street, Notting Hill,

Bayswater Road and Oxford Street. These roads were cut through densely wooded country, known at a later date as the Forest of Middlesex, and there seems to be little doubt that, before the time of the Romans, both Edgware Road and Bayswater Road had been British trackways.[1]

Mr. Reginald Smith, F.S.A., of the British Museum, considers that another trackway, not marked on this map, followed the high ground nearer to the river. This also probably was developed by the Romans, and subsequently became the road through Knightsbridge, Kensington and Hammersmith. These two roads joined at Brentford.

At Notting Hill Gate the Great West Road ran on the edge of a terrace ninety-five feet above the sea. The forest was not so dense here as it was further to the north, and the high land across the Thames would be visible. It has been suggested that a beacon may have been placed at Notting Hill Gate to correspond with another on the hill-top south-west of Egham.[2] Except for the name of High Street (Street being derived from *Via Strata*, the paved way), there seem to be no actual relics of the Roman period within the boundaries of Kensington parish. It has, however, been claimed that a trough of broken masonry, now

---

[1] In 1916 placards posted in the stations of the Central London Railway stated that Holland Park Avenue was the Via Trinobantia of the Romans, the chief road of the late Celtic Kingdom of the Trinobantes whose capital was Colchester.

[2] *Roman Roads in Britain*, by Thomas Codrington, 1905.

preserved in the garden of St. John's Vicarage, Ladbroke Grove, may have been part of a Roman sarcophagus. This stone trough was discovered about 1850 when the foundations of No. 1, Ladbroke Square were being prepared : a likely position for a Roman grave close to a main road. Being a coffin burial the date would be after A.D. 250.

The final departure of the Romans early in the fifth century was followed by a period of disorder. Middlesex lay between the quarrelsome kingdoms of Mercia and Wessex and was in a disturbed condition for many years. But, probably, somewhere about A.D. 700, a party of Saxon immigrants, " sons of Cynesige," discovered a favourable spot above the marsh lands of Chelsea and Fulham. And here, on the hill-top between the old roads, they founded their little " tun " or village. For Chenesitun, the Kensington of those days, only consisted of a few wooden homesteads with barns and cattle sheds, surrounded by a rough stockade : an island of cultivation in the midst of woodland and common.3 About the same time Poedings, or " sons of Padda," settled close to Watling Street, and another Saxon family, the Cnottingas, or " sons of Cnotta," may have made a clearing for themselves in the denser wood to the north.

No less an authority than Dr. Walter W. Skeat suggests this Saxon solution for the name of Notting

3 See *Kensington Picturesque and Historical,* by W. J. Loftie, 1888, and *Kensington,* by G. E. Mitton, 1903, in the *Fascination of London* Series.

Hill. Other writers have thought that the encampment was founded by followers of King Knut. Whether Saxon or Danish in its origin the little colony seems to have been entirely wiped out before the Norman Conquest ; nothing but the name remaining to testify to its former existence.4&5 The popular belief that Notting Hill owes its name to the nut bushes which grew upon its slopes is a pleasant, but untenable, tradition. The name occurs in the Patent Rolls for A.D. 1361. There it is " Knottynghull," proving that the " k " is original as is also the double " t."

The Forest of Middlesex has already been mentioned. William Fitz-stephen's well-known description, written about 1170, tells of " densely wooded thickets, the coverts of game, red and fallow deer, boars and wild bulls." There are no records of such game in this district, but remains of a wood can be traced on St. John's Hill, and there is other proof of forest land within the present area of North Kensington. At the British Museum is a Deed of the time of Edward the Confessor, which states that Thurstan, Chamberlain or Master of the King's Household, bequeathed his share of the Manor of

---

4 See *Kensington News*, April and May 1917.

5 The old village of Knotting in Bedfordshire is thought by some antiquaries to derive its name from " Noding," a Danish term for a cattle pasture. In the Cotswolds there is an entrenched camp known as Notting Hill.

Chelsea for the benefit of King Edward's new religious foundation at Westminster. Among lands belonging to Chelsea was a detached piece of woodland, given specially to supply faggots for the Abbey fires, and acorns for the Abbot's pigs. This portion of wood-land, 137¾ acres in extent, is now covered by the houses of Queen's Park Estate and Kensal Town. Chelsea Outland is shown on the map of 1833 on page 40, where also are seen many local names recalling the trees : Acton, or " place of oaks," Old Oak Common and Six Elms, Wormholt or Wormwood Scrubbs and the names ending in " den," like Neasden and Harlesden, which were valleys where swine might be fed.

At the date of the Deed mentioned above, the Manor of Chenesitun was held by Edwin, one of Edward the Confessor's " thegns." " Edwin the Thegn suffered the fate of most Saxon noblemen," [6] for, before the Domesday Book was drawn up in 1086, the Manor of Chensitun had been granted by William the Conqueror to Geoffrey, Bishop of Coutances, under whom it was held by Aubrey de Vere. It became Aubrey de Vere's freehold property during the reign of William Rufus. The Survey of the Manor in 1086 may be read both in Latin and English in Mr. Loftie's book. A picture is there drawn of the priest or rector, the eighteen farmers and seven slaves with their families, 200 to

[6] See *Kenna's Kingdom*, by R. Weir Brown, and *Kensington Picturesque and Historical*, by W. J. Loftie.

240 persons in all, cultivating some 1,400 acres, and living near the church, which was practically if not actually on the site of St. Mary Abbots. For the pasturage of their cattle there were about 500 acres of common land, making 1,900 acres as against the 2,290 acres of to-day. " But while the men went forth to follow the plough, to sow their seed or garner their corn, the women and children drove ' the cattle of the town ' to the pasture, and their herd of 200 pigs to pick up beech mast and acorns in the woods to the northward."

Aubrey de Vere and his successors owned the Manor of Kensington from the reign of William I to that of James I, a period of over five hundred years. " De Vers " had been amongst the noblest of the old Norman aristocracy. Later on they were created Earls of Oxford, and held many important State Offices. They took part in the Crusades, they fought at Crecy, Poictiers and Agincourt. Twice at least their lands were forfeited to the Crown, but were restored to subsequent holders of the title, and the twelfth Earl of Oxford and his son were beheaded. But, as they were always absentee landlords, it is probable that everyday life in Kensington was not deeply affected by the fate of the heads of the house. [7]

During the life-time of the first Aubrey 270 acres of land, extending from Church Street to Addison Road,

[7] Further details of this mighty family will be found in histories of Kensington, especially in W. J. Loftie's book.

was granted to the monastery of Abingdon, and became the independent Manor of Abbot's Kensington. Gradually the remaining portion of the parish was divided into three parts : the separate manors of Earls Court, covering what is now known as South Kensington, the Manor of West Town, originally called " the Groves " and consisting of fields west of Addison Road, and the Manor of Notting Barns with which these Chronicles are chiefly concerned.

The story of how the De Veres parted with this northern division of Kensington is so characteristic of the times that it must be given in some detail. When John the twelfth Earl of Oxford and Aubrey his eldest son were beheaded in February 1462, by order of Edward IV, on account of their allegiance to the House of Lancaster, their lands, including the Manor of Abbot's Kensington and Notting Barnes, valued together at twenty-five marks, were forfeited to " the Lord the King." Shortly after this for-feiture the King's brother, afterwards Richard III, was receiving " the issues and profits " from these lands, as if they had been granted to him ; whereas, evidence given in 1484 and in 1496 proves that " Richard, Duke of Gloucetir " only enjoyed and retained them " of his inordinate covetyse and ungodly dispocion." Added to this " by compulsion, cohercion and emprisonment " he had forced the widow of the beheaded Earl to release to him divers other lands, thus reducing her and her daughter-in-law to a state of absolute want.[8] Meanwhile " John Veer," the thirteenth Earl, was in exile and was suffering many hardships. When, however, Henry Tudor, Duke of Richmond, felt himself strong enough to make a bid for the throne of England, the Earl of Oxford joined his company. In 1485 they fought side by side on the fateful Field of Bosworth, and shortly after Henry VII had become King, the whole of the Vere family were reinstated in their lands, honours and dignities.

But, although he had been made Constable of the Tower, the Earl was so impoverished that he found it necessary to realize money on his estate, and in 1488 " the Manor of Notingbarons " passed into the hands of William, Marquis of Berkeley, Great Marshall of England. By means of a somewhat secret transaction with Sir Reginald Bray, the Manor was then sold for four hundred marks to Margaret, Countess of Richmond and Derby, mother of the King. Probably " Lady Margaret " hoped in this way to ease the burdens of a staunch supporter of her son's cause. Shortly after the purchase was completed this Manor, valued at £10 per annum, was joined with other properties in the county of Middlesex, making in all the " yerely valow " of £90. These properties were conveyed by the Countess to the Abbot, Prior and Convent of Westminster, with the specification that after her death the income should

---

[8] See *Paddington Past and Present*, by William Robins, 1853, and Loftie's book on Kensington, 1888.

be spent on masses for her soul in the Abbey Church of Westminster, and for the upkeep of the professor-ships which she had founded at Oxford, and in St. John's and Christ's Colleges, Cambridge. At the death of Lady Margaret in June 1509, in the midst of the Coronation festivities of her grandson, Henry VIII, these lands became the property of the Abbey, and were held by the Abbot " as of his Manor of Paddington by fealty and twenty-two shillings rent."

When the Earl of Oxford had parted with the Manor of Knotting Barns in 1488 it comprised " a messuage, 400 acres of land fit for cultivation, 5 acres of meadow, and 140 acres of wood in Kensington : 545 acres in all." Another 140 acres, forming the Norland Estate, and certain fields called North Crofts lying along the old Roman road, belonged to the Manor of Abbot's Kensington. These lands with the Manor of Knotting Barns seem, practically, to have covered the irregular triangle of North Kensington. In a Deed of 1526, " The Manor called Notingbarons, alias Kensington, in the Parish of Paddington " is described as including " dyvers lands and tenements in Willesden, Padyngton, Westburn and Kensington in the countie of Midd ; which maners, landes and tenements the said Princes late purchased of Sir Reynolde Bray, Knight."

Mr. Robins, see note 8, believed that all this land and more was included in the parish of Paddington. A simpler explanation seems to meet the case. By the middle of the fifteenth century the forest in this part of Middlesex had almost disappeared, and was being replaced by pasture land, used either for grazing purposes or for hay. The scattered meadows, purchased to increase the property which Lady Margaret was about to place in the hands of the Abbot of Westminster, may well have been grouped together under the name of the principal farm, which was in Kensington, while the holder of the property lived in Paddington. This at least was the condition of affairs some thirty years later.

All this is distinctly puzzling. Naturally there is also much variety in the forms of the name. Knottyng-hull, the steep hill on the high road, is mentioned a century earlier than the Manor House with its spacious barns which stood amidst the pastures to the north.[9] But in 1462 Knottyngesbernes is met with, and Knottinge Bernes in 1476, whilst the Manor appears as Notingbarons 1488, Notingbarns 1519, and Nuttingbars 1544. Other varieties occur later on.

After the death of Lady Margaret the Abbot promptly leased the Manor to a wealthy citizen of London described variously as Roper, Fenroper, Fenrother, etc. Alderman Robert Fenrother held the post of Sheriff in 1512 and again in 1516. A member of the Goldsmiths' Company and a Yorkshireman, he owned estates in various parts of England, but lived in the heart of the City, and when he died in 1526 he was buried in the Church of St. John Zachary

[9] *The Place Names of Middlesex*, by J. E. B. Gover, 1922.

at the corner of Mayden Lane. The Wills of Robert and Juliana, his wife, afford much information on the life and surroundings of a rich and worthy merchant family in the early sixteenth century. The Fenrothers had three daughters, Audrey, otherwise Etheldreda, Julian and Margaret, the eldest of whom married Henry White, gent., who was a sheep farmer.[10]

At the time of their marriage, about 1518, Nottyng Barnes was given over to the young couple for their use, and was to become their property after the death of Mistress Fenrother. But, whereas in 1488 the Manor had covered 545 acres, in 1526 it was reckoned at 420 acres, though the value was still £10 per annum. It now consisted of 40 acres of arable land, 140 acres of meadow, 200 acres of wood, 20 acres of moor, 20 acres of furze and heath and 40s. rent. A farm-bailiff may have been put in charge of the Manor farm, for the Whites made their home at Westbourne or Westbourne Place,[11] a house which stood on ground now covered by the Lock Hospital.

In 1527, a year after his father-in-law's death, " Henrico White, pastur in padington " in conjunction with William Person, obtained from Lord Sands, owner of Chelsea Manor, a lease for twenty-one years

---

[10] See *Notes from the Parish Church Registers,* in Kensington Parish Magazine for 1884 and subsequent years, by Mrs. Henley Jervis. Mrs. Jervis, who was an indefatigable investigator, came to the conclusion that in the fifteenth and sixteenth centuries Kensington South as well as North was a wool-producing district.

[11] This house was superseded by the handsome mansion of the same name built for himself by Isaac Ware in 1794.

of the four pasture closes, or fields, adjoining Notting
Barns, and covering the whole area of the detached
portion of Chelsea.   Up to the fourteenth century
this had been forest land, known as Kingsholt in 1365.
Before 1535 both Henry White, Esq., and his wife
Etheldreda had died, probably from some infectious
disease, and when Mistress Fenrother passed away
at her house in Mincing Lane, early in the year 1536,
Notting Barns with other estates was placed in trust
for the orphan grandchildren, Robert, Frances, Albone,
or Alban, and Elizabeth White, until they should
marry or become of age.   The young Whites lived
on at Westbourne for another seven years.

An Ecclesiastical Valuation, carried out at the
King's command in 1535, had opened the eyes of
Henry VIII to the extent and character of lands
belonging to the Church, and he determined to seize
this rich booty.   First the smaller religious houses
and then the larger monasteries were despoiled.   By
the year 1540, the Lady Margaret's munificent gift
to the Abbot and Convent of Westminster had become
vested in the Crown, and the King, as owner of these
lands, confirmed Robert Whyte, the eldest son of
Henry White, in the " messuage called Westbourne-
place with certain lands therto belonging."   In
1541 Master Whyte attained his majority, and paid
a tax of 15s. on his lands in Kensington.

Five years before this date the King had ousted

Baron Sands from the Manor of Chelsea, and had granted him in exchange a Priory in Hamptonshire. In 1543 the Manor of Chelsea was assigned as a marriage portion to Catherine Parr. Robert White owned some house property in Chelsea, and the lease of the four fields granted to his father in 1527 had not yet expired. It may be that King Henry became aware of the attractions of Knotting Barns when examining into the titles of the proposed gift to his sixth bride, for, in that same year of 1543, Robert White was forced to surrender his lands and the home where he and his brother and sisters lived, and to accept instead the Manor of Overburgate. In the Deed of Exchange the transaction is thus described : " Robert White, esquire, bargained and sold to the King his manor of Knotting Barns, in Kensington, with all messuages, cottages, mills, etc., to hold to the King, his heirs and successors, in exchange for the Manor of Over Burgate in the county of Southampton." Another deed states that " The said Robert White, Esq., having bargained and sold the Manor of Nuttingbarnes, with the appurtenances in the county of Middlesex, and the farm of Nuttyng-barnes, in the parish of Kensyngton, and the capital messuage with the appurtenances called Westbourne in the parish of Paddington, in the same county, and also the wood and lands called Nuttyngwood, Dorkyns Hernes, and Bulfre Grove, in the parish of Kensington, as also two messuages and tenements in Chelsaye, with

all other the possessions of the said Robert White, in
the same places and parishes ; and in consideration
of £106 5s. 1od. had other lands conveyed to him by
the King."[12]

It has usually been taken for granted that the young
Whites were defrauded of their home in order that
the land might be added to the royal park then being
formed on the north side of London,[13] but these
preserves " sacred to the King's owne disport and
pastime," do not appear to have extended so far to
the west.   In any case there is no record that
Henry VIII hunted or hawked in the thickets of
Kellsal Greene or Nuttyngwood.   And in 1547 he
died.

The description of the estate as given in the deeds
of 1543 is most valuable.   The spelling of the name
of the *Manor, in the parish of Kensington,* differs in
the two documents.   *The Farm of Nuttyngbarnes* no
doubt stood " in the midst of meadows surrounded by
spacious barns and outhouses," as it was standing
in 1800, and continued to stand until about 1880.
It is shown on most of the maps, see also the illustrations on page 10.   Both Lysons, 1792, and Faulkner,
1820, definitely state that the farm and the Manor
House were one and the same.   *The wood called*

---

[12] The sum paid is given elsewhere as £126.
[13] *Kensington Picturesque and Historical,* by W. J. Loftie, followed by
G. E. Mitton in the *Fascination of London* Series, 1903.

Nuttyngwood covered St. John's Hill, and seems to have extended in the shape of a wedge between North-lands and North Crofts down to the old Roman road. This area would account for the 200 acres of wood mentioned in 1526. A few elms, known from the rings of growth to be over 250 years old, have survived till recently in the garden to the south-west of the church, and fields called Middle Wood and North Wood once occupied part of the hill. See later.

The *lands called Dorkyns Hernes and Bulfre Grove* are less easy to trace, but some information is obtained from two lists of the fields belonging to Chelsea Outland, dated respectively 1544 and 1557. These four pasture closes possessed the quaint names of Darkingby Johes or Darking Busshes, Holmefield, Balserfield and Baudelands. Probably a man named Dorking, pronounced Darking, had owned the land, for Dorkinghernes, or Dorkyns corner (Middle English " herne " or " hurne," a corner), lay to the west of Darking Busshes and seems to have covered the most northern part of Kensington parish. A meadow called Sunhawes (" haw," a hedgerow) occupied the slope with a southern aspect and abutted on " the close of Nottingbarnes." Covering the site of Westbourne Park Station was arable land called " Downes." " Bulfre Grove " may have been named after some private owner.[14] Possibly this " land " abutted on the Norlands Estate, for it is not mentioned

[14] Suggestions made by Mr. J. E. B. Gover.

in connection with the Chelsea fields.   The *messuages*
on the estate were Westbourne Place and the Manor
farmhouse.   The *cottages* will be referred to later.
The *mills* have not been traced.

In these deeds of exchange no mention is made
of the " 20 acres of moor, and 20 acres of furze and
heath " which existed on the estate in 1526.   Even
now the fringe of Wormwood Scrubbs invades the
north-west corner of Kensington.   Rough uncultivated
land was unimportant as compared with " 140 acres
of meadow."   Reading this description there is no
doubt that the bleating of large flocks of sheep and
the merry shouts of haymakers resounded on the
slope now occupied by gas-works and a vast array of
tombstones.

In the year of Henry VIII's death " the messuage
called Westbourne with the land purchased of Robert
White " was demised to one Thomas Dolte, at a
rental of one hundred shillings a year.   Some
connection with Knotting Barns was maintained, for
the Parish Registers show that on February 27, 1614,
the bodies of two tramps : " William, a poore boy,
name unknown " and " Dorothy Daggers," both of
whom died in Westbourne Barne, were brought
to Kensington for burial.   The Chelsea fields were
already in other hands.

In 1549 Edward VI granted the Manor of Knotting
Barns to Sir William Paulet, Lord St. John of Basing,
a man seventy-four years of age, but who, shortly

after this date, became Lord High Treasurer and
Marquis of Winchester : " that gallant Lord Treasurer
of whom Queen Elizabeth playfully declared that,
but for his age, she would have found it in her heart
to have him for a husband before any man in
England." [15]   He held the Manor for thirteen years,
until in 1562 " being indebted in sundry sums to her
Majesty " he surrendered this and certain other
properties.   Elizabeth then granted Knotting Barns
to William Cecil, Secretary of State, created Baron
of Burghley (Burleigh) in 1570, and Lord High
Treasurer on the death of the aged Marquis in 1572.
There seems to be no authenticated account of either
of these Lord Treasurers having lived in North
Kensington.   But a curious letter exists, dated 1586,
in which Lord Burleigh describes his interview with
a group of officers who were searching scattered
houses between St. John's Wood and Harrow for the
fugitive Anthony Babington and other conspirators in
the plot to assassinate Queen Elizabeth and place
Mary, Queen of Scots, on the throne.   This interview
may well have taken place at Lord Burleigh's own
farmstead of Knotting Barns.   In any case the story
proves that patches of forest remained, and that this
part of the country was very secluded.[16]

Lord Burleigh died in 1598.   In March 1599

[15] *Old Kew, Chiswick and Kensington*, by F. Lloyd Sanders, 1910, and
other histories of Kensington.

[16] The incident is picturesquely described in *St. John's Wood, its History*,
etc., by Alan M. Eyre, 1913.

Sir Walter Cecil, Knight, as one of his trustees, sold
the Manor for £2,000 to Walter Cope " of the Strand."
But, as a debt on the estate was owing to Queen
Elizabeth, a " licence to alienate " had to be obtained
by Sir Thomas Cecil and Lady Dorothy, his wife,
heirs of Lord Burleigh.   Walter Cope also was
obliged to pay £6 for a " pardon."   This Walter,
afterwards Sir Walter Cope, is a very important
figure in local history.   Between 1591 and 1610 he
gained possession of almost the whole of the parish
of Kensington, and built for himself the magnificent
house first known as Cope's Castle and afterwards
as Holland House.   But apparently he bought Notting
Barns merely as a speculation, and, in November 1601,
he sold it to Sir Henry Anderson for the sum of
£3,400 ; this being a handsome profit on his expendi-
ture of £2,006.

Sir Henry Anderson, Knight and Alderman,
belonging to the Worshipful Company of Grocers,
was Sheriff of London in the year 1601.   He was a
man of similar type to Robert Fenrother, though he
was not so wealthy.[17]   Four years later he died leaving
a son Richard, aged nineteen, as his heir.   In the
Inquisition after the death of Henry Anderson, farms
and a wood of 130 acres are mentioned, and the Manor
was still held of the Crown by fealty and a rental of two
or three pounds.   " A manservant " died " at Notting

[17] Interesting extracts from his Will have been given by Mrs. Henley
Jervis.   See Note 10.

Barnes " in March 1603–4. This death may have occurred during a visit of the family to their rural farmhouse. For, as there seem to be no entries relating to the Andersons in the Parish Registers, they cannot usually have made their abode in Kensington.

In 1675 a second Sir Richard Anderson was in possession, probably a son of the youth who succeeded to the estate in 1605. These seventy years, beginning in the reign of James I and ending in that of Charles II, were years of stress and of great development in the life of the nation. At some time during this period the Manor of Knotting Barns ceased to belong to the Crown and became the property of the Andersons. Yet, in 1672, when a Presentment of Homage was made by the tenants to the Lord of the Manor, the whole of the northern portion of the parish was included in Abbots Kensington, and Sir Richard appears as freeholder of 400 acres. " This," writes Mr. Lloyd Sanders, " is a curious illustration of the way in which the Great Rebellion had obliterated old memories. Notting Hill is treated as if it formed an integral part of the Abbot's Manor, which it never did, and among the freeholders appears Sir Richard Anderson, its owner. Possibly he did not care to assert manorial rights against his powerful neighbour at Holland House, who at that time was Robert Rich, Earl of Holland." [18]

[18] *Old Kew, Chiswick and Kensington,* by F. Lloyd Sanders, 1910.

With the Sir Richard Anderson of 1675 the olden times come to an end.   For this reason the names of the known owners of the Manor down to the eighteenth century have been grouped together in the illustration forming the Frontispiece.

From the beginning of the seventeenth century the population of Kensington increased rapidly. About 1650 it became the custom to add the name of the district to the entry in the Parish Registers, and at once this " Charter of the Poor Man," as the Parish Registers have been called, provides information about the cottagers at Notting Barnes.   Between 1650 and 1680 six young couples with the surnames of Brockards and "bronckard," Ellis or Ells, King, Breteridge and Fell, brought infants to be " baptised at the Font," and some of the same children were buried in the churchyard.   It must have been a risky proceeding to carry a baby of a few days old along muddy field paths all the way to Kensington Church.[19] Some delicate children were registered as baptised at home at " Noting-barns " and also at " Canselgreene "; but it is quite evident that many births were never recorded.   In the corresponding list of burials between the years 1654 and 1676 appear the names of Alse or Alice Welfare, Thomas Williams, Elizabeth Hihorne and Richard Whitte, each described as of Noting-

_____

[19] This was the second church ; it was built in the fourteenth century and served the parish until a larger brick church took its place in 1696.

barns, and Mary Davis, widow, who was buried from the house of Edward Fell. A pathetic little story can be built up round Daniel and Elissabeth King. An Elissabeth King, no doubt their baby daughter, died in 1660. Her father died in the following year ; and after his death another little Elizabeth was born, who only survived for a few months. Then poor " Widdo King " took someone else's baby into her desolate home, for a " nurse child " was buried from her cottage in 1663.

Just west of the detached portion of Chelsea, was a small collection of houses, the beginnings of the hamlet of Kensall or Kellsell Greene.[20] These cottagers were chiefly " parished in Wilsdon," but in the middle of the seventeenth century four families are met with in the Registers of Kensington Church. Their names were Rippon, Shepparde, Cox and Beale. Each household possessed children, many of whom died in infancy. These families must have lived close to a crooked lane, the " Way from Paddington to Harlestone " (Harlesden). This ancient " Horse Tract " has become the Harrow Road, and forms the boundary between Kensington and Willesden. On the fields now covered by Kensal Green Cemetery there was a tenement with three acres of land, the freehold property

[20] It is suggested by Mr. Gover (see note 9), that Kensal Green may originally have been derived from Kelshall, a fairly common surname. Mr. Loftie's derivation from *The Green of the Kensings' Holt* seems very far fetched.

in 1672 of a certain Widow Nichols. And at least
one other little house stood on the south side of the
boundary lane. In the year 1820 Faulkner wrote,
" At Kensal Green is a very ancient public house,
known by the name of the ' Plough,' which has been
built upwards of three hundred years ; the timber
and joists being of oak, are still in good preservation."
No doubt the oak joists came from the neighbouring
woods. The " Plough " stands there yet, though,
in the modern brick house at the junction of Ladbroke
Grove and Harrow Road, there is little to remind the
passer-by of the low-timbered building seen opposite,
or the rustic charm of the more fanciful drawing
on page 14. This wayside inn may go back as
far as Faulkner suggests, for the Parish Registers
show that " Marget, a bastard childe, was borne in the
Ploughe, and was baptised the 30th day of August,
1589." A family named Ilford are said to have been
landlords of the " Plough " for several generations.
Further details of this family are given in Chapter II.

It must be remembered that the information from
the Parish Registers is over one hundred years later
in date than the description of Knotting Barnes as
given in the Deed of Exchange. After about 1680
there seems little to record for another hundred years
of the northernmost part of the parish of Kensington.

KENSINGTON GRAVEL PITS AND NORTHLANDS

DURING the period of disorder which followed the Roman occupation of Britain, the forests were allowed to encroach, and in many places stretches of road became decayed and were ultimately overgrown by trees. This evidently happened between Brentford and Shepherd's Bush. As the road through the Saxon villages of Hammersmith and Kensington remained intact, this southern portion received the Roman name of the Great West Road, whilst what is now Bayswater Road, the London end of the original Great West Road, was given different names at different periods. Among these names are the Way to Acton, the King's Highway, Oxford Road, the North Highway and Uxbridge Road. It appears to have been unsuspected that the two roads, since known as Kensington High Street, and High Street, Notting Hill, originally joined. But, in the middle of the eighteenth century, Dr. Stukeley, the antiquarian Vicar of Bloomsbury, pushed his horse with some difficulty " through a narrow straight way," and was able to trace, fairly correctly, the course of the Roman Road from Turnham Green to its junction with the " Acton Road at a common and a bridge a little west of Holland House." When the Goldhawk Road was constructed in 1834, all doubt on the subject was removed, for a Roman causeway was uncovered, and coins and other small objects were found.[1]

This break in the Great West Road certainly influenced the development of Kensington. The royal route from Whitehall to Windsor lay along the southern road, and more historic events probably happened on the " Waye to Reading " than on the " Waye to Uxbridge." However, there must always have been a considerable amount of traffic on the northern highway : two-wheeled carts and loaded farm-wagons, groups of folk on foot or riding astride coming to market at the periodical fairs, droves of sheep and cattle, or a string of pack-horses with men and dogs in attendance ; all the ordinary wayfaring life of the Middle Ages, with now and then the move-ment of troops, a religious pilgrimage or a lordly progress.

But the portion of road between what is now Shepherd's Bush and Notting Hill Gate was not always safe for travellers. Like other " coverts " round London, Knotting Wood was probably the

[1] *Historical Notices of Chelsea, Kensington, Fulham and Hammersmith*, by Miss Isabella Burt, 1871.

resort of robbers and outlaws. The first mention
of the district tells how William Lovel robbed Thomas
de Holland of a cart and a cap of Stratherne and other
goods in the cart at Knottynghull, before Michaelmas
in the thirty-third year of Edward III's reign. Two
years later, 1361–1362, Lovel was pardoned by the
King for this and other outlawries on account of
good service rendered in the Wars of France.[2] Acts
of Parliament had to be passed to enforce the widening
of roads through forest land so that no evilly disposed
person could lurk behind dyke or bush within two
hundred feet on either side of the way. The earliest
of these Acts was in 1385, twenty-five years after the
attack on Thomas de Holland. The great width
of road shown in Rocque's map at this spot, see
page 36, is a significant fact. Robbers may have
killed Sir Manhood Penruddock, knight, who, in
January 1607, was " slaine in Notting wood in fight."
But his death perhaps was the result of a duel.

Some stone cannon balls and ancient clay tobacco
pipes, which were unearthed in the garden of No. 1,
Ladbroke Square, when the stone trough or sarcophagus was also found (see page 3), may betoken
some ambush of troops placed in the wood during
the Parliamentary struggle. Those were troublous

---

[2] *Patent Rolls*, vol. xi, page 545. Thomas de Holland, K.G., married
Princess Joan Plantagenet, " the fair maid of Kent," neice of Edward II.
Sir Thomas de Holland, Earl of Kent, died in 1360, between the date of
the outrage and the pardon. He was succeeded by his son, a child of the
same name, but the widowed Countess at once became the wife of her cousin,
Edward the Black Prince.

times for Kensington, and especially for the owners of Holland House. In September 1651, two and a half years after the execution of Sir Henry Rich, Earl of Holland, for his adherance to the cause of Charles I, the Lord Protector Cromwell was conducted in state from Acton to London along the North Highway, accompanied by a train of over three hundred carriages.

On the south side of what is now Bayswater Road and Notting Hill Gate, and in scattered patches north as well as south of the road, were the famous Kensington Gravel Pits.

Deposits of gravel and sand occur along the flanks of the lower part of the Thames Valley. They rest on the stiff blue clay and the solidified mud, known as loam or brick-earth, which cover the old river basin. But the thick beds of gravel and sand, on which Brompton, Earl's Court and parts of the town of Kensington are built, do not appear to be so rich in colour or of such good quality as the earlier gravels left in " pockets " at a higher level on the slopes of the clay hills, and farther from the present river bed.

Evidently gravel had been worked in Kensington from quite early times, for the Rev. Mr. William Wigan, in making a return to the Bishop of London in 1672, stated that the glebe of the Vicarage, though at that time only thirteen acres, " appears to have been more. For, according to the composition [made between the Abbot of Abingdon and the Vicar of Kensington in

1260], it was bounded on the north side by the King's highway ; of which it is now much short, it having in times past, been dug away for gravel, and the Lord of the Manor claiming and enjoying the pit of many acres, as waste, on which several houses are now built." [3] This was an encroachment on the rights of the Church, and also on those of the tenants of the Manor of Abbots Kensington, who, by " ancient custom," were allowed to cut turfs or to " dig sand, gravel and loom " upon the " Commons " or common lands of " Notting Hill, the waste by the highways and the gravel pits."

Cope's Castle, afterwards Holland House, was commenced in 1607, and Campden or Camden House, and Sheffield House on the site of Berkeley Gardens, belonged approximately to the same date. These large houses, with their enormous retinues of servants, provided protection for humbler folk, and small dwellings began to make their appearance along the adjoining highway and among the gravel pits of the lane leading to Kensington, now known as Church Street.

In 1652, twenty years before the date of the " Return " made by the Vicar of Kensington, " the impaled ground called 'Hide Parke,' " along with other Crown lands, was sold for ready money. For this purpose the Park was divided into three lots. One of these, the Gravel Pit Division, was described as

[3] *Kensington Picturesque and Historical,* by W. J. Loftie.

"adjoining or lying near to the Great Gravill Pits upon Acton Road." One of these pits seems actually to have survived as a picturesque hollow until about 1830, and the site must be covered by the Children's Playground on the right-hand side of the Broad Walk in Kensington Gardens.[4]

The pits gave their name to a large undefined district bordering the road from Craven Hill to Notting Hill Gate. Included among them were the valuable gravel pits belonging to Mr. Orme, print seller of Bond Street, who made a fortune out of the soil, about the year 1814, before building Orme Square, St. Petersburg Place and Moscow Road. Gloriously golden gravel was exposed and sold when Dr. Davidson's house on the Bayswater Road was pulled down in 1888, in order that the houses of Palace Court might be built over the walled garden. Within the bounds of Kensington parish it is difficult to trace the working of gravel on the north side of the highway, though a large pond which was in the garden of Linden Grove House, may have begun as a pit, and two acres of land, now covered by the houses of Clanricarde Gardens and six shops facing the Bayswater Road, are still known as the Gravel Pits Estate.

This estate has a somewhat strange history. Originally it seems to have formed an outlying portion of the wide lands owned by Sir George Coppin, whose property included the house which, in 1631, passed

---

[4] See *Recollections of a Royal Academician*, J. C. Horsley, 1903.

into the hands of Sir Heneage Finch, Recorder of London, and at a later date became Kensington Palace. In June 1651 the field " at the Gravel Pits in Kensington containing two acres " was in the occupation of a certain Richard Barton, but belonged to Thomas Coppin, Esq., the second son of Sir George. He sold it to the twelve Trustees who administered the Charities founded by Viscount and Lady Campden in 1629 and 1644, " for the use, good and benefit of the poor of the town of Kensington " and to pay for the apprenticeship of one or more poor boys. The £45 employed in purchasing the field was an anonymous benefaction to Kensington, though tradition has ascribed it to Oliver Cromwell, and it has been called " Cromwell's Gift." The Lord Protector held some land in the south of the parish, but there is no real evidence to connect this sum of money with him. Several branches of the Cromwell family lived in the neighbourhood, and the gift may with equal probability have come from one of these.[5] At first it was intended that almshouses should be placed on this land, but the project was not carried out, and for many years this field, held by the Campden Charity Trustees, remained under grass.

In the second half of the seventeenth century, " Near Kensington Gravel Pits " was used to

[5] See *Antiquities of Middlesex*, by J. Bowack, 1705 ; *Old Kew, Chiswick and Kensington*, by F. Lloyd Sanders, 1910 ; *Fulham, Old and New*, J. C. Feret, 1900, etc.

distinguish the whole district of North Kensington,
from Campden Hill to Kensal Green, besides being
the recognized name of the village which bordered
the high road.   It was only in the nineteenth century
that Kensington Gravel Pits became a " blotted out
locality." [6]

Between 1654 and 1685 nearly one hundred families
with different surnames can be traced as living in the
northern half of the parish or in the village along the
North Highway.   There were also a good many
temporary residents.   Of the seventeen persons who
" presented the homage to the Lord of the Manor "
in 1672 for properties " In the Gravel Pits " (see page
19), one lived in Kensell Green and one in Notting
Hill.   The Parish Registers tell of five or six other
families who inhabited Notting Hill ; the term being
apparently interchangeable with the " Gravel Pits," in
respect of houses in what is now Notting Hill Gate
and Campden Hill.

Traffic along the road evidently played a very
important part in the life of the " long but discontinued
village " of 1675.   At that time there may have been
three inns besides the " Plough " at Kensal Green.
Robert Davenport and his wife were living in another
inn of that name.   A trade token, " found in the
neighbourhood " bears on one side the representation of
a plough, with the words " Robert Davenporte at "
and " God speed the Plow," and on the reverse side,

[6] See *West London Red Book*—" Indicator " Offices.

"Kinsington Gravell Pits. His halfpenny. R.M.D."
R. Davenport owned three tenements, for one of which
he paid the quaint rental of " two shillings and a couple
of capons yearly." Thomas Hill and his wife, Joan,
meanwhile occupied the " Harrow," a house that must
have been very insanitary, for between 1676 and 1679
the Hills lost three daughters and two soldier lodgers.
The third innkeeper, Petter Sammon, does not appear
in the list of tenants of the Manor. Probably he and
his wife, Susanna or Susance, only rented their house.
Two of their children died of plague in 1666. Peter
himself died in 1678. His token, dated 1667, bears
his name and the representation of a large dog, a
" Talbot passant," one of the faithful hounds who
guarded the wares, and on the reverse " In Kinsington
Gravel Pits, his Half Penny, P.S.S." [7] Local trade
tokens were much in use at this period, for scarcely
any copper money was minted during the Common-
wealth. But this irregular coinage was suppressed
by Royal Proclamation in the year 1672.

The most important of the innkeepers was John
Ilford, who held one cottage by lease on the north
highway near the Gravel Pits, for ninety-nine years.
As already stated, the Ilfords are said to have been
landlords of the little inn on Harrow Road ; but this

[7] *Tokens issued in the Seventeenth Century,* by William Boyne, 1858.
Faulkner's *History of Kensington,* 1820. *London & Middlesex Note Book,*
edited by W. P. W. Phillimore, 1892.

cottage on the North Highway is very suggestive of
the " Plough," now No. 144, High Street, opposite
Campden Hill Road, though that tavern is not known
to have existed prior to 1769. An earlier John
Ilford and Katherine, his wife, mentioned in the Parish
Registers, may have been at the " Plough " at Kensal
Green before the end of the sixteenth century, but
there are indications that it came into the possession
of a Robert Ilford of Paddington parish. This
Robert lost his wife, Amy, and their twin babes in
1639 and 1640. Probably this is the same man
whose marriage to " Alse parker " is recorded two years
later. Five or more children were born to this couple,
but in 1665 Ales Ilford died at the " Plough " of
plague. Already other branches of the Ilford family
had suffered terribly from contagious disease, presumably plague, as the deaths occurred in the years of
special virulence, 1603, 1625 and 1665.[8] Mistress
Ilford of the " Plough," succumbed in the third and
worst outbreak, and her daughter Elizabeth died in
1666. Robert Ilford did not long survive his wife
and daughter.

Taverns are always liable to infection, being houses
of call for all and sundry, and it must be remembered
that wealthy citizens of London were then fleeing into

---

[8] It has been reckoned that in 1603 about one-third of the 49 deaths
recorded in Kensington were from plague, in 1625, about one quarter of the
80 deaths, and in 1665 nearly one half of the 74 deaths, though in 1666 only
one-sixth died of this disease.—Dr. S. D. Clippingdale, *Kensington News*,
May 14th, 1915.

the country to escape " the tyrant malady," some with the plague already on them. Also no doubt the many tramps, in tattered garments and begrimed with dirt, who wandered through the land were especially dangerous at such a time. Such persons, when too ill to travel farther, would creep into outhouses or barns to die. Others died by the wayside or " in the cage," a low two-roomed shed by the churchyard gate, which served as the parish lock-up and casual ward. Since the year 1601 Overseers of the Poor had been appointed, empowered to relieve the aged and infirm born in the parish or settled there for a year. But this humane statute sometimes resulted in " out-dwellers " being hounded on, lest they should become chargeable on the rates. The number of tramps mentioned in the Parish Books is astonishing, and in North Kensington during the first half of the seventeenth century, besides the two deaths in Westbourne Barn (see page 16), " a strange woman " died at Notting Barns in 1638, and the deaths of two others occurred at Nor'lands in 1634 and 1640.

But to return to John Ilford, born in 1649, who succeeded to the business on the death of his father. He was a solid man, a Churchwarden, and Overseer of the Poor, although he signed the " Presentment of the Homage " in 1672 with his mark. Six years later two sick soldiers died at John Ilford's house " at ye Plow near ye Gravellpits " ; these were John Gentleman and Robert Collingwood. Evidently the

" Plow " served as country lodgings as well as a house
for refreshment. On August 1, 1678, an " Act for
Burying in Woollen " came into force, the object of
the Act being " to lessen the importation of linen from
beyond the seas, and to encourage the woollen manufacture of this kingdom." It was enjoined that an
affidavit should be presented to the clergyman that
the body was interred according to law. John
Gentleman died within two or three days of the enforce-
ment of the Act, and no certificate was forthcoming.
This was notified to John Ilford, Churchwarden, by
C. S., or Charles Seward, curate of the parish. As the
death occurred in his house, it may be that John
Ilford had to pay the fine and to distribute his own
money in relief of the poor. When Robert Collingwood died in the month of November naturally a
certificate was presented in due form.

It has already been stated that one hundred and forty
acres of land lying north of the main road belonged
to the Manor of Abbots Kensington. Abbots Kensington passed into royal hands at the Dissolution of
the Monasteries, and in 1595 was leased to Robert
Horseman, gent. In spite of this lease, Queen
Elizabeth sold the freehold of the Manor to Walter
Cope. Robert Horseman was extremely unwilling
to give up possession. At last, in November 1599,
by special intervention of the Queen, a compromise
was arrived at. Walter Cope, Esq., took that portion

of the Manor on which he afterwards built Holland House, whilst Mr. Horseman retained the house called the Parsonage and about 200 acres of land, after payment to Walter Cope of £665 9s. 8d.

Included in this 200 acres were " all those several closes and wood-grounds called Norlands, lying on the north side of the said highway leading to Acton, and abutting upon a wood called Notting Wood, on the east ; upon a farm called Notting Barnes farm on the north ; and upon the common sewer on the west. And also two closes called North Crofts, on the north side of the said highway, leading from London to Acton ; near unto the Gravel Pits of Kensington."

In April 1600, five months after the date of this deed, Robert Horseman died, leaving his widow guardian of their three children.   No special mention is made of the detached lands in his will, and shortly after his decease, their connection with the parsonage ceased.   A glimpse of these lands at an earlier date is obtained from the Parish Registers, for, on November 14, 1582, " Annes, a bastard child " was buried " from Robert Croxson's house at Northlands."

The *several closes and wood-grounds called Norlands* extended from a lane which led " to Noten Barnes," now Pottery Lane, to the boundary stream described, in the deed of 1599, as the *Common Sewer*, along what is now Norland Road—see the map of 1833 on page 40, and on page 30 a piece of one of John Ogilby's beautiful road maps, published in 1675.

The *two closes called North Crofts* lay to the east, divided
from Norlands by *Notting Wood*.   It may be that the
Gravel Pits estate, now covered by Clanricarde Gardens,
was part of these closes or fields.   It is difficult to
understand the statement, made by Faulkner in his
History of Kensington, that Sir Walter Cope died
possessed of " all that wood called Notting Wood or
Knutting Wood," for his death took place fifteen
years after he had parted with the northern portion
of Abbots Kensington, and thirteen years after he had
sold the Manor and *farm of Notting Barnes* to Sheriff
Anderson.

The next known owner of Northlands was John
Arnold.   The Arnolds " appear to have been the
chief bourgeois of Old Kensington." [9]   (In the time
of Queen Elizabeth many new and vigorous yeoman
families came to the front, partly because parcels of
land formerly in Monastic hands might now be bought
by laymen).   The heads of the house were William
and Mary Arnold who inhabited a large farm at
Earl's Court.   Their sons were William and John
and probably also Samuel.   In 1623 William Arnold,
Junior, married his cousin Elizabeth Arnold, and the
young couple continued to live at " Erls Court."   In
November 1632, Samuel, then a yeoman bachelor,
aged twenty, was granted leave by the Bishop of
London to marry Elizabeth Paulet of Wilsden, a

[9] *Notes from the Parish Registers,* by Mrs. Henley Jervis, printed in the
Parish Magazine.

spinster aged sixteen, daughter of the late John Paulet, gentleman, with the consent of her mother and brother. The " allegation " was made by William Arnold of Kensington, yeoman. In the marriage license " we catch the Arnold family . . . emerging from the chrysalid or yeoman stage of existence, into full-blown gentility. They were freeholders in the neighbour-hood, they married with the gentry and were presently recognized . . . as gentle-folk themselves " (see note 9).

About the same time, John, son of William Arnold, Senior, also married, and subsequently went to live at Northlands. His eldest child was born in 1633, and by 1651 the family had numbered thirteen or fourteen children, many of whom had died in infancy. Mean-while thirteen children arrived at Earl's Court. The names of William and John and their respective wives, Elizabeth and Lidya, occur with amazing regularity among the entries of baptisms. The Parish Registers give no indication of the date at which John Arnold obtained the freehold of Northlands, but either his wife " Liddia," or a daughter, aged twenty, who bore the same name, died at Northlands in 1665, and the family were then established in a house of some size and pretensions. Before 1665 John Arnold had passed away and his son John was in possession of the estate. It is interesting to note that, in the middle of the seventeenth century, branches of this family held farms all along the western boundary

of Kensington parish : the John Arnolds were at
Northlands, a Richard Arnold was connected with
West Town (the Addison Road district), the William
Arnolds were established at " Earlescourt," and
Samuel Arnold inhabited Coolhearne House in Little
Chelsea (now represented by Coleherne Court, West
Brompton).

John Arnold, the younger, born in 1638, had in
1661 married Mistress Elizabeth Sanders ; who was
probably a lady by birth.   Four years later their little
son, another John, died at Northlands of the plague.
When he signed the Presentment of the Homage
John Arnold was the third largest landowner in
Kensington, being freeholder of 140 acres, and copy-
holder of half an acre in Green Lane.   By 1675 he
had acquired another 125 acres in or near Green Lane,
and 30 acres in the Manor of Earl's Court.   It seems
probable that Green Lane here means the south end
of Portobello Road, and that the 125 acres included
the North Crofts.   John Arnold took an important
part in local public affairs and, like his grandfather,
William of Earls Court, and his father, John of Northlands, he acted as one of the trustees of the Campden
Charities.   This was in 1682.   He was living in
1684, and possibly until 1700 when " Mr. Arnold
had a handsome pleasant seat at the Gravel Pits." [10]
John Ogilby's map (see page 30), shows a large
building close to the high-road where Norland House

[10] *Antiquities of Middlesex*, by J. Bowack, 1705.

is known to have stood in later days ; and in subsequent maps the walled grounds, with a tower at the north-west corner, and a well-laid-out garden, are clearly seen.

By 1745 (see map on page 36), the house belonged to Mr. Green, and Green's Lane, not to be confused with Green Lane, ran beside it. In the year 1656 Mistress Elizabeth Arnold, one of the numerous daughters of John and Liddia, had married Mr. John Greene of Margaret's Westminster, and it is said that their sons William and Thomas, ultimately succeeded to Northlands. It was doubtless the sister of William and Thomas, Mistress Mary Green, who with her uncle, Tanner Arnold, the youngest of the children of John and Liddia, presented a painted east window in 1705 to the renovated parish church.[11] The Mr. Thomas Greene who owned Northland House in 1745, married Miss Mary Rose, step-daughter of Sir Hans Sloane, the famous physician. He was a brewer and seems to have been followed by his son, for the Rate Books show that in 1761 Master William Greene had built a second malt house. On William Greene's death in 1772 the Norlands estate was divided up and sold.

As in the case of Notting Barns the Parish Registers of the seventeenth century tell something of life in the farm cottages. One cottage was inhabited by Robert

11 See the views of the interior of this church in *Old and New London*, by E. Walford, 1897.

and Elizabeth Bird and their six children. Mistress
Bird also had a nurse child, for in 1674 Henry, the son
of Henry Somerset, Esq., was brought from Robert
Bird's house at Northlands and was buried " in ye
Alley near ye font."   In 1680 a child died at Thomas
Welfare's house.

Thomas and Elizabeth Austin, Philip and Elizabeth
Cobb and Bartholomew and Annie Glasse lived at or
near Nor'lands, and, with the exception of the Cobbs,
they all took in lodgers. The visitors came for the
sake of the " free " country air, but they did not
always find health. In the autumn of 1683 some
epidemic attacked the household of Bartholomew
Glasse. During the months of October and November
his little daughter Annie and two lodgers died, and
Thomas Atkins, " a poore man," died there in the
following March.

On Ogilby's map the road west of Norlands is clear
of buildings almost as far as " Shepperds Bush " ;
two bridges cross the Boundary Rill at the bottom of
the hill, and two or three more bridges are shown
further on towards Acton. Dr. Stukeley, in manuscript notes on Middlesex written about 1760, gives
the names of these bridges as Northlands Bridge, at
the bottom of Noding Hill, and Mile End Bridge
beyond Shepherd's Bush. Mile End Bridge was on
the boundary line of the Manors of Fulham and
Hammersmith. See Millen Bridge on the map.   In

this map Holland House is confused with Campden House and Park, but both houses are marked correctly in the map of the road though Kensington and Hammersmith. There seems to have been a strange vagueness about these two houses, for Dr. Stukeley mentions " Holland or Camden House . . . now generally called Holland House."

During the second half of the seventeenth century, Kensington, with Hammersmith, Knightsbridge and Chelsea, was becoming increasingly popular as " a summer residence of the nobility, gentry and wealthy citizens " of London. It was thought that the emanations from the carts bearing the newly turned gravel to London were peculiarly beneficial, and that the country air was as good as that of Hampstead, and better than that of Essex or of Kent. In 1699, Dr. Samuel Garth wrote a poem called " The Dispensary," in which he extolled the health-giving properties of Kensington Gravel Pits.[12] As a matter of fact the salubrity of the district is due rather to its elevation above the sea than to the character of its soil. On this subject Dr. S. D. Clippingdale wrote : " The popular notion that it is better to live upon a gravel than upon a clay soil is probably fallacious, certainly so far as London is concerned." He adds that this can be proved by comparing the statistics of the Registrar-General with a geological map of the

[12] Quoted in *The Old Court Suburb,* by Leigh Hunt, 1855

areas of London.   In the Parish of Kensington it will
often be found that the air is clear and dry on Notting
Hill and Campden Hill, which are lumps of clay
about one hundred feet above the level of the Thames,
whilst it is gloomy and damp in Earl's Court and
Brompton which lie upon gravel not more than twenty
feet above the river.[13]

It was quite natural that William III and Queen
Mary should seek for a home in this fashionable
and healthy suburb, as soon as it was recognized that
" the Smoak of the Coal Fires of London much
incommoded his Majesty, who was always troubled
with an Asthma, and could not bear lying in Town."
But it is hardly necessary to accept the assertion that
" Kensington was a small poor village till the Court
came there ; " nor that between 1689 and 1714, it
had " become a large Town . . . fit for the Entertainment of the greatest Quality." [14]

Another cause besides the arrival of Royal
inhabitants had favoured the growth of its population,
for, at this juncture, springs containing Epsom or
Glauber Salts were discovered in the neighbourhood.
One spring was at Earl's Court, another close to what
is now the south end of Ladbroke Grove, and a third
in Lady Bedford's Walk, now Bedford Walk.   But
the most noted of these springs, and the only one to

[13] See *Kensington News*, May 1915.
[14] *A Journey Through England in Familiar Letters from a Gentleman here
to His Friend Abroad*, by John Macky, or Mackay, 1714.

be exploited, rose among the fields which had taken the place of the common land on the top of Notting Hill, fields which may then have belonged to the Campden House estate. It was a time when Mineral Water Spas were very much in vogue. The mildly purgative springs on Notting Hill (now Campden Hill) seem to have been acquired by a small company of doctors, Dr. Wright and Partners, and a " Wells House " was built in 1698. In 1705 Kensington was " a handsome populous place . . . resorted to by persons of quality," especially in the summer time when it was " extreamly filled with Lodgers for the pleasure of the Air, Walks and Gardens round it " ; and the Gravel Pits village then contained " several handsome new-built houses and a famous Chalybial Spring much esteemed and resorted to for its Medicinal Virtues." [15]

But " Kensington Wells " never attained the popularity of the more potent Wells at East Acton, and shortly after 1720 the Wells House was a private dwelling, a " Villa at Nottin Hill," owned by Edward Lloyd, Esq., afterwards to become Sir Edward Lloyd, Secretary of War.[16] Remains of three wells were found in 1873 and 1914 under the beautiful eighteenth century building now called Aubrey House. The original ground belonging to this house covered the present garden, the site of Aubrey Road and Campden

[15] *Antiquities of Middlesex*, by J. Bowack, 1705.
[16] *Springs, Streams and Spas of London*, by Alfred Stanley Foord, 1910.

Hill Square, formerly Notting Hill Square, and the house itself was long known as Notting Hill House. It is this house which the Rev. W. J. Loftie, in his book on Kensington, claims to have been the Manor House of Notting Hill.   No such Manor ever existed, and no building is known on this spot before the year 1698.

CHAPTER III

IN THE EIGHTEENTH CENTURY

THE commencement of the village of Kensington Gravel Pits has already been described. Under present conditions it is difficult to realize how countrified the place remained during the whole of the eighteenth century. In Kip's *Britannia Illustrata*, published in 1714, there is a bird's-eye view of the Palace seen from the south.[1] Surrounding the royal demesne is a wall which crosses the picture and hides the high-road. Beyond this wall are fields with hills forming the background. This artistic background must not be taken too literally, but the configuration of the ground corresponds in a remarkable degree with the view that may still be seen from the top floor of the highest houses on St. John's Hill. A hundred years after this engraving was published Faulkner wrote : " The views to the north of Kensington Gravel Pits embrace much rural scenery, comprehending Harrow in the distance with the rich intervening pastures ;

[1] A reduced facsimile of this engraving is given in *The Historical Guide to Kensington Palace*, by Ernest Law, B.A., 1899.

and on the right Hampstead, Highgate and Primrose
Hill." And again : " The whole of the north side
of the north highway is laid down with grass, except
an inconsiderable quantity of acres adjoining Portobello
Farm." [2] Rocque's map, 1741 to 1745, on page
36, agrees with this description. A set of etchings
of places round London was published about this time.
Two of these are sometimes called Old Kensington
and sometimes Notting Hill. One has been adapted
into a pretty drawing of " Notting Hill in 1750,"
which appears in *Old and New London* (see note 9).
The other etching is of a still more rustic scene with
two or three men hanging about a country lane and
a pond and a pig in the foreground.

The wide lane on Rocque's map which joins the
highway on the north side, is now represented by
Portobello Road, and the end of Pembridge Road.
Even the sharp bend is seen where one road turns into
the other. This bend, no doubt, was caused originally
by some obstruction such as a clump of trees or a
pond. Until the middle of the nineteenth century
Portobello Lane was " one of the most rural and
pleasant walks in the summer in the vicinity of
London," and within living memory it led " through
fields to Kensal Green . . . cornfields and meadow
land on each side. . . . Charming views could be
obtained," and it became the favourite walk not only
of the inhabitants of " Notting Hill, but also of many

[1] *History of Kensington*, by Thomas Faulkner, 1820.

from the great city." 3   Considering that there were few cornfields elsewhere in the neighbourhood, it is interesting to find that land to the east of Portobello Lane, on the site of Archer Street, was at one time known as " Barley Shotts " ; 4   a " shot " being a small division of field land.   Portobello Lane, on some old maps, is called Green Lane (see page 38), but the chief Green Lane in the district was the winding track from Harrow Road towards Paddington Green.   It has developed into Great Western Road, part of Cornwall Road, and Westbourne Park Road.

Portobello Farmhouse stood where the lane from the North Highway to Kensal Green became merely a footpath.   Faulkner states that Portobello Farm was the property of " Mr. A. Adams, the builder, at the time that Porto Bello was captured."   Puerto Bello with its fine harbour in the Gulf of Mexico, close to the present Panama Canal, was taken from the Spaniards by Admiral Vernon in November 1739, the news reaching England in the following March. The name of Admiral Vernon is perpetuated in Vernon Mews, Portobello Road.5

It is strange that there is no sign of Portobello

---

3 *Kensington, Notting Hill and Paddington*, by " An Old Inhabitant," 1882.

4 From notes by Mr. Ernest Swain.

5 A good account of the taking of the town is given in a little pamphlet, *The Interesting History of Portobello Road*, by Ernest P. Woolf ; and the popular excitement over the victory is described in *Beau Brocade and other Poems of the Eighteenth Century*, by Austin Dobson.   The town of Portobello near Edinburgh is said to owe its name to the same event.

Farm on Rocque's map, and as Puerto Bello was taken
for the second time in the year 1819, by Sir George
McGregor, it has been suggested that this capture
might have been referred to.   The earlier date, however, is correct, as the farm appears on Fadon's map
of 1810 shown opposite.   In 1795 the Kensington
Rate Books mention an Abraham Adams as owning
over 200 acres in this district.   He was probably
the grandson of the builder of the farmhouse.

During the whole of the eighteenth century the
knoll, called in these pages St. John's Hill, was covered
with trees : a survival of Notting Wood.   Faulkner
thus describes the scene.   " The ascent near Holland
House is clothed with wood, and affords a variety of
picturesque views," whilst " the sister hill of Holland
House " was " of great height and entirely free from
wood."   He continues, " The valley on the north
(of St. John's Hill) is laid down with grass, and the
whole of the district appears to have undergone but
little alteration, in respect to culture and division of
the land, for several ages.   Although the distance
from London is scarcely three miles, yet the traveller
may imagine himself to be embosomed in the most
sequestered part of the country, and nothing is heard
but the notes of the lark, the linnet or the nightingale.
. . . In the midst of these meadows stands the Manor
House of Knotting Barns."

In 1767 Mr. Edward Lloyd let his " Villa at Nottin
Hill," now Aubrey House (see page 43), to Lady

Mary Coke. During her tenancy, which lasted from 1767 to 1788, she wrote a copious and delightful journal, which throws much light on the state of the district at this period.[6] Lady Mary Coke often speaks of the seclusion of Notting Hill. On one occasion when riding back from town she met " nothing but women who had been working in the fields, and they talked to me not very civilly, I thought." In July 1770, when an Installation of Knights was taking place, she writes : " The crowd and bustle at Windsor I suppose is great, and all here is such a state of silence that it seems a deserted country ; nobody riding in the great roads ; nothing appears but the stage coaches. I walked in view of one of the great roads just now, and did not see a creature pass."

It was along this road that one of her cows, named after an old friend, made an adventurous expedition. " Miss Pelham (my black and white cow) took a frisk this morning, got out of my grounds, and went very near as far as London before I heard of her. I believe she thinks my place too retired, for she was found among a great herd of cattle."

This seclusion was caused in part by the state of the roads. In spite of Turnpike Acts, which had been in existence since 1663, highways and byways all over England remained in a deplorable condition. The

---

[6] See *Aubrey House,* by Florence M. Gladstone, 1922, and *Letters and Journals of Lady Mary Coke,* 4 vols., edited by the Honble. J. A. Home, 1889–1896.

roads both south and north of Hyde Park were often
almost impassable with mud, and streams, which are
now carried in sewers underground, crossed the
surface. The North Highway was liable to be flooded
at the depression where the Westbourne or Bays
Water crossed the road. In 1675 this stream was
spanned by a brick bridge, which was replaced by a
stone bridge before 1769. From Lancaster Gate
the ground rises to Notting Hill Gate Station, and
then falls some seventy feet before the western boundary
of the parish is reached. At Shepherd's Bush floods
were even more severe than at " Bayswatering." In
1624 the low-lying ground, now occupied by the
West London Railway at Uxbridge Road, was called
the Marsh.7 In later days this marsh became three
lakes, which may be seen on various maps in this
book, and even now water rises in the Electricity
Generating Station east of Wood Lane. Rills and
bridges on the north side of Shepherd's Bush have
already been mentioned. See page 40. By 1769
the wooden bridge across the boundary stream had
been replaced by one of brick.

The autumn of 1768 was exceptionally wet. Lady
Mary Coke records : " When I got up this morning
I saw two rivers, the grounds two or three miles off
being all under water, and the Thames made a fine

---

7 This is shown on an interesting old Plan of the Land given by Edward
Latymer, Esq., for Charitable Purposes, preserved at the Latymer Foundation School, Hammersmith.

appearance. My servants tell me two houses at Knightsbridge have been washed away, and one of the bridges upon the King's Road." In the afternoon of the same day water was so deep in the lane leading to Hammersmith, now Shepherd's Bush Road, that a friend feared she would be drowned when driving through the flood in Lady Mary's chaise. (There was flooding in this district as recently as the summer of 1917). In 1772 the trouble recurred and a strange picture is given of the manners of the time. Lady Mary, then a widow of forty-six, had been dining with Lord Spencer at Wimbledon. In that house they had a " terrible custom " of serving too much liquor to the waiting servants. On the return journey, after ten o'clock at night, when they reached a " little bridge between Hammersmith and the Acton rode, the postillion turned short about and drove the open chaise into deep water." After debating whether to stop in the chaise or to get out and walk, Lady Mary determined to remain where she was. So she ordered the relatively sober footman to walk at the heads of the horses, and to hold the postillion on if he could. In this fashion they at last reached home. Contemporary newspapers tell the same tale. In 1788 " Mr. Salmon of Bond Street, in attempting to cross the hollow near Kensington Gravell Pits in a single horse chaise on his way to Acton, nearly escaped drowning, so large a body of water being collected as to bear up the horse and carriage, and it was with extreme difficulty that he was rescued from the pending danger."

An Act of Parliament had been passed in 1714 to authorize the collection of tolls "for repairing and amending the highways between Tyburn and Uxbridge." But keeping in repair was not all that was needed. The preamble to a later Turnpike Act states that the road between Tyburn and Kensington Gravel Pits is "frequently infested in the night-time with Robbers and other wicked and evil-disposed Persons, and Robberies, Outrages, and Violences are committed thereon, which might in a great Measure be prevented if the said Highway was properly lighted and watched." The case was not over-stated. It was a time of much lawlessness. In Notting Hill, thefts from garden, orchard and poultry-yard constantly occurred. Strange cattle would be driven during the night to graze in fields bordering the high road, and farmers had their sheep carried off, or the carcases left behind minus skin and fat. Highway robbery took place on all the roads round London, and the fear of attack was a cruel strain on the nerves of respectable citizens.

Newspaper reports of local crimes are preserved at the Public Library. To travel from Acton to Shepherd's Bush was a hazardous proceeding. The most critical part between Shepherd's Bush and Tyburn is said to have been at what is now Lancaster Gate, for robbers could hide themselves under the shade of the trees which overhung the wall enclosing Kensington Gardens. Here, in 1753, a specially brutal attack was made by a footpad one Sunday night on two friends. " On their making Resistance, he ran an iron skewer into the body of one of the Men, and got off, though pursued by the other. The man who was stabbed " afterwards lay " dangerously ill at a Publick House at Bayswater." But the piece of the road between the sister hills near Holland House was also very lonely and unprotected. On this portion of the road, in 1751, two gentlemen were robbed of their watches and money by men in black masks " who swore a great deal and appeared to be in liquor." An upholsterer of Piccadilly had his watch and £3 stolen in 1768, and another man lost £5 and some silver in 1769. Lord Holland's Lane, now Holland Walk, was the scene of a serious robbery at three o'clock one October afternoon in 1772, and shortly afterwards a highwayman was shot " on the outer road " at the bottom of Lady Mary Coke's grounds between nine and ten o'clock at night. She heard the report of the pistol while reading in her library. In July 1774 her neighbour, Mrs. Lahoop, was robbed on the same part of " the Acton Road within a hundred yards of her own house." On this occasion the two thieves remained in the neighbourhood all night, and stopped a poor woman early next morning. As she had no money they would have stripped her of her clothing, but, someone coming by, they made off.

It must be remembered that roads were unlighted, and that the inefficient police system and the prevalence of bribery made the detection of crime a difficult matter.   Consequently when a rogue was caught he suffered as a warning to others.   Terribly degrading scenes were connected with the public executions at Tyburn, which were continued until the year 1783. It became the practice to expose the bodies of felons near the scene of their crimes.   In 1745 gibbets stood by the Uxbridge Road at Starch Green, at Shepherd's Bush and at Tyburn, a distance of little more than three miles.   The hanging place at Shepherd's Bush was known as Gallows Close.   Two highwaymen were hanging here in 1748, and remains of the gallows are said to have existed until the year 1800.[8]

But brutal forms of punishment had little deterrent effect on evil doers.   Carriages were still held up, and murders committed by highwaymen.   It was in an Inn at Shepherd's Bush, reputed to have been the only house between Acton and Kensington Gravel Pits, that the notorious Jack Rann, or " Sixteen String Jack," was finally arrested.   The " Coach and Horses," now 108, High Street, Notting Hill Gate, and the " George Inn," 61, Church Street, were known to harbour these gentry.   Probably the walls of several inns in the neighbourhood could have told tales of

[8] *Histories of Kensington and Hammersmith,* by T. Faulkner, 1820 and 1839, and *MS. Notes,* by T Butler Cato, Esq.

" coaches robbed and plunder shared between Knights of the road and obliging landlords." 9   Beggars and other undesirable characters congregated round the recognized stopping places.   One of these regular halts is shown on Leddiard's Plan of the Road, 1769, page 30, just where the " Duke of Clarence," opposite Royal Crescent, still preserves its old-world character, with sign post and stone mounting blocks.

Such was the condition of affairs when the Turnpike Act of 1769 came into force.   As the result of this Act the care of the road was vested in trustees, who met at the George Inn, Acton, four times a year. Toll gates and toll houses were erected, and glass lamps placed at intervals along the dark parts of the road, whilst " fit and able-bodied " watchmen were appointed to endeavour to prevent murders, robberies and other outrages.   Fines and imprisonment were to be inflicted if lamps were broken, and should anyone refuse to pay toll, the toll-keeper was empowered to seize his beast or goods and sell them, giving the owner the balance of the profits, " after reasonable charges " had been deducted.   A note or ticket was provided on payment of toll.   No tolls were to be exacted on the day of a Parliamentary election, nor from citizens riding or driving to divine service on Sundays.   By 1801 the whole of London was parcelled out into Turnpike Gate Trusts.   Bayswater Gate, near the Swan Inn, a picturesque rustic building standing

9 *Old and New London*, by E Walford, 1897

beside the bridge over the Westbourne, as well as
Kensington Gravel Pits Gate and other toll-gates
further to the west, belonged to the Uxbridge Trust.
One ticket freed the traveller for the day at all these
gates. Kensington Trust covered a large area south-
west of Hyde Park.[10] There was a Gate at Tyburn
even before the execution of criminals ceased at this
spot.

Paul Sandby, one of the original members of the
Royal Academy, who lived in St. George's Row facing
the north side of Hyde Park, made many charming
water-colour drawings of the neighbourhood. Two
drawings now in the Albert and Victoria Museum,
dated 1790, show the wall of " Kensington Garden,"
and Bayswater Toll Gate with two or three small
dwellings beside it. A wide country road stretches
towards London and a coach is seen in the distance.
In one drawing [11] carts and men on horseback are
grouped by the " Old Swan Inn," and four young
women are seen walking into town with flat baskets
on their heads, baskets probably containing fruit picked
in market gardens on the west side of London. This
part of the road is in the parish of Paddington, but
the description of Kensington Gravel Pits thirty years
later agrees with Paul Sandby's pictures. This
description was meant to prove what a busy place it

[10] See *Survey of the High Roads from London,* by J Cary, 1790 and 1801.
[11] Reproduced in *The Eighteenth Century in London,* by E. Beresford
Chancellor, 1922

had become. Faulkner writes : " The principal street runs along the north high-road for about three furlongs . . . and lying in the direct road from Uxbridge and Oxford it is enlivened every hour by the passage of mail coaches, stages and waggons."

The Kensington Gravel Pits Gate, since then known as Notting Hill Gate, was the first of three successive turnpikes at this spot, and crossed the road east of the site of the Metropolitan Station. It seems probable that the toll-keeper's house occupied the corner where that station is set back from the road. The very interesting view of this gate by Paul Sandby, R.A., dated 1793 (see page 54), faces west, and apparently shows the end of Portobello Lane and the Coach and Horses Inn.[12]

By this time a cluster of houses with gardens behind them stood opposite the end of the lane leading to Kensington, now Church Street. Between Nos. 50 and 60, High Street, the houses still show eighteenth century characteristics, although shops have been built out on to the present line of road. Two of these houses belong to the year 1790, and have curious brick bays. Unfortunately the remains of these handsome old buildings will soon disappear, as will also the picturesque, though tumbledown, shops at the north end of Church Street. In 1711 the Gravel Pitts Almshouses were placed on the south side of the road, between Church Street and the Mall, in what was

[12] From the original water-colour, owned by Herbert E. Friend, Esq.

known as Greyhounds Row.   But these tiny dwellings
were demolished in 1821, when in a very dilapidated
condition.

Beyond Portobello Lane the village straggled on
past Montpelier House, a good-sized private residence,
now Nos. 128 and 130, High Street, to the Plough
Inn, the predecessor of the large tavern bearing that
name.   See Cruchley's map on page 100.   Pictures
of several of these buildings are grouped together on
page 58, and a drawing of the " Academy " by
Mr. W. Cleverley Alexander, appears on page 92.

The Kensington Rate Books become available for
research from the year 1760.   By this time all trace
of the Manorial system had disappeared, and the larger
estates were being divided.   It is only possible in these
pages to follow up three or four of the most important
landowners, and their properties.

In 1675 the Manor of Knotting Barns belonged to
Sir Richard Anderson, and covered 400 acres.   Before
1820 the Manor House had passed to Sir William
Talbot, indeed it would appear that the Estate had
been owned by the Talbot family ever since 1712.
Apparently Knotting Barns Farm had been let to
Admiral Darby, who was succeeded by his son William
Thomas Darby, Esq., " the proprietor " in 1795.[13]
Probably in 1795 Mr. Darby died, for " Darby's

---

[13] *Environs of London*, by the Rev D. Lysons, 1795, and Faulkner's
History of Kensington, 1820.

Land," to the extent of some 230 acres, was acquired by three men : Abraham Adams, John White, and Bright Hemmings. Mr. Adams of Portobello Farm soon got the largest share into his own hands, and eventually, seems to have gained possession of nearly two-thirds of this northern pasture land. He only held it until 1816 when William Wise took over the property, the Talbots remaining as ground landlords. (The further history of Portobello Farm will be given in Chapter IX.)

In 1820 the Manor House of Knotting Barns was "occupied" by William Smith, Esq., of Hammersmith, who had been paying rates on 27 acres of "Darby Land" since 1771. In 1797 Mr. Smith became possessed of other land in the neighbourhood, and he continued to add field to field, until in 1809, he paid rates on at least 264 acres in the estates of Knotting Barns and Norlands. In 1811 Mr. William Smith, Churchwarden, and Mr. John Hall each advanced £200 towards the repair of Kensington Church, which amounts were afterwards refunded. Mr. William Smith's name appears on the Rate Books until 1828, but it will be shown in Chapter X that Mr. Salter was probably then renting Notting Barns Farm. In 1828 Mr. Smith's estate in Notting Barns was rated at 150 acres.

Already another important ground landlord had appeared on the scene. This was Richard Ladbrooke, Esq., who in 1760 owned two farms on the north

side of the high road. The name is stamped all over
the district which formerly had been covered by Notting
Wood. Richard Ladbrooke must have been a son
of Sir Robert Ladbroke, head of the firm of Messrs.
Robert Ladbroke and Co., goldsmiths and bankers
in Lombard Street in the year 1736. He was also
Colonel of the City Militia, Member of Parliament,
and Lord Mayor of London in 1747. The arms
" azure, a chevron ermine," which appear on the gate
of the path from Kensington Park Gardens into
Ladbroke Square, are those borne by the Father of
the City. The original Warwickshire family bear
a plain chevron.[14]

In the year 1784, when he made his will, Richard
Ladbroke of Tadworth Court, in the County of Surrey,
Esq., owned lands in the parish of Reigate, and in
Kensington, Paddington, Notting Barns, Westbourn,
South Mimms, St. Sepulchre's and Enfield Chase, etc.
Being unmarried, he left his estates in trust for his
mother and his four sisters. The freehold and copy-
hold property was to pass to his nephews, who were
enjoined to adopt his surname. Failing male issue
it was to descend to his executor and cousin, Robert
Ladbroke and his heirs. Richard Ladbroke of
Tadworth Court died in 1794, and was succeeded by
Osbert Denton Ladbroke, the son of his youngest
sister, who died " a bachelor " in 1810, and by Cary

[14] The information on this family is chiefly gathered from an abstract
of the title to some property in Pembridge Villas.

Hampton Weller Ladbroke, also a bachelor, who died in 1819, and his brother James Weller Ladbroke, sons of Mary Ladbroke and the Rev. James Weller. Mr. James W. Ladbroke had married in 1803, but he left no sons. At his death in 1847, the property, therefore, passed to a distant cousin, Felix Ladbroke of Hedley, in the County of Surrey, Esq., born in 1802, a grandson of the Robert Ladbroke mentioned in the will. James W. and Felix Ladbroke will appear in the subsequent history, but no member of the family seems to have resided in Kensington.

In 1763 Richard Ladbroke Esq., let part of Ladbrook's Land to Mr. John Hall, who probably brought his wife and child to a farm-house on this property. Mr. Hall at once began to buy up piece after piece of land from different owners. In 1791 he died, and was succeeded by his son of the same name, then a man of twenty-nine years of age, having been born one year before his father moved into the district. John Hall, Junior, still further added to his possessions until his leasehold property equalled, if it did not exceed, that of Mr. William Smith. A house and large farm belonging to Mr. Hall was let, 1808–1812, to Colonel Lowther and family, and another was occupied by Lord Valencia in 1812. Already John Hall has been mentioned as advancing money for church purposes. "John Hall, Esq., of Halkin Street, Grosvenor Place, and of Notting Hill in this parish," died on August 10, 1816, aged 54 years.

" An elegant marble tablet surmounted with an urn "
was placed to his memory on the west wall of the old
church, " over the Christening pew." The inscription is given in full by Mr. Loftie.   It is a happy
example of the laudatory epitaphs of the period, and
describes a worthy man : " One, who in life by good
works, and by fervent faith in death, proved that the
source of virtue is in the love of God."   The name
of Christopher Hall appears in the Rate Books from
1817 onwards.

" Notting Hill Farm was the residence of the late
Mr. John Hall," writes Faulkner in 1820.   Loftie
and later writers have asserted that this farm was " an
unpretentious homestead " on the hill-top.   This is
incorrect.   There was no solid building on the summit
of the hill until the Church of St. John the Evangelist
was placed there in 1845.   The farm-house, which was
of a fair size, was either a little way off the main road
or was on the main road where the Mitre Tavern,
No. 40, Holland Park Avenue, now stands.   A small
oil-painting of this farm, very carefully restored by
Mr. Herbert Jones, hangs in the North Kensington
branch of the Public Library.   See illustration opposite.   It is there said to be Notting Barns Farm ;
but it is entitled " Notting Hill Farm " and may depict
the scattered farm buildings on the highway and
the south end of the " public road " through the
farmyard, now represented by Ladbroke Grove.
This sketch is ascribed to William Mulready, Junior.

This is quite possible, for the farm-house does not seem to have disappeared much before 1830. Rocque's map of 1745, on page 36, and Fadon's map of 1810, on page 48, show the buildings of Notting Hill Farm, and also show how few other houses existed at this time north of the Oxford or Uxbridge Road.

No doubt the nature of its soil had much to do with the slow development of North Kensington. Wells sunk in gravel which rests on clay are soon supplied with "pure" water, whilst wells sunk in the clay itself only catch water from the surface, and this water is hard and often contaminated. The earlier settlers in and around London naturally chose sites where a good supply of drinking water was easily obtainable. It is only when water is brought from a distance, and domestic wells can be dispensed with, that a town is able to expand irrespective of its subsoil. Professor Prestwich worked out this point for the whole of London in his Presidential Address to the Geological Society in the year 1872, and he stated that this was the reason why such clay districts as "Regents Park, St. John's Wood, Westbourne Park and Notting Hill received town populations much later than . . . Paddington, Kensington and Chelsea, which were situated on gravel."

It is true that long before the end of the eighteenth century water was being conveyed to the Palace and

to the more fashionable parts of Kensington. In
1908 a wych-elm pipe was dug up in Uxbridge Road,
near Palace Gardens, belonging to about 1620, when
Sir Hugh Middleton brought the New River water
from Hertfordshire to London. Kensington had in
more recent times been supplied with Thames water
by the Chelsea Water Works Company, first started
in 1723, and the West Middlesex Water Works
Company inaugurated in 1809, but it is improbable
that water was laid on north of the high road. The
boundary stream was useless as a source of supply,
for it is significantly called " the common sewer " as
early as 1599. Evidently the inhabitants depended
on shallow wells and rain water cisterns, and these
were becoming inadequate for the population.

At this juncture a man of public spirit and resource
came into the neighbourhood.

It has already been stated that after the death of
Mr. William Green in 1772 the Norland Estate was
divided up. When Cary published his Road Maps,
in 1790 (see note 10), Norland House and its large
walled garden was being used as "The Prince of
Wales's Military Academy." This was a boarding
school for boys under fifteen years of age, conducted
by Thomas Marquois, Professor of Artillery and
Fortification. An interesting prospectus of the
Academy at Norlands may be seen at the Kensington
Public Library. Lewis Vulliamy of 98, Pall Mall,
clockmaker to the Court, seems to have bought the

place about 1794.[15]   He may not have lived in the
house, for, in the second edition of Cary's Maps,
1801, the house still appears as the Military Academy.
This, however, may be incorrect.   It seems more likely
that personal experience of the difficulty of obtaining
good water determined his son, Benjamin Vulliamy,
to sink a deep well similar to those in use in the Province
of Artois in Northern France.   In November 1794
a shaft four feet in diameter was dug through the
clay for 236 feet, after which a $5\frac{1}{4}$-inch borer was
inserted.   When the depth of 261 feet was reached
water rose to the surface at the rate of 46 gallons per
minute.   It has been claimed that this was the first
Artesian well to be sunk in England.   The interest
which it excited is shown by the elaborate description
of " Mr. Vulliamy's Overflowing Well " given in
Faulkner's *History of Kensington*.[16]   The " spring "
stood in a square enclosure close to the road, and was
leased for one guinea per week to three persons, who
formed themselves into a small company under the
pretentious title of the " Notting Hill Water Works."
These persons sold the water at 2s. 6d. a ton or $\frac{1}{2}$d.
a pailful.   The advertisement of the Company stated
that the water was specially good for washing purposes :
an indication that the ordinary domestic supply was

---

[15] An ancestor of the Vulliamys had come over from Switzerland in 1704
to study English clock making.   He married the daughter of his employer
and succeeded to the business which remained in the family until 1854.

[16] *Dictionary of National Biography* and *Springs, Streams and Spas of
London*, by A. S. Foord, 1910.

" hard " water.   Part of the shaft of this well, now
covered by concrete, exists in the garden behind
No. 130, Holland Park Avenue, but the remains of
the engine room, visible in 1909, seem now to have
disappeared.[17]   The well was covered in between
1830 and 1844.   In 1812 Mr. Henry Drummond,
banker, of Charing Cross, became tenant of Norland
House, though Mr. Benjamin Vulliamy continued to
pay rates on the spring until 1819, and the names of
Lewis and Benjamin, and Benjamin Lewis, and
Mrs. Sarah Vulliamy are connected with this and
neighbouring house property as late as 1838.

Although the following incidents belong chiefly
to the first quarter of the nineteenth century, it seems
best to finish this chapter with an account of the
establishment of a little colony of brickmakers and
pig-keepers on the low ground situated in the north
part of the Norlands Estate.   The soil in this district
is almost entirely composed of the malleable yellow
clay from which London stock bricks are made.   In
1781 a portion of land, perhaps seventeen acres in
extent, had been taken for a brickfield by a certain
James Watson, and some poor buildings were already
put up.   By 1818 part of this brickfield and eight
or nine acres of adjoining land, was in the hands of

[17] Many years later Mr. John Treeby sank a well just beyond the eastern
bounds of Kensington parish.   This well gave its name to Artesian Road.
It was known as the " Western Water Works," and water was distributed
as late as 1853.   Then the well was filled in.

Samuel Lake. Next year William Adams bought up the remainder of the original brickfield, and had a house on his land. It is impossible not to connect William Adams with Abraham Adams, the owner of Portobello Farm down to 1816. Adams' Brickfield lasted for many years in Notting Dale, and probably it was Mr. W. Adams who started the "Norland Pottery Works," with its well-known kiln for the manufacture of tiles, flower-pots and drain-pipes, which still stands in Walmer Road. See illustrations on pages 66 and 88.

The coming of the pigs is connected with Samuel Lake, a chimney-sweep and night-man of Tottenham Court Road, who had moved, in 1818, to this bare land beyond the outskirts of London, in order that he might continue his unsavoury profession without being a nuisance to his neighbours. A year or two later Lake invited a bow-string maker to share his solitude. This man, Stephens by name, is said to have purchased part of Lake's property for £100, and, giving up his former trade, to have taken to keeping pigs. In his enquiries after pigs, etc., he became acquainted with the troubles of a party of pig-keepers who inhabited land now covered by Connaught Square. These men fed their animals on broken food collected daily from houses in Mayfair. It can be readily understood that the gruesome memories connected with Tyburn for many years prevented the extension of London on the north side of the Park.

But at last good houses were being built,[18] and the pig-masters of the " West End Establishment," as they called themselves, recognized that the time had come when they must move elsewhere. Stephens offered these men a share of the refuge which he and his friend Lake had found in Norland Row. The offer was gladly accepted, and many of the " masters either bought or rented small plots of land from the original proprietor, and removed their establishments of pigs and children to this favoured spot, where Lake assured them everybody should do as they liked, and he'd see that nobody meddled with them." [19]

Mrs. Bayly, who wrote a charming account of the beginnings of the slum area known as Kensington Potteries and afterwards as Notting Dale, thought that the pig-keepers preceded the brickmakers, and that they arrived in the early years of the nineteenth century, but the Rate Books suggest that they settled on " Brickland " about the year 1820. The first houses were one-storied dwellings built by their owners and planted down " in no street in particular." Tucker's Cottage (see page 136), may be taken as a typical specimen. The illustration is from a drawing made shortly before it was pulled down in 1855. It consisted of " two apartments, one for the family, the other for domestic purposes and such animals as

---

[18] See *Old and New London*, E. Walford, and *History of Paddington*, by W. Robins, 1853.

[19] *Ragged Homes and How to Mend Them*, by Mrs. Mary Bayly, 1859. Squatting rights still exist in Pottery Lane.

were thought indispensable to the general welfare."
Its plot of ground was enclosed by a thick mound of
earth, the domain of poultry, pigs and the donkey.
In the rear was a pond overhung with willows, into
which " flowed the foul streams of the province," for
there was no proper drainage, and wells sunk in the
back yards soon became contaminated. The means
of approach from the main road was by " the public
way to Notting Barns," afterwards Pottery Lane.
Most of the settlers had their own horse or donkey-
cart, and would make their way townwards early in the
morning to collect kitchen refuse from houses or hotels
in the West End. How this broken food was treated
may be given in the words of old Mrs. Tucker :
" When we come home, we sorts it out ; the best of
it we eats ourselves, or sells it to a neighbour, the
fat is all boiled down, and the rest we gives to the
pigs." (The boiling down of fat, including offal of
various kinds, was a local industry until very recent
times.)

These people, though uncouth and unlettered, were
a self-reliant and a sober race, honest and industrious.
Their nearest neighbours were either at " the farm
opposite Holland Walk," that is Notting Hill Farm,
" where the men sang at their work as they stacked
the hay and the corn," or at the other farm on the site
of Royal Crescent, " where milk could sometimes be
obtained for the children." See map of 1831 on
page 100. The brickmakers, on the other hand, were

chiefly Irish labourers of a low type.   A woman who
had lived most of her life in the place once remarked
to Mrs. Bayly.   " Now pig-keepers is respectable, but
them brick-people bean't some of them no wiser than
the clay they works on."   The drawing of the Kiln
(on page 66) is dated 1824, and " The Kilns " are
marked on the map of 1833 (see page 40).   After
1837 certain buildings are shown along the road which
already was called Pottery Lane.   But the little colony
of brickmakers and pig-keepers kept themselves to
themselves and were studiously left alone by their
neighbours.

CHAPTER IV

DURING THE EIGHTEEN THIRTIES

THE first encroachment on the rural character of Notting Hill was the cutting of the Paddington Branch of the Grand Junction Canal. Several artificial waterways had already been constructed among the manufacturing towns in the north of England, and the canal system was being rapidly extended, when, in 1783, Parliamentary powers were obtained for the making of " a Navigable Cut from the Grand Junction Canal in the precinct of Norwood, in the County of Middlesex to Paddington," in order to connect the Midlands with the Metropolis. At the London end of its course this canal was to cross the northernmost part of Kensington, then, after skirting Harrow Road and curving through Westbourne Green, it was to become a huge basin covering much of what is now Praed Street and the Paddington Station of the Great Western Railway.

In the half-mile within the boundaries of Kensington parish the canal crossed a small portion of the Notting Barns farm-land, then called " Smith's Farm," and the corner of a large farm owned by Mr. John Watkins,

probably Red House Farm, shown in the map of
1833. Subsequently the Canal Company paid rates
on this land. The canal was opened for traffic on
June 1, 1801, and on July 10th of the same year there
was a public inauguration, and a barge with passengers
from Uxbridge arrived at Paddington Basin amid
the ringing of bells and firing of cannon. It is said
that 20,000 persons gathered on this occasion " to
hurrah the mighty men " who offered to the Londoner
a new mode of transit for his goods. See illustration
opposite. For the first few years the canal was an
enormous success, but the carriage of goods was
considerably reduced when the Regent's Canal was
completed in 1820, and further reduced when railways
were built. The traffic, however, on this " silent
highway " was still considerable, and is so at the
present time.

In early days passenger boats went five times a week
to Uxbridge, and pleasure trips, first by barge and
later by steamboat, continued for many years ; whilst
a generation ago row-boats could be hired near Carlton
Bridge. Among " Single Day Excursions from the
Metropolis " Mr. John Hassell, water-colour artist
and engraver, in 1818 recommends a journey by
water to Harrow-on-the-Hill, and gives charming
descriptions of the scenery along the route.[1]   This

---

[1] *Picturesque Rides and Walks Ten Miles round London,* vol ii, by
J. Hassell, 1818. See also, *The Tour of the Grand Junction Canal,* by
John Hassell, 1819.

excursion was made on the Canal Accommodation Boat, a huge barge which was often uncomfortably crowded. Many drawings and caricatures of life on the canal by Rowlandson and others are in existence. A good selection may be seen at the London Museum. There are also pictures of ladies and gentlemen walking on the banks of the limpid stream where, from about 1840, the " Flora Tea Gardens," now No. 525 Harrow Road, formed a pleasant retreat for a summer afternoon. See maps on pages 76 and 194.

The Canal Company supplied water for domestic use until the year 1811. In that year the Grand Junction Water Works Company was formed, and an engine house and reservoir were placed in the centre of Paddington. But this water, coming chiefly from the Colne and the Brent, proved unsatisfactory, and the Thames was reverted to for the source of supply. By the year 1825 the works were at Kew Bridge and on Campden Hill. But the old name was retained and was used until 1904 ; thus showing the original connection between the Grand Junction Water Works and the Paddington Branch of the Grand Junction Canal.

The map of 1833 shows that the meadows north of St. John's Hill were crossed by two brooks, tributaries of the " Rivulet " or boundary stream. This stream, after a course of four miles with a fall of 150 feet, discharged (and still discharges) itself into the Thames at Chelsea Creek. Further information can be obtained from a rare map of 1827 or earlier which is preserved at the Public Library.[2] One of the tributary brooks rose near the " Plough " on Harrow Road, and passed south-west of Notting Barns Farm ; the other commenced close to Portobello Farm and, running in marshy ground at the foot of the north slope of St. John's Hill, joined the main stream further to the south. The connection with the ditch on the eastern boundary of the parish, suggested in the map of 1833, may be a mistake.[3]

The hill, originally Notting Wood, was now pasture land, divided into seven meadows. These are shown in a plan attached to a deed of 1840. The names of these meadows are most interesting. To the east of the footpath, now Ladbroke Grove, lay " Pond Field," on the site of Ladbroke Square, " Middle Wood " was round about Stanley Gardens, and " North Wood " on the northern slope of Kensington Park Road. On the other side of the footpath, from Hanover Terrace on the south to Cornwall Road on the north and extending as far west as Clarendon Road, were " Ploughed Field," " Hilly Field," " Middle Field " and the " Eighteen Acre Field."

---

[2] " Plan of Districts drained by Watercourses discharging into the River Thames under the jurisdiction of the Commissioners of Sewers of Westminster." A later edition of this map, corrected to 1844, may also be seen at the Library.

[3] In *Old and New London*, E. Walford mentions a trout stream running from Notting Hill Manor towards Hay Hill, Berkeley Square. This stream is imaginary ; it would have crossed the watershed. Possibly a tiny tributary of the Westbourne from near Colville Terrace is referred to.

Certain other field names are known. The " Meads " and the " Marshes " were important holdings in " Norland Row," and may have covered Royal Crescent and part of Norland Town. " Longlands " and the " Hooks " lay between Westbourne Grove and the south end of Portobello Lane. " Barley Shotts," a field on the site of Archer Street, has already been mentioned.

Probably several small springs rose on the crest of the hill. Some of these springs still give trouble in the basements of houses in Kensington Park Road, Ladbroke Square and Ladbroke Grove, and there are traditions of others. But there is no foundation for the statement, occasionally met with, that a vast lake underlies the district.

At this time, as no doubt for centuries before this, the North Kensington fields were crossed by footpaths, forerunners of the principal cross roads of the present day. With the exception of Portobello Lane, all these paths were means of communication with the Manor Farm of Notting Barns, or connected Notting Barns with Portobello Farm. Most of these paths, but not all of them, are shown on the map of 1833. An ancient footpath " from Kensale Green to Uxbridge Road " started from Harrow Road, and was carried by a small bridge over the canal. This was the northern end of the " public road " which passed through the Manor farmyard and emerged on Uxbridge Road east of the Norlands estate. This cart-track has already been mentioned under various names. The northern portion has disappeared, but the southern end is now represented by Walmer Road and Pottery Lane. The footpath across Wormwood Scrubbs from Acton Wells, and another path which joined it from Willesden Green, have become merged in St. Quintin Avenue and St. Mark's Road. Cambridge Gardens is practically along the line of the pathway, bordered with elm trees, which connected Notting Barns with Portobello Lane, and was continued east of the lane till it joined the road to Paddington, now known as Westbourne Grove. Another path open to the public branched off at the present junction of St. Mark's Road and Cambridge Gardens, and, continuing in a south-easterly direction, crossed the hill by the curve of Stanley Crescent and descended to Uxbridge Road by Ladbroke Place, as the north end of Ladbroke Grove was called in the year 1835. When Faulkner wrote his history in 1820 this " public road " led through the farmyard of Notting Hill Farm and communicated with Kensington by Lord Holland's Lane. This was the path that was the cause of strife in 1837.

In 1833 North Kensington was absolutely rural, but a scheme was already formulated which would connect this district with the Metropolis. The rapid increase in the population of London and its suburbs during the eighteenth century had brought about the need for more space in which to bury the dead. Existing graveyards were terribly over-crowded, and burials within churches had become an abomination. The " Act for Amending the Burial of the Dead in the Metropolis " was not passed until 1852, but over twenty years before this date a Company was founded by Mr. George Frederick Carden, and Parliamentary powers had been obtained, for the formation of the Cemetery of All Souls at Kensal Green.

The plot of ground chosen by the General Cemetery Company for this pioneer enterprise lay between the canal and the north boundary of Kensington parish on the Harrow Road. Here in 1832, fifty-six acres were enclosed by a stone wall, and in 1833 the Bishop of London, in spite of his former opposition to the scheme, consecrated thirty-nine acres of this land, fifteen acres being reserved for the burial of dissenters. A Nonconformist chapel, built in the classic style with Ionic columns, was placed at the east end of the cemetery enclosure, and an Anglican chapel, flanked by colonnades with Doric columns, occupied the western extremity and stood on the highest ground in Kensington, 150 feet above sea level. These buildings, with the so-called catacombs and the imposing gateway, with its semicircle of Doric columns, on Harrow Road, all belong to 1832. The enormous entrance must have looked strangely out of place by the side of a country road, but the cemetery appealed to the taste of the period, and " marble

obelisks and urns began to rise among the cypresses
in all the variety which heathen and classical allusions
could suggest." [4]

Some sentences may be quoted from a pamphlet
written in 1843. After describing the condition of
existing graveyards, the writer continues : " What
an escape from the atmosphere of London burial-
places to the air of Kensal Green. . . . The surrounding landscape, so rich in cultivation, in character
so diversified, in extent so sweeping. . . . It is
scarcely ten years since the sheep were driven from
their pasture, and already have there been about six
thousand interments within that noble and spacious
enclosure." [5]

A farm-house and an " Academy " had stood close
to the " Plough " on the south side of the Harrow
Road. In making the cemetery these buildings
were pulled down and the beginning of the ancient
footpath from Kensal Green was lost. It had branched
off from the road where the large entrance to the
cemetery was placed. From the south end of the
high bridge near the " Plough," now in Ladbroke
Grove, a new path was made which joined the ancient
path on land afterwards covered by the gasworks.
The ground plan of the cemetery is shown in the
maps of 1841 and 1850 on pages 76 and 120. The

4 *Old and New London,* by E. Walford, 1897.
5 *The Cemetery at Kensal Green ; the Grounds and Monuments, with a
Memoir of H.R.H. the Duke of Sussex,* by Laman Blanchard, 1843.

illustrations on pages 214 and 218 belong to about the year 1845.

The cemetery grounds were in process of being laid out when the question of bringing two railway lines into London was under discussion. About 1832 it had been suggested that a line from Bristol (the Great Western Railway) should join the London and Birmingham Railway (the London and North-Western Line) near Kensal Green, and that a joint terminus should be placed at Euston Grove. Royal assent for this project was granted on August 31, 1835; but the proposed junction of the lines was abandoned, and a site for the terminus of the Great Western Railway was chosen adjoining the basin of Paddington Canal. This change of plan necessitated making a tunnel under the extreme north-western corner of the cemetery for the " London and Birmingham Railroad," and running a double line of rails for the Great Western Railway right across the fields south of the canal. On June 1, 1838, an experimental train carrying a large number of directors and their friends ran from Paddington to Maidenhead. A tiny Great Western train crossing Wormwood Scrubbs is included among the drawings on page 110; it is taken from the background of one of Henry Alken's pictures of the Hippodrome, in 1841.

A writer in the *Mirror* of April 28, 1838, speaking of the Birmingham railway which crosses " the Harrow

Road at the end of the village of Kensal Green,"
contrasts " the clear, yet chilling note of the Cemetery
Chapel bell with the almost undescribable noise of the
approaching engine and its train upon the railway
many yards beneath." He then turns to view a
glorious sunset in order to reflect " how puny are the
proudest triumphs of Art in comparison with the
Majesty of Nature."

From about 1836 to 1840 another railway line was
in course of construction from Willesden Junction
to what was known as the Basin of Kensington Canal.
Subsequently it was extended as far as Chelsea. This
line, called at first the Bristol, Birmingham and Thames
Junction Railway, is now known as the " West London
Junction Railway." It runs on an embankment along
the course of the boundary " rivulet," just within the
limits of Hammersmith parish. When this railway
was built part of the boundary stream was shifted
considerably to the east, so that it now runs in a straight
line along Latimer Road, St. Ann's Villas, and Holland
Villas Road. See map of 1841 on page 76. Two
openings were made in the embankment between
Willesden Junction and Uxbridge Road, at those
points where the old footpaths crossed from Wormwood Scrubbs to Notting Barns. For some un-
explained reason this was known as Punch's Line.

Houses stood in a solid line along the north side of
Uxbridge Road, and a second row, called Weller

Street, now Ladbroke Road, already contained some fair-sized houses with spacious gardens, when an attempt was made to establish a regular series of race-meetings and a training ground for horses " on the slopes of Notting Hill and the meadows west of Westbourne Grove." The race-course existed only from 1837 to 1841, but it determined the future aspect of the whole district.[6]

The Hippodrome, as it was called, seems to have been the individual enterprise of Mr. John Whyte of Brace Cottage, Notting Hill. He was the " projector," although he associated with himself other gentlemen interested in this form of British sport.[7] Negotiations were entered into with Mr. James Weller Ladbroke, who owned the property (see page 60), and nearly 200 acres of meadow land were surrounded by a wooden paling, seven feet high. This enclosure was bounded on the east by Portobello Lane, on the north by a line between the present Cornwall and Lancaster Roads, apparently along the course of the brook from Portobello Farm, on the west by the " public way " from Notting Barns, and on the south by the line of the present houses in Ladbroke Square, continued in Hanover Terrace.

6 *Old and New London*, by E. Walford, 1897, and Loftie's *Kensington Picturesque and Historical*, 1888. An excellent account of the Hippodrome appeared in the *Home Counties Magazine* for March 1912, written by T. Butler Cato.

7 Mr. John Whyte may have been related to Mr. James Christie Whyte, for in the *History of the British Turf* by that gentleman, frequent mention is made of the Hippodrome, Bayswater.

Three tracks, the steeplechase course, the race-course and the exercise course, encircled the enclosed ground. The chief public entrance was situated in Portobello Lane, at the point where Kensington Park Road now joins Pembridge Road, but subscribers and pedestrians might use a gate at the end of Ladbroke Terrace, corresponding with the present gate into Ladbroke Square Garden. The saddling paddock and stabling for seventy-five horses occupied the south-west corner of the ground. Here horses could be hired for riding, or hunters might be trained. Even " ponies and donkeys " were provided for the use of invalids and children. The space inside the race-courses was to be used for training purposes and riding exercise, or it might be let on non-racing days for revels and public amusements, such as archery, " shooting with bow and arrow at the popinjay, cricketting, etc., etc." In the centre the grassy mound "a sort of natural grand-stand," now crowned by St. John's Church, was railed in as a hill for pedestrians.[8]　See plan of Hippodrome Park, and the illustrations on pages 82 and 84.

The scheme was quaintly advertised in the *Sporting Magazine*, early in 1837, as "a racing emporium more extensive and attractive than Ascot or Epsom. . . . An enterprise which must prosper. . . . It is without competitor, and it is open to the fertilization

[8] It is often stated that the grand-stand occupied the summit of the hill. This is incorrect, though there may have been a refreshment buffet on that spot.

of many sources of profit. . . . A necessary of London life, of the absolute need of which we were not aware until the possession of it taught us its permanent value." It is stated to be eminently suitable for horse exercise especially " for females," for whom " it is without the danger or exposure of the parks," whilst the view from the centre is " as spacious and enchanting as that from Richmond Hill, and where almost the only thing that you cannot see is London."

In spite of opposition from all classes of residents in the locality, opposition based on various points of view, the project was successfully carried out. The opening ceremony on June 3, 1837, was attended by a brilliant company. There were " splendid equipages " and " gay marquees with all their flaunting accompaniments " ; but there were " no drinking or gambling booths," and the prices charged were strictly moderate. Prizes of £50 and £100 were competed for, and among the stewards were such " dandies " and leaders of society as Lord Chesterfield and Count D'Orsay.9

But the race-course had been planned without taking into consideration the footpath from north to south across the hill. It is evident that persons on foot avoided crossing " Kensington Potteries," and that

9 The Earl of Chesterfield owned a large racing stud, and was " a sincere and generous patron of British field sports." Alfred, Count D'Orsay, " the sportsman, the exquisite, the artist " had recently come to reside in Kensington and was sharing Gore House with " the gorgeous Lady Blessington."

the path over the hill was being more and more used.
About this time Pottery Lane was nicknamed Cut
Throat Lane, and it was possible, and sometimes
advisable, to hide in the ditch beside the track.
Indeed on a plan of 1837, preserved at the Kensington
Public Library,[10] it is stated that there was " no
thoroughfare " along the old public way to Notting
Barns Farm. The stoppage of the hill path was,
therefore, a serious matter, and already had been
strongly criticised.   Early on the morning of the day
of opening a party of the claimants for the right of
way, " with hatchets and saws " broke down the strong
paling at Ladbroke Place, where Ladbroke Square
crosses to Hanover Terrace, and fairly made their way
over the course.   Of the 12,000 to 14,000 persons
said to have been present on that day " some thousands
thus obtained gratuituous admission."   During the
following days Mr. Whyte tried to block the path
with loads of clay and turf.   So, on June 17th, local
inhabitants and labourers, led by the parochial surveyor
and accompanied by the police, cleared away these
obstructions and made wide apertures in the palissading
on the north as well as on the south side of the hill.
Before leaving they halted on the summit and gave
three deafening cheers for " the Parish of Kensington."

The footpath people " seem as a rule to have been
orderly enough, but gipsies, prigs (thieves) and

[10] Plan of the Hippodrome with the Intersecting and Surrounding Ancient
Footpaths and Roads.

hawkers did not neglect the opportunity of mingling with the nobility and gentry." [11] People using this path may be seen in the picture on page 84. A year later the pathway was fenced off by an iron railing, and, before the beginning of the season of 1839, Mr. Whyte gave up the contest and renounced the eastern half of " Hippodrome Park," thus releasing the disputed pathway.

Meanwhile local feeling ran very high. Petitions were prepared, and the whole question of the race-course was discussed by the Court of King's Bench and also before Parliament. In order to pacify opposition Mr. Whyte and his friends promised to reform certain evils on the premises, and to admit the public free on Sundays, and for a charge of twopence on certain holidays. This was considered by many as a desecration of the Sabbath. It was also pointed out that restrictions on gaming and drinking within the Hippodrome would not " prevent these evils in the purlieus . . . where already gambling houses, gin-shops, beerhouses, etc.," had increased in number ; and it was maintained that " the scum and offal of London assembled in the peaceful hamlet of Notting Hill." [12] As a result of the opposition the " Notting

[11] *Cremorne and the Later London Gardens*, by Warwick Wroth, 1907. Much interesting information from contemporary newspapers is preserved at the Public Library.

[12] In one of the *Brownrigg Papers* Douglas Jerrold ridicules the controversy, and the arguments brought forward, especially by the " Scholastic Establishments on Bayswater Road."

Hill Enclosure Bill" was quietly dropped in
September 1838, and, as already stated, a large piece
of the ground was given up. To make good this
deficiency the race-course was extended to the north-
west, just avoiding the footpath from Wormwood
Scrubbs, now St. Quintin Avenue. Hippodrome
Park thus became a huge bulb-shaped piece of land
which reached as far as Latimer Road, and the race-
course formed a loop on the western side of the training
ground. The arrangement will be best understood
by comparing the plan from the *Sporting News* with
the other on page 80.[13]

Portobello Lane was now connected by road with
a new entrance on the top of the hill. (Part of this road
was unearthed when a potato patch was made in
Ladbroke Square Garden in 1916.) In thus
" remodelling the Establishment " the old public way
from Notting Barns to Uxbridge Road seems to have
been cut through and done away with without any
protest.

But the question of the footpath over the hill was
only one of the difficulties which beset this " spirited
enterprise." The second race-meeting in June 1837
had to be suddenly relinquished on account of the
death of William IV. The sale of the royal stud
after the king's death was a serious blow to horse-
racing in general, but " Meetings " took place in

---

[13] Maps of the period represent the race-course as still running round the
enclosure. It would have been impossible to race over St. John's Hill.

September and November 1837 and at intervals during 1838. The Hippodrome was then renamed after the youthful Queen, and became Victoria Park, Bayswater. In order to pay for the extensive alterations the charges for admission had to be doubled. Pedestrians paid two and sixpence instead of one shilling, and a four-wheeled carriage cost ten shillings instead of five. A still more important objection to the place consisted in its deep, strong clay soil, and this drawback could not be got over. It was found that the training ground was only serviceable at certain periods of the year, and leading jockeys soon refused to ride.

In 1839 a group of foreign notabilities " condescended to visit the London Epsom." On this occasion a gold cup was offered by the Grand Duke of Russia. The attendance was very large. Only two race-meetings, however, are recorded in 1839, and already there were signs of failure. It is true that a successful steeplechase was held on June 2, 1841, commemorated in four large coloured prints by Henry Alken, Junior. Two of these prints are shown on page 88.14 But the end was approaching.

In May 1842, Mr. John Whyte, who had lost heavily over the scheme, announced that it would be impossible to run the races advertised for that year : the land having been taken possession of by mortgagees

---

14 These drawings have already been referred to on account of local details in the backgrounds. A set may be seen on the walls of the North Kensington Branch of the Public Library.

for building purposes. So the gates closed, and the summit of the hill for pedestrians quickly reverted to open country.[15]

For several years the piece of ground which had been added on in 1839 seems to have been used for "schooling hunters in jumping."[16] But to this day signs of the existence of the race-course are not wanting. Houses built in the village of Notting Hill between the years 1837 and 1841 have a large amount of stabling accommodation. Especially is this the case with the hostelries of the period ; "Prince Albert Tavern" at Notting Hill Gate, the "Ladbroke Arms" with its tall sign-post in Ladbroke Road, and others. St. John's on the Hill was long known as the Hippodrome Church, and a small turning connecting Portland Road with Pottery Lane is Hippodrome Place, though locally it is called "the Posteses," because, until recently, posts prevented the passing of vehicles. The mews off Hippodrome Place is still "the Racing Stables." But above all, there is the laying out of the whole area in one plan with a remarkable succession of fifteen or sixteen common gardens, the houses having also private gardens of their own : a beautiful example of an early Garden Town Planning Scheme.[17]

[15] See *Kensington, Notting Hill and Paddington,* by "An old Inhabitant," 1882.

[16] In *Old and New London,* Mr. E. Walford confuses these fields with Portobello Gardens. See Chapters IX and X

[17] Articles on this theme have appeared in the Press ; by Sir Alexander Binnie, in *The Times* ; by Frank E. Emmanuel in the *Architectural Review* October 1915, etc.

Before, however, considering the laying out of the Kensington Park Estate, it is necessary to describe the development of buildings along the Uxbridge Road during the first half of the nineteenth century.

CHAPTER V

THE PEACEFUL HAMLET OF NOTTING HILL

AT the beginning of the nineteenth century, the village of Kensington Gravel Pits extended for three-eighths of a mile along the North Highway. The name seems to have been used for scattered buildings as far east as Craven Terrace or Westbourne Green Lane, now called Queen's Road. When the pits disappeared the name was changed. No definite date can be given for this, but it is safe to say that, after 1840 the whole of the northern division of Kensington Parish was known as Notting Hill, and that the streets built near the turnpike both south and north of the main road were distinguished as Notting Hill Gate. They have continued so to the present day.

The boundary line between Kensington and Paddington, now so complicated and devious, a hundred years ago followed a fairly direct course at the edge of fields, and was indicated by a ditch. The tiny Boundary House opposite Kensington Palace

Gardens now covers the spot where the ditch emerged on the highway. (It has been a boot-shop since 1852.) See illustration on page 166. In 1760 a malt-house occupied the Kensington side of the boundary. At Michaelmas 1786 the Gravel Pits Estate, on which the malt-house stood, was let for eighty-one years at £38 per annum to Mr. John Silvester Dawson, with the covenant that two houses and outbuildings should be placed on it. (A Mr. Dawson had a house on Bayswater Road in 1790.) The buildings erected were Stormont House, with a courtyard entered by an iron gate (this was on the site of No. 1, Clanricarde Gardens). And an adjoining brewery called the " Sun," which apparently, from the Rate Books of 1812, was owned by Messrs. Trews & Co. Stormont House possessed a square staircase and good reception rooms. In the year 1808 it was a boarding school for young ladies kept by Miss Martha Tracey. She was there for nearly twenty years, but in 1827 Miss Elizabeth Tress seems to have taken over Miss Tracey's school.[1] By 1812 there was another school for young ladies nearby on the Uxbridge Road. This school, belonging to Miss Elizabeth Wilson, may have been at the " Academy " opposite Church Lane (see page 92), or it may have been at the Hermitage, Linden Grove, which a generation later was in use as a girls' school.

---

[1] Can there be any connection between Messrs. Trews of the Brewery Miss Tracey and Miss Tress ?

Miss Wilson's " Semenary " had a large garden, for the house and land were rated at £94.   See illustration on the opposite page.

The brewery built on the Gravel Pits Estate in 1800 had a short life.   Before 1820 its grounds were covered with small " tenements."   They formed a turning off the main road called Campden or Camden Place.   To this double row of dwellings short side streets were added, named Anderson's Cottages and Pitt's Cottages.   In 1838 Thomas Anderson was paying rates on nine houses.   From early days these cottages seem to have been overcrowded, and by the middle of the century Camden Place was a notorious rookery, known as " Little Hell."   Two ladies living at Kensington Palace, Miss Desborough and Lady Gray, started a Ragged School in Camden Place. This probably was held in Stormont House, as about the year 1860, Mr. Gray of 4, Linden Grove, nick-named " Gaffer Gray " (father of the Rev. E. Ker Gray, see page 220), used to hold penny readings in a large room in that house ; really two rooms thrown into one.   At the side of the house there was then the drying ground of a laundry.   In the eighteen sixties nursemaids, on their way to Kensington Gardens, would hurry their charges past the end of this evil alley.   (The writer well remembers the scene and the tiny shops and narrow pavement at this part of the high road.)   It was only in 1867, when Mr. Dawson's lease of the Charity Land fell in, that the whole place was cleared and Clanricarde Gardens was built on the site.

Across the road was the red brick wall surrounding the kitchen gardens belonging to the Palace. Somewhat further to the west the Mall ran at right angles from Uxbridge Road to Church Lane. It does so still. Here, besides one or two good houses, were some picturesque cottages known as Robinson's Rents, and a row of three houses built in the time of Queen Anne by a Mr. Callcott. (These houses were pulled down to make room for Essex Church.) John Callcott, the musician, and Sir Augustus Wall Callcott, the painter, inhabited these houses early in the nineteenth century, and it was largely through the influence of the Callcotts that a group of artists settled in this suburb of London. Thomas Webster, R.A., afterwards Sir Thomas Webster, lived in the Mall, and the Horsleys, the musician father and the artist son, were at No. 1, High Row, Church Lane. Delightful reminiscences of these artists with many details of local interest are given in the autobiographies of W. P. Frith, and J. C. Horsley.[2]

In the early years of the century a man named Mulready brought his family from Ireland and settled as a leather breeches maker in a shop between the Mall and Church Lane, close to the Gravel Pits Almshouses.

---

[2] *Autobiography of W. P. Frith*, 1887, 2 vols. *Leaves From a Life*, by Frith's daughter, Mrs. Panton, 1908, and *Recollections of a Royal Academician*, J. C. Horsley, 1903.

One of his sons was William Mulready, R.A. (1786–
1863).   On a moonlight night, about the year 1805,
as young Mulready was returning home along the
Bayswater Road from his art classes at Somerset
House, and had reached the end of Westbourne
Terrace, then a country lane, a man came out of the
shadow of a tree and, presenting a pistol, demanded
his watch and money.   Mulready did not possess a
watch but gave up the silver in his pockets.   On
reaching home he drew the man's face from memory,
and took the drawing to the police at Bow Street.   A
fortnight later he was called upon to identify the thief
in a sailor who had been arrested for the murder of
the toll-keeper at Southwark Bridge.   At the age of
seventeen Wm. Mulready married a sister of John
Varley the artist.   In 1809 the young pair were living
in Robinson's Rents, but in 1828, on the advice of
Sir A. W. Callcott, Mulready moved to No. 1, Linden
Grove, a charming, low house with a good garden at
the far end of a quiet lane.   This house is now
represented by No. 42, Linden Gardens.   There
were four sons, Paul, Michael, William (see page
62) and John, all of whom eventually gave drawing
lessons.   In Linden Grove, in 1840, Mulready
designed the penny postage envelope for Sir Rowland
Hill, and he died there in 1863.   (After his death the
house was occupied by Alfred Wigan the actor, and
it was used for the wedding reception of Sir Henry
Irving.)   Two paintings of the Mall, Kensington

Gravel Pits, by W. Mulready, dated 1812 and 1813, are at the Victoria and Albert Museum.

The secluded and unlighted lane of Linden Grove also contained the Hermitage, already mentioned, and a few other two-storied houses, the largest of which was inhabited in 1827 by Thomas Allason, Esq. It is said that much house property between the Marble Arch and Notting Hill was built by this well-known architect. Linden Lodge or Linden Grove House was on the west side of the lane. At one time this was the home of one of the Drummonds, bankers. It was taken by Thomas Creswick, R.A., the landscape artist, in 1836. There this kindhearted and jovial man and his sweet wife gave charming dances for the children of their artist friends. A small oil-painting of the house was made by Thomas Creswick for Mr. Thomas Allason. A copy by Mr. Herbert Jones hangs at the Public Library, Kensington. It is said that the Allasons lived there after Creswick's death in 1869. Through the marriage of Miss Louisa Creswick Allason the property passed into the hands of Arthur Bull, architect, and his brother a surveyor. They pulled down " the old house, filled up the lake, and built Linden Gardens and the shops in front on the site of the house, meadow and gardens. The Metropolitan Railway paid a considerable sum for permission to run under the estate." [3] George

3 *Some Recollections of Bayswater, Fifty Years Ago,* by the Rt. Hon. Sir W. Bull, M.P., in *Bayswater Chronicle,* August 4, 1923.

Grindle, Esq., was the last occupant, and the iron gates into Linden Gardens represent the gates into his drive.

The regular village of Notting Hill seems to have begun west of the Mall and Linden Grove. In 1840 it was still very countrified, with more cows than people, and with chickens scuttling across the road. There were few shops, and those were very small. Only two " were above one story high ; " one story over the shop. A graphic description of the place is given in a pamphlet by " An Old Inhabitant " who came into the neighbourhood in the year 1844[4]. The following account is chiefly built up from his recollections, but valuable manuscript notes collected by Mr. T. Butler Cato have also been made use of, and other details are added from talks with local residents. The buildings mentioned can be fairly well traced on the maps in this book, but at the Public Library the actual number of houses and many other details may be discovered from the quaint plans in a book entitled *Diagram of the Parish of St. Mary's, Kensington, for the Year* 1846.

The Happy Family who inhabited the village about 1844 included Mr. Fenn the tailor, who lived at the south-west corner of Linden Grove, and Mr. Brewer,

[4] *Kensington, Notting Hill and Paddington,* by " An Old Inhabitant," 1882. This pamphlet may be seen at the Public Library in Ladbroke Grove.

who transacted the largest business of the village in the grocery, cheesemongery, and corn-dealing line. There was a candle-maker, who might be seen making candles in his cellar. His shop was reached up four stone steps. And there was a butcher's shop, owned by a man named Price, which was entered by a gate at the top of three steps. When Mr. John Short came to see the place in 1858, with a view to taking it, he found Mr. Price seated on the steps fast asleep, with a pipe in his mouth. (That shop has developed into a very large business.) Another of the villagers in the forties was a Mr. Burden, rag and bottle merchant, who was an orator and a great man on the Kensington Vestry ; he was also a proprietor of Bayswater omnibuses. His wife kept a green-grocer's shop. Poor woman, she was of such proportions that when she died the coffin had to be lowered by ropes from the bedroom window. Most of these shops were situated in what had been Greyhound Row between the Mall and Silver Street, the name then given to Church Lane.

The Swan Inn, with its trough and signpost, standing back from the road at the corner of Silver Street, which is seen in the drawing of the second Notting Hill Toll Gate (see page 96), was faced at the opposite corner by a little butcher's shop, and next to this was a brush shop, the proprietor of which, a most intelligent man, was a Chartist, and a great friend of Fergus O'Connor. Close to " Brewer's

Cottages," in what he loved to call " Pittman's Corner,"
Mr. Matthew Pittman, stationer and newsagent was
born, about the year 1842, and here he spent almost
the whole of a fairly long life.   Here too stood the
Hoop Inn, projecting at an angle still occupied by
licensed premises.   Behind the houses on this south
side of the road was   a brickfield owned by a
Mr. Clutterbuck, and it was here that Mr. Ernest
Swain, the house agent, remembered bonfires being
lighted and guys burnt in the early fifties.

In 1844 shop windows were of common glass and
the shops were lighted with oil lamps or candles.   A
crowd assembled night after night to see the illumina-
tion when the first shop was lighted with gas.   This
was Mr. King's Italian warehouse, one of the four
shops built about 1844 over the front garden of " Elm
Grove," a later name for the " Academy."

The village pump stood on the site of the Metropolitan Railway Station.   When a proposal was made
that it should be removed, public " Indignation "
meetings were held and fierce threats were made of
legal proceedings.   Finally a tap supplying Water
Company's water was placed a few yards further to
the west.   For years this tap existed in front of No. 71
or 73, High Street.   The " Old Inhabitant " suggests
that an inscription might be placed on one or other of
these houses with the words : " Here stood the Village
Pump."   He also suggests that a tablet might mark
the position of the Village Pound, which harboured

" many a disconsolate donkey, horse or goat." This Pound occupied the east corner of Johnson Street on Uxbridge Road. The house afterwards built on this spot was known as " Pound House," but the name is not to be seen on the shop opposite the Coronet Theatre. Adjoining the Pound was a blacksmith's forge with a low gate, across which boys could watch the smiths at work and the fascinating sparks struck from the anvil. Uxbridge Street lay behind the houses on this side of the way, and was connected with the high road by Turnpike Farm Street, now Farmer Street, and Johnson Street which crossed what had been Johnson's Brick Fields. Semi-rural dwellings may still be traced in this quarter, but relics of the past are fast disappearing.

The Notting Hill Toll Gate crossed the high-road close to the village pump. The picture of the gate as it appeared between about 1835 and 1856, on page 96, is adapted from a well-known drawing which hangs in Kensington Public Library. This gate was replaced " in the fifties " by a toll-house in the middle of the road at the end of Portobello Lane, and gates crossed the road diagonally from No. 79, High Street, as shown on page 124. Bars or subsidiary gates were placed across turnings off the high-road in order that the payment of tolls should not be avoided. One bar was in Silver Street, opposite Campden Street, and others at Portobello Lane, now Pembridge Road, at Addison Road and at Norland Road. Some of

these bars were removed earlier than others, but all
the remaining gates and bars were done away with
by Act of Parliament on July 1, 1864. Old inhabitants of Notting Hill can remember the public
rejoicings and the procession of vehicles which passed
through the gates when they were opened at midnight
on that day. The last people to drive through Notting
Hill Gate were Mr. and Mrs. Randall of 4, Lansdowne
Crescent.

But to return to the north side of the road. The
shops west of Linden Grove were in Kensington
Terrace and Elm Place. The numbering of the
houses in these short terraces was most erratic and
far from consecutive. The late eighteenth century
house with two bays (see page 58), was reckoned as
part of Elm Place. It has a quaint circular staircase
and the doors are curved. In one room is a fireplace
with a coat of arms belonging to the Pilkington
family. Part of it is now used as the West London
Branch of the Society for Teaching the Blind.5 It
is known as Vestris House because Lucia Elizabetta
Bartolozzi, Madam Vestris (a granddaughter of the
famous engraver), " that most incomparable of singing
actresses," at one time lived here. Madam Vestris,
the first woman to become the lessee and manager
of a theatre, was born in 1797. In 1838 she was

5 The Notting Hill Institute for the Blind began about 1876 in two
shops in St. John's Place (Penzance Place), Norlands. In 1880 it was
reconstituted and renamed, but it has been until recently an entirely
Kensington Charity.

married at Kensington Church to the actor, Charles
James Matthews, and in 1856 she died. Her portrait
appears on page 58. Another house, which was
demolished when the Metropolitan Railway was made,
was known as the Vicarage. It was well-built and
had a fine staircase, but was inhabited in the eighteen-
sixties by the family of a postman named Brownridge.

Beyond Elm Cottages, now represented by Pembridge Gardens, a farm occupied the site of the station
of the " Tube " or Central London Railway. (Was
it Turnpike Farm ?) In 1840 this property was
owned by John Hall, Esq., probably a son of
Christopher Hall (see page 62), but before 1840 the
farm had been replaced by a house known as Elm
Lodge. The charming garden and orchard of this
house were bounded on the west by the hedgerows
of Portobello Lane, and the fruit was often stolen.
Elm Lodge was inhabited by the Rev. J. W. Buckley
and his family.[6] Mr. Horsley, in his Recollections,
tells how " Willy Buckley " watched all night in the
garden, and caught a man with a sack stealing apples ;
how he pushed the man before him through the house,
the paved yard and entrance gate, without waking the
family, and finally handed him over to one of the
" newly-invented constables " whom he found asleep
" leaning against one of the newly-invented lamp-
posts." In 1844 Elm Lodge was the residence of

---

[6] One son became Sir Henry Buckley, the judge ; and a daughter,
Arabella Buckley, is well known as a writer of excellent scientific books.

the Rev. Mr. Holloway, minister of Percy Chapel, Fitzroy Square. After his death it was occupied by the Rev. Mr. Gordon, a Presbyterian minister who for some years held services in a building attached to his house. The " Devonshire Arms " was afterwards built on part of the Elm Lodge grounds.

The group of " Elms " : Elm Place, Elm Grove, Elm Cottages and Elm Lodge, have disappeared with the elm trees. Mulberry Walk is Palace Gardens Mews, and the limes of Linden Place on the south side of the main road, and Linden Grove on the north side, are now only recalled by the collection of houses comprised in Linden Gardens.

The junction of Weller Street, now Ladbroke Road, and Portobello Lane, now Pembridge Road, was widened to accommodate the entrance to the Hippodrome. The " Prince Albert Arms " and the " Hope Brewery " were placed just outside the gates. It is at this corner that a portion of the old-world village can be seen practically in its original state. Probably few residents in the neighbourhood know of the existence of the quaint lane called Bulmer Place, with its tiny cottages and gay front gardens. It is reached by a covered passage at each end. The local fire-engine was kept in " Tucker's Shed " at the upper end of Ladbroke Road.[7] Later on, when firemen ceased to be a voluntary body, a fire station was built

---

[7] Mr. Noakes, a gardener, foreman of the local firemen, lost his life at a disastrous fire in Archer Street in the year 1869.

further down the road next door to the police station, which was just above the present palatial erection.

The " Coach and Horses," No. 108, High Street, was still a small and primitive tavern. The proprietor, Mr. Drinkwater, got into trouble for selling spirits on the Hippodrome grounds without a sufficient license, but the tavern itself was reputed to be quiet and respectable, instead of being a refuge for highwaymen as of old. It was rebuilt in 1863. In 1870 Mrs. Drinkwater was in possession, and this was the office for coaches to Hillingdon and Hayes, and for omnibuses to Hanwell. Somewhere between the years 1810 and 1825 Montpelier House, Nos. 128 to 130, High Street (see illustration on page 58), became the residence of Joseph Hume, F.R.S., sometime surgeon in the East India Company, one of the leaders of the Radical Party in Parliament. Philosophic and literary discussions must also have taken place here, for, before 1830, Charles Lamb and his friends Hazlitt, the essayist, and Godwin, the philosopher, are said to have been constant guests at this house. Joseph Hume married the daughter of a wealthy East India proprietor, and had six children. (Mrs. Augusta Webster, poetess and social worker in Kensington, was a granddaughter.) He died in 1855 four years before Peter Alfred Taylor, M.P., came to live at Aubrey House ; but Joseph Hume had been closely connected with P. A. Taylor the elder, in the Corn Law agitation of the eighteen-forties.

Almost next door was the " Plough," equally removed in character both from the original inn on the North Highway, and the large modern building at 144, High Street. The map of 1831, on page 100, shows that the ground at the back of the " Plough " was arranged as a tea garden. Bayswater abounded in public open-air resorts, but this seems to have been the only place of the kind in Notting Hill. These pleasure grounds had none of " the romantic associations and historic dignity " of such eighteenth century gardens as Vauxhall or Ranelagh. They were used by " the lower orders." In the tavern garden a man might sit with a friend, or whole families might assemble to take a modest repast. According to a London Guide of 1846, in such places the amusements were innocent, the indulgence temperate, and a suitable mixture of female society rendered them both gay and pleasant.[8]

Between the " Plough " and Ladbroke Terrace stood a large white house in a garden surrounded by a high wall overhung with ivy, against which, about the year 1850, an old woman used to sit selling apples. Bellvue House was inhabited by a Dr. Barnes, but by 1870 it had disappeared.

Across the main road the winding pathway of Plough Lane climbed the hill. Plough Lane ended in

[8] *Cremorne, and the later London Gardens,* by Warwick Wroth, 1907. An excellent account of such tea gardens is given by Charles Dickens in *Sketches by Boz,* under the heading London Recreations.

Campden Passage, a footpath between the premises of the two water companies. At the corner (now occupied by Messrs. Pearson's ironmongery stores), was a dairy farm called Notting Hill Dairy, locally known as " Shoesmith's " ; and a little way up the hill was a good old house which seems to have ended its career as a laundry. Below this house, at the north-west corner of Plough Lane, Mr. R. T. Swain, in 1848, built a cottage to which he brought his young family from a house in Shepherd's Bush. Here, in 1849, he established the business of auctioneer and house agent, a business which is still carried on in Notting Hill Gate. The Lodge, as it was called, had a large garden full of fruit trees and roses, but, although it was so near to the waterworks, and built for his own use by a house agent, all water needed for domestic or garden purposes had to be fetched from a pump in the main road. The Lodge was demolished in 1870 to make way for the much-needed thoroughfare of Campden Hill Road.

The village of Notting Hill ended at Ladbroke Terrace, as High Street, Notting Hill Gate, ends there still. But building was being carried further west. By 1824 Mr. Christopher Hall had given up Notting Hill Farm, rated at £520, though probably property at Notting Hill Gate was held by the family. A man named Paul Turley purchased Mr. Hall's farm—and for building purposes. The farm-house was pulled down and a terrace of little houses facing east, Nos. 11 to 19, Ladbroke Grove, was built. According to one of the leases these houses appear to have been inhabited by the year 1825. Before 1827 a most charming row of houses on the main road, known as Notting Hill Terrace, now forming part of Holland Park Avenue, extended almost as far as Ladbroke Place, now Ladbroke Grove. In 1827 Mr. Turley's name disappears, and it is the ground landlord, Mr. James Weller Ladbroke, who pays the rates on the Notting Hill Farm property.

Notting Hill Terrace was faced on the south side of the road by Notting Hill Square and certain villa residences. Hanson's or Notting Hill Square, now Campden Hill Square, was commenced between 1823 and 1825 on part of the Notting Hill House estate. It was built by Mr. Joshua Flesher Hanson, the purchaser of Notting Hill House ; first the houses on the east then those on the north, and lastly those on the west side.9 A delightful picture of the scene, as it appeared in 1834, three years before the making of the race-course, is provided in the comic drawing, " The Flight of the Hunted Tailor of Notting Hill," by Henry Alken, Junior, shown opposite. (Mr. Alken's pictures of the steeplechase, in 1841, have already been mentioned.) The legend runs that

9 See *Aubrey House*, by F. M. Gladstone, 1922. Mr. Lloyd Sanders in *Old Kew, Chiswick and Kensington*, antedates this square. Mr. J. F. Hanson also built Regency Square, Brighton, and some of the houses in Hyde Park Gate, S.W.

one Sunday morning a tailor went out to shoot birds. In doing this he unfortunately broke a window, besides breaking the Sabbath. For these misdemeanours he is shown in the picture being chased by the populace past the houses of Notting Hill Terrace. A country road, evidently Ladbroke Grove, joins the thoroughfare, St. John's Hill appears in the distance, and a man in the foreground is seen climbing over the palings of the square garden.

Each map or plan of the forties and fifties gives variations in the naming of the new streets, and the complication of small " terraces " and " places " is most confusing.   It is a matter for thankfulness that they are all now included in Holland Park Avenue. A series of mews runs behind all the terraces on the north side of the road, showing how necessary it was at this period to own a private vehicle.   Boyne Terrace and Grove Terrace lay west of Ladbroke Grove. See map on page 100.   For awhile the south end of Lansdowne Road was called Great Circus Street or Liddiard's Road, and Clarendon Road was Park Street.   Portland Road, the road to the Hippodrome stables, was chiefly known as Norland or Hippodrome Lane.   Beyond Pottery Lane was the Norland Nursery, covering what had formerly been a large pond.   On this nursery ground the three houses of Castle Terrace were placed in 1861.   Views of this part of the road are shown, page 116,[10] but before 1857, the date of these

[10] These engravings were published in a booklet containing six views.

quaint engravings, shops had been added over the front
gardens of many of these houses. The grounds of
Holland House then reached down to Uxbridge Road,
and were enclosed by a rustic paling, but a year or
two later thirty-seven acres of the estate were bought
by the Messrs. Radford Brothers, and the twin rows
of large houses known as Holland Park were commenced on land formerly occupied by oaks and may-
trees.[11]

The map on page 120, shows the position of Norland
Terrace and Norland Place, rows of houses facing
the high road, separated by Norland Square. This
square was built between 1837 and 1846 on part
of the site of Norland House and its walled-in grounds.
Norland Place was divided by Addison Road North
(since 1915 called Addison Avenue). At the north
end of this attractive road the church of St. James's,
Norland, was placed in 1845, the architect being
Mr. Lewis Vulliamy, a son of the Benjamin Vulliamy
who had sunk the famous overflowing well nearly
fifty years earlier. See illustration on page 110.
Lewis Vulliamy had also been the architect of
St. Barnabas, Addison Road, a church known as
Kensington Chapel when built in 1827. The name
of Addison is, of course, derived from Joseph Addison,
the writer, who married the widow of the sixth Lord
Holland. He died in 1719. Two small terraces,
some cottages and stables and the coaching inn, the

[11] *Kenna's Kingdom*, by R. Weir Brown, 1881.

Duke of Clarence, stood beyond Addison Road on the
south side of the way, faced by Norland or Royal
Crescent.   Both names were used when the crescent
was being built in 1846.   See illustration on page 110.
Between Royal Crescent and Norland Road the main
road turns slightly to the north, and here were placed
the twelve little houses of Union Terrace.

The boundary " rivulet " already ran in a sewer
under Royal Crescent Garden (see page 80), and
Norland Road had become the western boundary of
the parish.   Norland Market, the outstanding feature
of Norland Road, dates from the time when there
were few local shops, for it must be remembered
that the buildings along Uxbridge Road were all
private residences.   A row of small houses on the east
side of Norland Road bears on its central pediment
" Shepherd's Bush and Norland Market."   It is said
that " The Market " differs from other street markets
in that the stall-holders have no stands elsewhere.
With the passage of years, and the development
immediately to the north of a " deplorable quarter,"
this market has changed greatly, but, to those who are
familiar with the scene, Mr. Harold Begbie's description in *Broken Earthenware*, Chapter I, appears
unnecessarily lurid.

By 1844, the southern part of " Norlands " or
Norland Town had been laid out practically in its
present shape, although only a few houses were built
along the various roads.   Compare the difference in

this part between the map of 1841 (page 76), and the map of 1850 (page 120). Almost every house stood in its own garden. Princes Place and the other small turnings off Queen's Road, now Queensdale Road, St. Ann's Villas and Darnley Street belong to this period. The brick houses with charming diagonal work and stone facings in St. Ann's Villas were long known as the Red Villas. A tablet let into the front wall of Nos. 1 and 2, St. James's Square, announces that the first stone of this square was laid on November 1, 1847, therefore more than two years after the church was completed. For some years after 1847 there were no houses on the north side of the square : the garden abutted on open ground.

St. Catherine's Road, now Wilsham Street, as late as 1850 was nothing but a footpath leading from the south end of Latymer Road to Pottery Lane ; one small terrace of houses, Cobden Terrace, stood at its western end. William Street, now Kenley Street, then a row of small semi-rural houses with long front gardens, was the only road north of St. James's Square. Well on into the sixties it was inhabited by the families of City clerks. A narrow footbridge across a small stream, which seems to have been connected with the open sewer in Norland Lane, gave access to the allotment gardens and marshy land which separated William Street from the Norland Pottery Works and the notorious colony of pig-keepers already described.

CHAPTER VI

KENSINGTON PARK

As buildings increase the story necessarily becomes more local. It is also impossible to avoid overlapping of dates. This chapter begins with the time when Mr. John Whyte resigned the eastern half of the Hippodrome with the footpath over the hill, and Mr. James Weller Ladbroke, the ground landlord, let this piece of land to a Mr. Jacob Connop. The date of this transaction was October 5, 1840. The plan, originally attached to the deed,[1] has already been mentioned as giving the names of fields. Mr. Connop no doubt had advanced money to Mr. Whyte, for, besides taking part of the race-course off his hands, Mr. Connop became " proprietor " of the race-course, when, in May 1842, the announcement was made that the land had been taken possession of by mortagees for building purposes.

Already, before the Hippodrome was closed, Messrs Connop and Duncan had started building operations. Kensington Park Villas, a terrace of small houses near the public entrance, houses now incor-

[1] This plan is now owned by Dr. Friend of St. Stephen's Crescent.

porated into Kensington Park Road, were amongst the earliest to be built.   By 1844 six large detached houses higher up the new road, the Swiss Villa, now No. 48, and its companions, the Italian, the Norman, the Elizabethan, etc., were in course of construction. The plans for these beautiful villas were exhibited at the Royal Academy.   A row of houses was also commenced to face "Mr. Ladbroke's common garden," these being No. 20 and Nos. 23 to 47, Ladbroke Square.   Perhaps the suburb was too remote from London for such large houses to be let readily.   Whatever the reason, in February and again in May 1845, Mr. Jacob Connop appeared before the Insolvent Debtor's Court, and "an assignee was appointed to carry the works to a conclusion."   The liabilities of Messrs' Connop and Duncan were then stated to be between £60,000 and £70,000.

The original area of the Hippodrome having reverted to the ground landlord, Mr. J. W. Ladbroke, he entrusted the planning of the whole estate to Mr. Thomas Allom, architectural artist.   "Kensington Park" was chosen as the name, and it was stipulated that houses put up by purchasers of building plots should be in accordance with the general scheme.   A large and elaborate plan of Kensington Park Estate is given in E. Daw's map of Kensington, 1846, a copy of which may be seen at the Public Library, but that shown on Wyld's map of 1850, on page 120, is sufficiently clear.   A comparison with the more modern conditions shown in the map on page xiv, and all maps after 1850 proves that much of the original design has been carried out, and, indeed, in the southern half of the estate the resemblance is remarkably close. A wide tree-lined avenue, now Ladbroke Grove, cuts through a series of roads curving round the hill, the culminating point being a House of God. As first planned these roads were confined within the limits of the estate, but this part of the scheme was altered, and the crescents were extended to the east across Portobello Lane, thus forming a connection with building which was in progress in Bayswater and the nearer parts of Paddington. In the northern half, instead of detached and semi-detached villas, solid rows of houses were built. But the western border remained self-contained, and between Clarendon Road and Notting Dale there is a group of blind alleys which are a source of annoyance to the present day. On the south Mr. Ladbroke had set aside nearly seven acres to form a pleasure ground, the largest common garden in London, and a road along the side of the square, called Ladbroke Road until that name was given to Weller Street, connected Kensington Park Villas with Ladbroke Terrace and Ladbroke Place. Another large space, which was to be called either Beaufort or Lansdowne Square, was afterwards cut across by the houses of Stanley Gardens.

Up to this period there had been no church in the parish of Kensington north of the main road.

Mr. Robert Roy, of Messrs. Blunt, Roy and Johnson, purchased and presented a site on the top of the " Hill for Pedestrians " for an Early English stone church, designed by Messrs. Stevens and Alexander, to accommodate fifteen hundred worshippers. The builder was Mr. Hicks. As too much stone and brick had been estimated for, the Vicarage and the adjoining house were built of the extra stone and Nos. 3 and 4, Ladbroke Mount, now Lansdowne Crescent, of the extra brick. At first " St. John the Evangelist " stood alone " in the hay-fields." See pictures on page 124, and 166. When viewed from Crescent Street or from Ladbroke Grove the church now is embedded among trees on the hill-top. Although " erected before Gothic details were fully understood . . . it is one of the best situated and best designed churches in the parish." [2]

St. John's was consecrated on January 29, 1845, six months before the smaller church of St. James's Norland. The parochial districts given to these two churches included the whole area of Notting Hill : one parish extended from the top of Campden Hill to Kensal Green, the other parish covered Norland Town. The first incumbent of St. John's, the Rev. William Holdsworth, 1845 to 1853, was succeeded by the Rev. E. Proctor Dennis who died

[2] *Kensington Picturesque and Historical,* by the Rev. W. J. Loftie, 1888. See also *The Church Index,* by William Pepperell, 1871. The writer well remembers, when a child, watching the enormous gilt weathercock being lowered to the ground in the arms of a steeple-jack.

of cholera in 1854, but from 1855 to 1878 the Rev. John Philip Gell presided over the parish. (Mrs. Gell was the only child of Sir John Franklin ; this fact accounts for the vertebræ of an Arctic whale which lay for many years in the Vicarage garden.) Mr. Gell was followed by the Rev. Crauford Tait, whose lamented death took place three months after his institution. (It is said that the double gates leading to the Vicarage were made so that the archiepiscopal carriage might drive in.)

The houses built before 1850 are clearly marked in the map on page 120. Upper Lansdowne Terrace, now Nos. 67–77, Ladbroke Grove, occupies the actual summit of the hill ninety-nine feet above sea-level. It has been asserted that the hill-top was originally somewhat further to the south, and that it was reduced by ten feet in order to level the road facing the church : Kensington Park Gardens. This seems unlikely. When first built the view from Upper Lansdowne Terrace must have differed little from that described by Thomas Faulkner in 1820. At the present time " from the housetops a splendid panorama may be enjoyed up the Thames Valley . . . as far, on a clear day, as Windsor Castle . . . while Citywards, one may discern St. Paul's Cathedral and Westminster Abbey." 3 The chief names of these early roads are Ladbroke, which explains itself,

3 *An Early Garden Town Planning Scheme in London*, by Frank E. Emanuel in *Architectural Review*, October 1915.

Clarendon, probably from the Earl of Clarendon who
figured in the Crimean War, and Lansdowne, either
from the noted politician of that name, or because the
Dowager Marchioness of Lansdowne, Mistress of the
Robes to Queen Victoria at the commencement of her
reign, was then living on the summit of Campden
Hill. Upper Lansdowne Terrace was faced by a
row of houses called Stanley Villas, now Nos. 42 to
58, Ladbroke Grove ; 42 and 44, Ladbroke Grove
was a single house with a central tower. There is a
tradition, probably inaccurate, that this house was
built by Mr. Ladbroke for his own use and was called
the Manor House. It is also said that, when King
Edward VII was a child, his parents were recommended
by their physician to send him to Notting Hill for
the benefit of his health, and that one of these villas
was prepared for him but was not used. Another
version relates that the then Prince of Wales, when
about nine years of age, spent some months in the
Manor House under the care of a medical man. The
story gains some degree of probability from the fact
that Sir James Clarke, the well-known physician who
advised Queen Victoria to go to the neighbourhood
of Braemar, recommended Ladbroke Square as the
healthiest place in London to another patient who con‧
sulted him on where to take a house. This lady bought
Hanover Lodge, Hanover Terrace, built in 1837 or
1839, and her descendants have lived there ever since.

The Hippodrome enclosure, as already stated,

NORTH KENSINGTON, 1922.

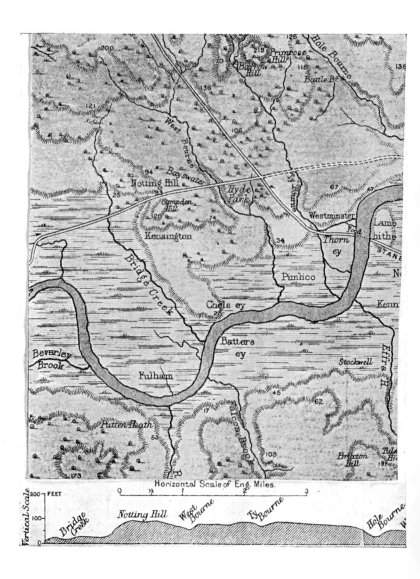

THE THAMES VALLEY IN ROMAN DAYS.

NOTTING BARNS FARM, ABOUT 1830.

Adapted by E. Woolmer from an old drawing.

THE PLOUGH, KENSAL GREEN.

(Is supposed to have been built about A.D. 1500, and remarkable for having been the favourite retreat of the celebrated Morland.)
By Mary and Robert Banks.

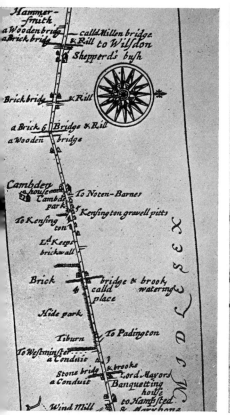

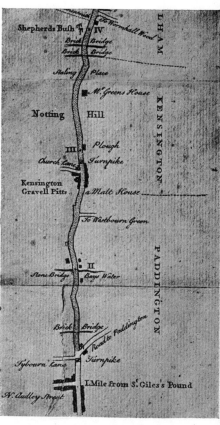

OM "BRITANNIA," BY JOHN OGILVY, 1675.

y republished by the Topographical Society, 1911, as "Roads Out of London."

FROM "A PLAN OF THE GREAT ROAD FROM TYBOURN TO UXBRIDGE."

Surveyed by Leddiard, Junr., 1769.

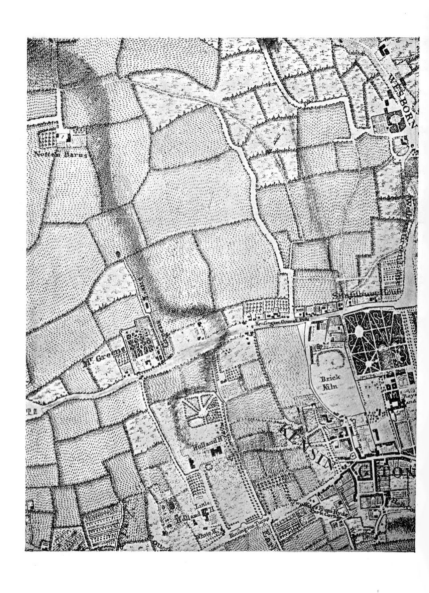

FROM "ENVIRONS OF LONDON," BY JOHN ROCQUE, 1741–1745.

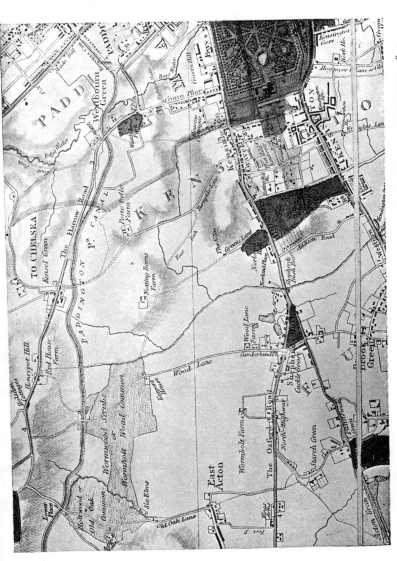

A NEW TOPOGRAPHICAL MAP OF THE COUNTRY IN THE VICINITY OF LONDON, JAMES WYLD, 1833.

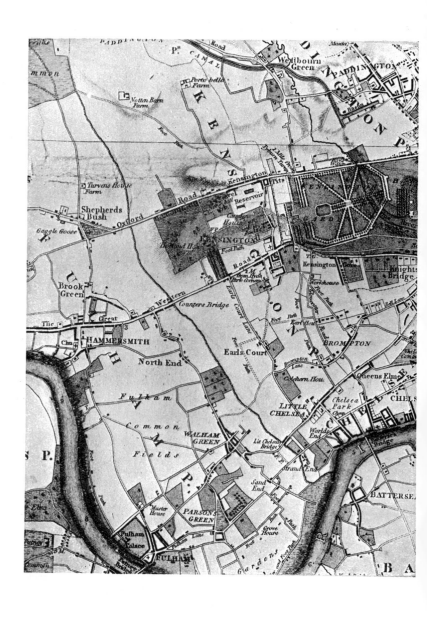

FROM "MAP OF COUNTRY IN THE VICINITY OF LONDON," W. FADON, 1810.

"NOTTING HILL TOLL GATE," LOOKING WEST.
From water-colour drawing by Paul Sandby, R.A., 1793.

Montpelier House
1776.

Madame Vestris
as Apollo.
1797 - 1856.

Kensington
Institute for
The Blind.
2. Elm Place 1790.

Some
18th Century Buildings
in
Notting Hill Gate

At The
Corner of Church Street

The Gravel Pits Almshouses.   Taken Down. 1821

Elm Grove, or
The Academy
Ethel Woolmer 1921

DRAWINGS BY MISS WOOLMER.

"NOTTING HILL FARM." OIL PAINTING ASCRIBED TO MULREADY, JUNR.

At Kensington Public Library.

ADAPTED FROM A DRAWING IN "OLD AND NEW LONDON" BY E. WOOLMER.

THE TILE KILN, 1824.

From an original sepia drawing.

OPENING OF THE PADDINGTON CANAL.

A view from the left of the first bridge at Paddington with the company and barges, on the
10th July, 1801.

(*Crace Collection, British Museum.*)

THE CANAL IN 1804.

(*Crace Collection, British Museum.*)

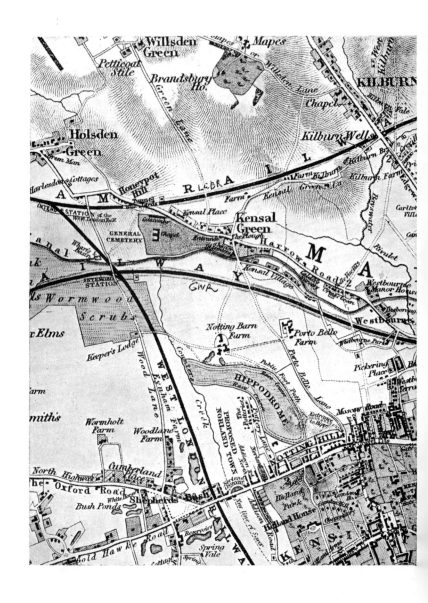

FROM "MAP OF KENSINGTON," B. R. DAVIES, 1841.

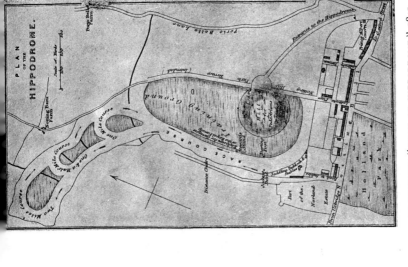

AN ALTERED "PLAN OF HIPPODROME," 1841.

From the Sporting Review.

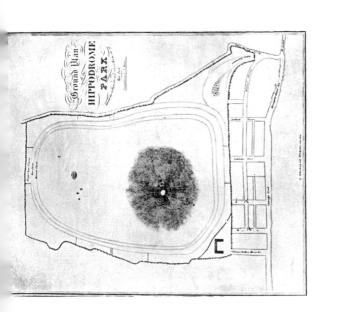

GROUND PLAN FROM PROSPECTUS OF HIPPODROME PARK, 1837.

THE HIPPODROME, 1838.

THE HIPPODROME, ABOUT 1840.

covered nearly 200 acres of land. A large part
of the central portion known as the Hundred Acre
Estate was bought from Mr. Ladbroke by Mr.
Charles Henry Blake, whose descendants still hold
property in the district. It was to Mr. Blake
that Mr. Thomas Allom dedicated the fine lithographic view of Kensington Park Gardens, shown on
page 128. Sixteen houses in the Gardens are due
to Mr. Blake, and were sold by him to Mr. George
Dodd in 1859 and 1860. The earliest houses in
Kensington Park Gardens were numbers 1, 2, 3, 5,
and 8. These were erected by Mr. William Henry
Drew, who also built and owned houses in Ladbroke
Road and Ladbroke Terrace. Mr. Drew parted with
his houses in Kensington Park Gardens in 1859–1860,
and many other houses changed hands about that
time. By 1858 the remaining houses of Ladbroke
Square (see page 112), and the houses on both sides
of Kensington Park Gardens were inhabited. Much
of the actual building of the roads between Notting
Hill Gate and Arundel Gardens was carried out by
Mr. John Dewdney Cowland and Mr. William
Wheeler. The site of Mr. Wheeler's own house
and grounds is partly covered by Victoria Gardens,
Ladbroke Road.4

4 See *Kensington News*, March 16, 1917. Valuable information has been
drawn from a letter to Mr. F. L. Emanuel from Mr. C. S. Baldwin, dated
September 1911. Mr. Baldwin helped his father-in-law Mr. Stevens in
building some of Mr. Blake's houses. The carpenter who worked for
Messrs. Stevens and Baldwin possessed the delightful name of Onisiphorus
Cox. He died in 1886 at the age of 84.

In November 1855, ten years after St. John's Church was opened, the foundation stone of St. Peter's, Bayswater, was laid. The church was consecrated in January 1857. St. Peter's is "an Italian basilica with a good colonnade of the Corinthian order." Mr. Thomas Allom made designs for this church, but the architect appears to have been " Mr. Hallam, a young practitioner of great promise who died early." The tower over the façade groups well with the surrounding houses (see illustration on page 166), and when viewed from the hollow in Portobello Road is said to resemble a scene in Portugal. The original ground plan was a parallelogram, with the present galleries extending to the east wall in which were three windows. Two of these windows have been placed in the west gallery. In 1878 it was decided to construct a chancel and apse, but the year 1887 had arrived before the "noble apsidal sanctuary" was completed, chiefly from the designs of Sir Charles Barry.[5] On the south wall of the nave is a marble memorial to the wife of the first rector, the Rev. F. H. Addams. She died in 1860 while nursing her five children with scarlet fever. (The ravages of scarlet fever was a tragedy which occurred in other houses in the district at this period, for extraordinarily little was known about the spread of infectious disease.) It is not, however, the first rector, but the Rev. John

[5] An interesting account of the church is given in *St. Peter's Year Book* for 1913. See also, *The Church Index*, by Rev. William Pepperell, 1872.

Robbins, D.D., who held the living from 1862 to 1883, whose personality is best remembered in connection with the earlier history of St. Peter's.

Among the first purchasers of land on the Hippodrome Estate was the Rev. Samuel Edmund Walker, of St. Columb Major in North Cornwall, who appeared in Notting Hill with the intention, so it was believed, of investing half a million sterling in house property. " He was not long in causing hundreds of carcases of houses to be built. If he had commenced his operations on the London side of the estate no doubt the houses would have been sold and a fine investment made, but as he preferred building from Clarendon Road (where roads were not made) towards London the land was covered with unfinished houses which continued in a ruinous condition for years, and the consequence was the investor was almost ruined." [6] The Old Inhabitant, perhaps here combines the work of various speculative builders, but it will be seen later on that Dr. Walker's scheme was of huge proportions. The history of two houses in Clarendon Road may be taken as typical of many others. No. 12, Clarendon Road has a charming long garden, and is still very countrified, but the ground floor is better built and is altogether superior to the upper stories. Mr. Hugh Carter, the artist, bought the house in 1866 from Mr. Henry Drew, who had taken it over as bankrupt

---

[6] *Kensington, Notting Hill and Paddington,* by " An Old Inhabitant 1882.

property. A photographer was the first tenant. No. 38, originally known as 28, Clarendon Road Villas, is one of eight well-designed detached villa residences facing west. There is reason for thinking that these houses were begun by the Rev. Dr. Walker, and were left in an unfinished state. In 1846, No. 38, Clarendon Road was handed over by James W. Ladbroke to Mr. Richard Roy, but he soon gave up possession. The close proximity of the " Piggeries and Potteries " was a sufficient reason why the western parts of the estate did not take the public fancy. Even in 1867, Mr. Lionel Clarke and other householders in Lansdowne Road were obliged to complain to the vestry of the boiling down of fat at an hour in the night when it was fondly hoped that the smell would not be noticed.

Fortunes were certainly made, but fortunes were also lost in developing Kensington Park, and " sad tales could be told of not a few who sank their all in bricks and mortar. Lawyers and moneylenders have in time past reaped a rich harvest at Notting Hill, but many a hard-working man, falling into their hands, has been ruined " (see note 6). The failure of Overend and Gurney's Bank in 1866 seems to have dealt a crushing blow to the estate. Few of the builders survived the ordeal, and of those few the " efforts were maimed " (see note 4). Even such an influential man as Mr. Drew became involved in mortgages, and some of Mr. Felix Ladbroke's ventures are believed to have been costly failures. The Hundred Acre Estate got into liquidation. The mortgage of part of it was then taken over by Richard Roy, Esq., already mentioned. (Rents charged for the use of some of the common gardens are still paid to the firm of Messrs. Roy and Cartwright.) Many persons, when recalling early impressions, refer to houses without roofs, or with holes for windows, black holes which seemed like staring eyes to the frightened child who hurried by. The row of un-finished carcases on the north side of Ladbroke Gardens came into the hands of Mr. Andrew Perston of 9, Kensington Park Gardens, and his sister-in-law, Miss Churchill, and a young architect, now Sir Aston Webb, P.R.A., put staircases into some of these houses. Other instances could be given ; but enough has been said to explain the mongrel condition of much of the building, especially on the fringes of the Hundred Acre Estate, and the large number of " made-down " houses which have always puzzled visitors to the locality.

Shortly after the Hippodrome was given up a row of small two-storied houses was built at the south end of Portobello Lane overlooking the garden of Elm Lodge. These houses were long known as Albert Place, but are now part of Pembridge Road. Most of them have been converted into shops, but they retain an old-world air, and two or three are in their

original condition, at least, externally.   In one of
these little houses, then No. 18, Notting Hill, Feargus
O'Connor, the "Lion of Freedom," spent the last
clouded days of his stormy public life.   He it was
who, on April 10, 1848, had commanded the vast
assemblage of Chartists at Kennington Common, when
troops under the Duke of Wellington were called out
to quell   the   rioters.   Feargus   O'Connor   died
August 30, 1855.   On September 11th, a great body
of his followers marched from Notting Hill Gate to
Kensal Green Cemetery, where a funeral oration was
delivered by Mr. Edward Jones.7   The grave is
marked by an obelisk.

In 1849 Horbury Chapel and school were placed
at the junction of Ladbroke and Kensington Park
Roads.   With Norman towers flanking the façade,
the chapel stands in a commanding position, indeed
this corner is one of the most effective points in the
whole neighbourhood.   See illustration on page 166.
" Horbury " was a " hiving off " from the crowded
congregation at Hornton Street, Kensington, but a
close connection was maintained with the parent
church.   The name is that of a village in Yorkshire,
the birthplace of Mr. Walker, deacon and treasurer,
to whom the success of the undertaking was largely
due.   During the ministry of the Rev. William
Roberts, the beloved pastor from 1850 to 1893,

7 This probably was *Edmund* Jones with whom he started a huge
Co-operative Land Co., in 1846.

" Horbury " was the centre of much congregational life.[8]   For awhile it was also the meeting place of the Kensington Parliament, a debating society which developed the powers of several well-known public men.

The buildings on the north slope of St. John's Hill are all of later date, though one row of small houses called Kensington Park Terrace was built in Kensington Park Road as early as 1853.   The name and the date may still be seen on the pediment facing Arundel Gardens.[9]   In 1862 a Proprietary Chapel was placed a little lower down the hill.   This iron building belonged to an Independent minister, known as Mr. Marchmont.   He was an eloquent preacher and attracted large crowds.   Services were conducted according to the form of the Church of England " to the great scandal of the neighbourhood."   One Sunday night in May 1867 a fire took place, and the building was gutted.   Ugly reports spread as to the cause of the conflagration.   A large brick church was soon commenced by Mr. Marchmont on the same site, but the Bishop of London intervened.   In 1872 this " carcase " was purchased by a body of Presbyterians who, for two or three years, had been worshipping in the Mall Hall, Notting Hill Gate. Peculiarities in the internal arrangements of Trinity

---

[8] *Congregationalism in the Court Suburb*, by John Stoughton, D.D., 1883.
[9] The windows of this terrace and neighbouring houses were shattered by the fall of a bomb in the garden opposite in 1917.

Presbyterian Church were due to its origin. This church had a series of remarkable pastors, among whom may be mentioned the first minister, Dr. Adolf Saphir, noted for his wonderful knowledge of the Bible, Dr. Sinclair Paterson, and the saintly Rev. J. H. C. MacGregor.[10]

A very undesirable music palace, called Kensington Hall, stood on the spot where is now the Kensington Presbyterian Hall, and somewhat further down the road was the Mission Room belonging to All Saint's Church. (The site is occupied by the Notting Hill Synagogue, founded by Mr. Moses Davis to meet the needs of a large community of Jews, chiefly Russian and Polish, who have come to live in the immediate neighbourhood.)

In 1867 a charming terrace of small houses was built in Blenheim Crescent originally called Sussex Road ; these houses were on the edge of the country, and the scent of new-mown hay used to be wafted in at the windows across the garden of the Convent. This Franciscan Convent of the Order of St. Clare was connected with St. Mary of the Angels, Westmoreland Road, Bayswater. It was founded by Cardinal, then Father, Manning, and had been placed in 1859 on low ground at the foot of the hill, where formerly withy beds showed the course of the stream running

---

[10] *History of Trinity Presbyterian Church*, Bryce, 1913. Published locally by " Tamblyn." In 1919 this church was closed as the congregation became united with the Presbyterian Church in Westbourne Grove.

west from Portobello Lane. The Convent buildings and the large garden in Ladbroke Grove cover one and three-quarter acres ; about thirty nuns are said to live within the high, encircling wall. Immediately to the north of the Convent stood a country inn with a skittle alley beside it. The " Lord Elgin " is still remembered by many local inhabitants. It is now represented by the Elgin Tavern at the corner of Ladbroke Grove and Cornwall Road.

In 1863 a modern Gothic church with bands of brick and stone, flying buttresses and a spire, was planted down in the midst of fields on the west side of Ladbroke Grove opposite the Convent wall. The site for " St. Mark's in the Fields " had been given by Mr. Charles Henry Blake, and Miss E. F. Kaye presented her nephew to the living. The Rev. Edward Kaye Kendall, formerly curate at St. John's, was " an enlightened and able minister," and St. Mark's became the centre of valuable parochial organizations, including an excellent National School. Where the Parish Hall now stands was then an allotment. In 1871, the average congregation numbered over one thousand persons belonging both to " the higher middle class and the poor." Many beautiful additions have since been made to this church, and three galleries have been removed. Before the completion of the church a Baptist chapel had been placed close by. Few people know of the quaint origin of the chapel in Cornwall Road. In 1862 Sir Morton Peto obtained a contract for the removal of the buildings of the Great International Exhibition in South Kensington, and he was presented by Messrs Lucas and Co. with the end of one of the transepts. This transept, "a long wooden and plaster object" was "stuck up" at Sir Morton Peto's expense as Ladbroke Grove Baptist Church. Later on it was entirely rebuilt. In spite of its shoddy origin this chapel " has been honoured by the ministry of several notable men," the first minister being the Rev. James A. Spurgeon, 1863 to 1867, brother of the renowned Charles Spurgeon.

The advance of buildings is indicated by the dates of these various places of worship. Before the days of the chapel in Cornwall Road, a boxing booth stood on this spot, run by the noted prize-fighters, Tom King and Jem Mace. Tom Sayers and another prize-fighter owned a circus which occupied the corner of Ladbroke Grove and Lancaster Road. The gardens behind Lancaster Road mark the boundary of the Hippodrome Estate. Kensington Park Hotel, No. 139, Ladbroke Grove, which is shown in the photograph of 1866, on page 184, is beyond the limits, as is also Lancaster Road. Of late years Lancaster Road has become the centre of an interesting group of philanthropic agencies including the Campden Technical Institute, a modern development of the Campden Charities, the Romanesque Church of St. Columb, originally a daughter church of All

Saint's, and the fine red-brick building of the North
Kensington Branch of the Public Library. Although
this building only dates from 1891, the Notting Hill
Free Library, from which it has sprung, was started
in the year 1874 at No. 106, High Street, Notting Hill
Gate, through the private exertions of Mr. James
Heywood of 26, Kensington Palace Gardens. Mr.
Herbert Jones, librarian-in-chief, was appointed as
assistant to Miss Isabella Stamp (a lady with the
regulation ringlets of the period) who presided over
this library at Notting Hill Gate. After Mr.
Heywood's death it was carried on for awhile under
the Public Libraries Act, by a committee of local
gentlemen. The corner of Ladbroke Grove and
Lancaster Road may be looked upon as the central
point of North Kensington.

Unfortunately a group of mean streets extends
from Cornwall Road to Clarendon Road. Hanover
Court, the strange circle of houses with radiating
gardens which fills up the north-west corner of the
original plan (see map on page 120), has been replaced
by a veritable slum area. It must be remembered
however that the houses were not built for the class
of people who now inhabit them.

Before leaving the subject of Kensington Park a
little more may be said about the development of the
portion on the top of St. John's Hill. When Ladbroke
Square was laid out Mr. J. W. Ladbroke arranged

for a rent charge of three guineas per annum on each
house over which he had jurisdiction.   This was for
the upkeep of the garden.   Other houses within the
radius of half-a-mile, on paying a rent, were allowed
the use of the common pleasure ground.   Mr. James
Weller Ladbroke died in 1847.   In 1864 his cousin,
Mr. Felix Ladbroke, parted with his interest in the
Square garden for the sum of £2,000, raised by
a hundred shares of £20 each.   Six trustees and a
garden committee of five persons, living within a
hundred yards of the Square, were appointed from
among the shareholders to collect and employ the
rent charges and subscriptions in order that the garden
or pleasure ground, the fences, gates and gardener's
lodge, the summer houses, furniture and property
might be kept up in perpetuity.   Surplus funds were
to be divided among the shareholders.   These
provisions are still carried out.   The original trustees
were Edward Langdon · Brown, M.R.C.P., William
Matthewson Hindmarsh, Q.C., an authority on
Patent Law ; Arthur Pittar, a diamond merchant
(who in 1860 had taken No. 4, Kensington Park
Gardens, the house formerly kept by Miss Killick
and Mrs. Lewis as a boarding school for young ladies) ;
and Alfred Waddilove, D.C.L., a probate lawyer, all
living in Kensington Park Gardens ; also Robert
Cocks of Wilby House, Ladbroke Terrace, a music
publisher, and Henry Liggans of Ladbroke Square,
author of a pro-slavery pamphlet.   The solicitor of the

company was Edward Young Western, whose father owned houses in Kensington Park Gardens and in Ladbroke Square. The firm still remains solicitors to the trust. The deed of conveyance, dated March 1, 1864, and the schedules attached to it throw further light on the earliest inhabitants, but it is not possible to tell who had any particular house. Much interesting information on the subject was furnished to the writer by Mr. Lionel A. Clarke, a former Master of the Supreme Court, who in 1916 was living at No. 5, Ladbroke Square, the house occupied before his time by the blind William Gardner, whose name will always be remembered with gratitude for his benefactions to those afflicted in like manner with himself. Evidently in 1864 men of position and intelligence were living on the breezy heights of Notting Hill, and merchants, lawyers, men of science, literary men and artists have continued to inhabit these comfortable mid-Victorian houses to the present day.

In the words of a modern writer : [10] " Leafy Ladbroke has a peculiar completeness as a quarter . . . and it gives me a stronger impression of social stability than any other part of London that I know." But whilst it may be admitted that the bulk of the dwellers in Leafy Ladbroke have been those " solid men, the backbone of the country " upon whom " the greatness of England is founded," men whose business it is

[10] *Now*, by Charles Marriott, 1910.

to buy something and sell it again at a profit, it is also true that the lump has been leavened by an admixture of less self-centred elements : men and women who have devoted their energies to furthering the welfare of their neighbours.

The following lines from " An Evening Song," by Henry S. Leigh,[11] belong to the period which has been described.

> Fades into twilight the last golden gleam
> Thrown by the sunset on upland and stream ;
> Glints o'er the Serpentine—tips Notting Hill—
> Dies on the summit of proud Pentonville.
>
> Day brought us trouble, but Night brings us peace ;
> Morning brought sorrow, but Eve bids it cease.
> Gaslight and Gaiety beam for a while ;
> Pleasure and Paraffin lend us a smile.
>
> Temples of Mammon are voiceless again—
> Lonely policemen inherit Mark Lane—
> Silent is Lothbury—quiet Cornhill—
> Babel of Commerce, thine echoes are still.
>
> *   *   *   *
>
> Westward the stream of Humanity glides ;—
> 'Buses are proud of their dozen insides,
> Put up the shutters, grim Care, for to-day—
> Mirth and the lamplighter hurry this way.

These light-hearted verses show how times have changed within living memory.   The strain and stress of modern conditions in " Uxbridge Road," are

[11] *Carols of Cockayne,* by Henry S. Leigh, 1869.

described in a most beautiful poem by Evelyn Underhill,[12] from which some lines are quoted:—

The Western Road goes streaming out to seek the cleanly wild,
It pours the city's dim desires towards the undefiled.

The torments of that seething tide who is there that can see?
There's one who walked with starry feet the western road by me!

He is the Drover of the soul; he leads the flock of men,
All wistful on that weary track, and brings them back again.

He drives them east, he drives them west, between the dark and
    light;
He pastures them in city pens, he leads them home at night.

Yet not unled, but shepherded by one they may not see—
The one who walked with starry feet the western road by me!

[12] In *Immanence,* a book of verses, by Evelyn Underhill.

CHAPTER VII

NOTTING DALE

BEFORE describing the streets to the east of the
Hippodrome Estate, connecting Notting Hill with
Bayswater and Paddington, it will be best to consider
the growth of the district which has had such a
disastrous effect on the development of the western
borders of Kensington Park. The name now in use
has been given to this chapter, but the area to be
described was originally known as Kensington
Potteries and Norland Town.

Already it has been told how a company of pig-
keepers established themselves in the early years of
the nineteenth century among the brickfields at the
foot of the hill. By 1840 the little colony was an
irregular group of hovels, which were more and more
taking the form of a self-contained village. See maps
on pages 76 and 120. There were two main streets,
James Street and Thomas Street.[1] James Street was
a portion of the old " public road," now included in
Walmer Road. Thomas Street later on became Tobin

---

[1] Also *Diagram of Parish of St. Mary's, Kensington,* 1846. See page 96.

132

Street. Notting Dale, a charming name were it not for its associations, at first was a small turning, apparently identical with Thresher's Buildings. This alley of low houses, with good back-yards, was described in 1904 as "a double row of cottages with a paved way between them that seem to have been lifted bodily out of a Yorkshire mill town and dropped with their quaint outhouses on the confines of Kensington." [2]

Very little of the primæval hamlet remains, though Heathfield Street and Mary Place and Hesketh Place, formerly known as Sidney Place, still have tiny front gardens and stabling with tiled roofs ; forming a curious little oasis in the midst of a London slum. The " Black Boy " and the " King's Arms " were the names of notorious public houses off James Street. By the side of the Kiln, which has been preserved as an historical relic (see illustrations on pages 88 and 110), was a range of sheds, and " Potteries " belonging to Mr. Adams also occupied the west side of Pottery Lane, where is now Avondale Park. Mary Place (dedicated not to Our Lady but to a Mary who kept pigs) ended in Mr. Stephen Bird's brickfield, and the row of Bird's cottages, close to the site of Sirdar Road L.C.C. School.

Brick-making was carried on chiefly during the five summer months, and the men worked fifteen or sixteen hours a day and for some hours on Sunday.

[2] " Off the Track in London," by G. R. Sims, *Strand Magazine*, 1904 ; republished in book form 1911.

The wives and elder children often helped in the work ; indeed children worked the same long hours as their fathers, carrying loads of wet clay on their heads, and looking like pillars of clay themselves ; until, through the efforts of Lord Shaftesbury, this form of child-slavery was abolished by Act of Parliament. A family party could earn large wages for those times : even £2 to £3 a week. But the work was very exhausting, and the men considered it necessary to drink at least seven pints of beer a day. Naturally this kind of life reacted on home conditions, and in winter a brick-maker's family might be penniless. At this period, however, drunkenness was almost unknown among the women. The Sunday amusements were cock-fighting and bull-baiting. Many dogs were kept for dog-fights and rat-killing. Neighbours were afraid of these dogs. Even the inhabitants did not venture out after dark, for, besides the dogs, there were the dangers of the unmade roads.

Meanwhile the pigs kept had grown in numbers ; until at one time, on the eight or nine acres of the district, there were 3,000 pigs and 1,000 human beings, living in some 260 hovels. With the increase of population sanitary conditions had become more and more unsatisfactory. An official report of the year 1849 states : " The majority of the houses are of a most wretched class, many being mere hovels in a ruinous condition, and are generally densely populated. They are filthy in the extreme and contain vast

accumulations of garbage and offal. . . . On the
north, east and west sides this locality is skirted by
open ditches of the most foul and pestilential character,
filled with the accumulation from the extensive
piggeries attached to most of the houses." [3]   Besides
these open sewers fetid pools formed on the surface ;
one sheet of water, known as the " Ocean " being
nearly an acre in extent.   The water in the wells was
black, even the paint on the window frames was
discoloured by the action of sulphuretted hydrogen
gas.   The inhabitants all looked unhealthy, with
sunken eyes and shrivelled skin, the women especially
complaining of sickness and want of appetite.

It is hardly to be wondered at that " nobody ever
cared to come nigh the place."   At last, in the early
forties, a small school was opened through the exertions
of Lady Mary Fox, of Little Holland House, and
another friend of the district presented the site for
St. James's National School.   But the first centre for
directly religious work was started by combined
members of Silver Street Baptist and Hornton Street
Congregational Chapels.   For several years services
were held and schools carried on in a house with
unplastered walls, the precursor of Notting Dale
Chapel and school in Walmer Road.   This little
Mission-room in the Potteries can claim to be the

---

[3] Quoted in a lecture on " Slum Areas in London," February 24, 1924,
by Lieut.-Colonel Cecil B. Levita, C.B.E., Chairman of the L.C.C. Housing
Committee.

earliest place of worship in the whole area of North
Kensington. By the middle of 1845 the churches
of St. John's-on-the-Hill, and St. James's Norlands
were established. And in 1847 the London City
Mission sent one of their missionaries to the district.

Such was the state of affairs when, in the summer
of 1849, London was visited by cholera. As was to
be expected Kensington Potteries suffered severely
from the epidemic. Then the infection spread to
more comfortable homes. Between September 11
and 22, 1849, seven deaths occurred "in Crafton
Terrace a quarter of a mile away." This was probably
Crafter Terrace on Latimer Road. See map of 1850
on page 120. The attention of the public was drawn
to the locality through these deaths, and Charles
Dickens brought it into further notice by an article
which appeared in one of the first numbers of *Household Words*. This article begins : " In a neighbourhood studded thickly with elegant villas and mansions,
viz.: Bayswater and Notting Hill, in the parish of
Kensington, is a plague-spot, scarcely equalled for
its insalubrity by any other in London ; it is called
the Potteries." These disclosures led to discussions
both in and out of Parliament. As a result " a good
road was made," no doubt Princes Road, and supplies
of fresh water were introduced. But the drainage of
the area was found to be a difficult problem on account
of the low level of the ground.

Seven years later the Medical Officer of Health had

to give a still worse account of the conditions of " one of the most deplorable spots not only in Kensington but in the whole Metropolis." The ground was still saturated by drainage from the badly paved styes of over 1,000 pigs, and all the wells were contaminated. Many of the houses were in a very dilapidated state, and old railway carriages and worn-out travelling vans might be seen converted into dwellings. The death-rate in 1856 was actually 40 to 60 per 1,000, and 87·5, or 43 out of every 50 deaths, were of children under five years of age. Smallpox was reputed to be ten times more fatal than in the surrounding districts. This statement is valuable in view of the heavy toll of life in subsequent epidemics. Not only was this the case in the outbreaks of cholera in 1849 and in 1853, when the Vicar of St. John's lost his life (see page 115), but in the bad attack of scarlet fever which occurred about 1870, and the devastating wave of influenza in 1889-1890. After the report of the Medical Officer in 1856 " great efforts were made to get rid of the swinish multitude altogether, but the shrewd chimney-sweep, Lake, seems to have foreseen this evil day, and ' for the purposes of pig-keeping ' had been inserted in the very leases which the people were able to produce. . . . Nothing but a special Act of Parliament could remedy the existing evil."

In the middle years of the nineteenth century a

wide-spread interest was felt in questions relating to
the welfare of the poorer sections of society, and
several fresh methods of philanthropy were introduced.
Two of these new methods came into being in this
" frowsy suburb."   And in the story of the establishment of the first Mothers' Meeting, and the earliest
Workmen's Institute, graphic pictures are given of the
early development of Notting Dale.4

It was at the suggestion of Mr. Parfitt, the City
Missionary, that Mrs. Bayly undertook the management of the " Mothers' Society."   This met for the
first time on the evening of Monday, November 3,
1853, and it is remarkable how closely hundreds of
Mothers' Meetings to-day conform to the scheme
evolved nearly seventy years ago.   When the numbers
in attendance became on an average eighty to one
hundred some of the women were formed into another
group.   By 1863 there were three Meetings in the
neighbourhood under the management of one Ladies'
Committee, besides a similar Meeting connected with
St. James's Church, conducted by the daughter of
Sir Edward Ryan in Phœnix Place off Queensdale
Road.   Until a trained Bible-woman was obtained
by the help of Mrs. Ranyard in 1860, Mrs. Trickett
acted as " Female Missionary."   Her name is known
in the locality through the wood-chopping business
inaugurated by her son.   Mrs. Swindler, in 1915,

4 *Ragged Homes and How to Mend Them,* 1859.   *Home Weal and Home
Woe,* by Mrs. Bayly and Miss Elizabeth Boyd Bayly, 1892.

told the writer that, when she was a young married woman living in Princes Road, she used to go on a Monday afternoon to Mrs. Bayly's " little chapel," which was behind the present police station in Sirdar Road. This was on the outskirts of the Potteries' village, and fields reached almost to the door. Allotments and small market-gardens lay all around, and a narrow stream on the north side of St. Katherine's Road, now Wilsham Street, had to be crossed in order to reach the Mothers' Meeting. Mrs. Swindler's little son used to take crusts to feed the baby pigs and the geese met with on the way.

The " Piggeries and Potteries " (a name said to have been invented by the Rev. Charles Spurgeon) were not confined to the eight or nine acres of the original estate, but had spread both to the south and to the west. St. James's parochial schools were surrounded by pig-sties in 1859, and the health of the Rev. R. N. Buckmaster, who nobly worked as curate from 1847 until after 1871, suffered severely owing to " exposure to so much damp, and the stench of the highways and byways." Here the Norland and Potteries Ragged School was opened by Lord Shaftesbury in 1858. (The work is still carried on in the same building under the name of the Holland Park Mission, St. James's Place.)

The building of the Birmingham, Bristol and Thames Junction Railway (The West London Railway) has already been mentioned. After that line was built about the year 1836, a track ran across the fields from Mortimer Terrace, now called Boundary Road, to the archway leading to Wormwood Scrubbs. See map of 1850, page 120. This track, afterwards Latimer Road, followed the course of the " rivulet " ; the actual boundary at this time being an open ditch which was crossed by plank bridges when houses were built on the east side of the road. Allotment grounds lay at the south end of this track or footpath ; and it was not until about 1860 that Norland Road North was made across these allotments to connect Latimer Road with Shepherd's Bush. The " Old Inhabitant " describing the state of affairs in the middle forties writes : " Beyond the Colony of pig-keepers at the end of Pottery Lane I discovered another in Latimer Road. . . . But what a place it was when I first discovered it—comparatively out of the world—a rough road cut across the fields the only approach. Brick-fields and pits on either side, making it dangerous to leave on dark nights. A safe place for many people who did not wish everybody to know what they were doing." In this desolate region the worthy man conducted services and established a day school. Unfortunately the position of this school, as well as the identity of the Old Inhabitant has, so far, eluded discovery.5

Latimer Road owes its name to Edward Latymer,

5 *Kensington, Notting Hill, and Paddington,* by " An Old Inhabitant," 1882.

Esq., citizen and feltmonger, son of a Dean of Peter-
borough, who, at his death in 1626, bequeathed
thirty-five acres of field land north of Shepherd's Bush,
with further property in Hammersmith, for the support
of six poor men and the education of eight poor boys
in the Charity School which he had founded in 1624.
The charity was added to in later years and now
provides for many pensioners and hundreds of day
scholars in the two Latymer Foundation Schools. A
small portion of the estate lies within the parish of
Kensington, and the benefits of the charity are devoted
indiscriminately to children from both parishes, but
the quaint provisions as to clothing and education
are no longer required of the recipients of the bounty.[6]
The " Latymer Arms " at the corner of Boundary
Road was within living memory a one-storied country
inn. The quartered arms of Latymer and Wolverton
appear on the present tavern, the property having
descended to Latymer through his great-grandmother,
Elizabeth Wolverton.

It must have been about the time when the " Old
Inhabitant " came into the district that Mr. James
Whitchurch, an attorney of West Southampton, then
known as Blechynden, bought fifty acres of land in
Hammersmith and Kensington, at the rate, it is said,
of £10 an acre. The " Fifty Acre Estate " abutted

[6] See *History of Hammersmith*, by Thomas Faulkner, 1838. Interesting
maps of the property are preserved at the Latymer Foundation School,
High Street, Hammersmith.

on the Latymer Estate, joined the property of
Mr. Stephen Bird, the owner of large brick-fields, and
spread some distance to the north. In this northern
portion an outlying group of roads was projected
shortly after 1846. These roads included part of
Lancaster Road, Silchester Road and Bromley, now
Bramley Road, and were bounded by the upper end
of Walmer Road, which followed the curved line of
the Hippodrome pallisade. Countrified houses with
dilapidated gardens, used as drying grounds for
linen, may still be found in these roads, but several
of these early houses were demolished to make way
for the Kensington Baths and Wash-houses. Mr.
Whitchurch built for his own use a house in Lancaster
Road, now No. 133, but he died near Blechynden.
He was not exactly an accommodating landlord, and
he was fully acquainted with " his rights and remedies,"
but he insisted on having wide roads across his property,
and the generous proportions of Latimer Road, and
the roads already mentioned, have since proved of
inestimable benefit.

The map of 1850 shows various buildings along
Latymer, now Latimer Road. The more respectable
residents had pig-sties in their back yards, the rougher
element in many cases inhabited mere hovels, where
the family and their animals, pigs, horses, dogs and
poultry, lived together in " squalid degradation."
The final eviction of pigs by order of the Vestry of
Hammersmith was not carried out until 1883. For

many a year this action was much resented in the locality.

Already gipsy vans were accustomed to make their appearance each autumn, to disappear again at the beginning of the following summer. The gipsies established themselves at the south end of Latymer Road, and half a mile further to the north where St. Helen's schools have been built. The dark coloured tents or " tans " were also pitched on Black Hill, now included in Avondale Park, but their chief encampment was on the low ground where St. Clement's Church was afterwards placed. This land had formerly been part of Bird's brick-field. In 1862 the gipsies of Latymer Road were reckoned at from forty to fifty families. The following incident illustrates the curious conditions which prevailed. Mr. Moore was the owner of a small farm on the west side of Latymer Road. One evening a young gipsy woman, whose tent was pitched on Mr. Moore's ground, came to him in distress, saying that a strange man must have got into her tent, for she could hear him snoring. On accompanying her, Mr. Moore discovered that the intruder was, not a man but, an old asthmatic sow of his own, which had strayed, and had found a soft corner in the gipsy's bed.

The patriarch of the tribe, known as " the King of the Gipsies," was a picturesque old man with the regular gipsy name of Hearn. He had fought through the Napoleonic Wars, and had wandered all over the country " chair-bottoming." In the early sixties, when more than ninety years of age, he settled down and made himself a little home out of an old advertising van with a tin pail for a chimney. It was at this time that mission work started among these gipsies. " Old Hearn " signed the pledge, and many other " travellers " gave up drunkenness and swearing and even abandoned the lucrative practice of fortune-telling. They sold their horses, which formerly had been fed at the expense of the public, took out hawkers' licences and, for reasons known to themselves, discarded the Romany language. Besides this some thirty-five couples went through the marriage service. The well-known evangelistic work of " Gipsy Smith " and his family is an outcome of this revival. A gipsy tea-meeting was a sight not easily to be forgotten. The writer can recall how, during the meeting that followed tea, a crying baby was hailed with joy, as it formed an excuse for a man to get up from the unaccustomed hard seat and pace the room with the child in his arms. At last a tent, to be used for religious and educational purposes, was pitched among the dark " tans." This tent was opened on a sultry afternoon in the summer of 1869. But it could not be used for long, as an outbreak of scarlet-fever occurred, and the local authorities insisted on the abandonment of the gipsy camps.

Ever since 1870 the gipsies in Notting Dale have ostensibly lived under roofs ; but many an inhabited van has been hidden away in back premises. Although a good deal of intermarriage with the ordinary population has taken place, beautiful dark-eyed children with massive hair may still be found in the elementary schools. Pictures of the gipsies of Latymer Road, appeared in the *Illustrated London News* in 1879 (see page 144), and Mr. G. R. Sims, writing in 1904, see note 2, tells of a genuine Romany funeral which had recently occurred.

Meanwhile in Kensington Potteries and Norland Town conditions had changed. When Mr. Goderich, M.O.H., made his report in 1856 men belonging to the building trades and other casual labourers had come to live in the district ; the number of pigs had declined, and many of those were fattened on commission instead of being owned by the pig-keepers. The winter of 1856 was one of unusual distress. Little unskilled work was to be obtained, and " had it not been that many of the women found employment as charwomen and laundresses, numbers of families would have had no resource but the workhouse." Through this simple and apparently praiseworthy action on the part of the women a trade was introduced which in time became the chief industry of Notting Hill, ousting the brickmakers and pig-masters.

At first, no doubt, a woman would take in washing from a family in one of the better-class houses, and the clothes would be dried in her garden. But later on small laundries, owned and managed by a man and his wife who employed about half-a-dozen women, became a distinguishing feature of the locality.   In the absence from home of a woman worker her baby had to be left to the care of a neighbour, often an old woman in a back kitchen, the other children ran wild or were locked in till the mother returned at night, when she tried to carry out her domestic duties after twelve hours at the wash-tub or the ironing board.   Standing in the atmosphere of steam frequently produces varicose veins and rheumatism.   It is not surprising, therefore, that many of these poor women resorted to stimulants, with the natural result of more miserable homes and less healthy children.   As the women became the principal wage-earners the district more and more was " infested with a contemptible set of men . . . loafers or worse," and it is well recognized amongst the poor that men move to North Kensington " for the purpose of being kept by their wives." 7   There is a local saying that " To marry an ironer is as good as a fortune."   Those who best know the laundry workers will acknowledge the many brave souls amongst them, but women's work away from home inevitably has a demoralizing effect.

These evils were of slow growth.   The women were still a sober race when, in 1859, a crusade against the drinking habits of the men was determined on. A " Rescue Society," afterwards known as the

7 *Some Kensington Problems*, by Miss A. M. Alexander, April 1904.

Temperance Society, was formed, the working-men
members being organized as district visitors to their
mates. It soon became clear that, if rough men were
to be saved from drink, they must have some place
where they could meet without being exposed to
temptation. Mechanics' Institutes had already been
founded : a public-house without drink seems to have
been quite a new venture. After some delay two
skeleton houses were purchased in Portland Road,
and were adapted for the purpose. A model of the
Eddystone Lighthouse was fixed outside the building,
and showed its light along the three roads converging
on the spot. The " Workmen's Hall " was opened
on March 12, 1861, by Dr. Tait, Bishop of London,
and was subsequently managed by a committee of
men presided over by Captain and Mrs. Bayly. By
the end of 1862 there were six or seven hundred
staunch teetotalers on the roll. The original Workmen's Hall was closed in 1866 owing to unforeseen
difficulties. But it had " lived long enough to found
a family " in subsequent coffee palaces and in the
Men's Institutes started by Miss Ellice Hopkins and
Miss Daniells.

Miss Boyd Bayly describes the frequenters of the
" Hall Haul All," " carpenters, shoemakers, brick-
layers, brickmakers, pig-feeders and plasterers . . .
including ' Jimmie the Devil,' the tall pig-feeder, who
had been a hard drinker from sixteen till over sixty,
and Taylor the navvy whose face, always bright,

positively radiated beams when he got ensconced among his mates at the Hall. . . . Compared with the splendours of the modern coffee palace, the Hall was almost a barn for plainness, but it was jolly there." [8]

Mr. Gell, the esteemed vicar of the parish, Mr. Roberts, pastor of Horbury Chapel, City missionaries and others took an active part in the work, and it is stated that from seventeen to eighteen hundred persons united themselves with various Christian communities in the neighbourhood. But the so-called " Chaplain of the Hall," was Mr. Henry Varley, the noted evangelist of later days, then a handsome young butcher in High Street, Notting Hill, who conducted services at the Notting Dale Chapel in Walmer Road. This little building became so crowded that in 1864, with the help of his father-in-law, Mr. Varley built the Free, or West London Tabernacle, which, when enlarged in 1872, was capable of holding twelve hundred worshippers, and actually had an evening congregation of over one thousand. (The " Tabernacle " and " Tabernacle Hall " which stood beside it in St. John's, now Penzance Place, are at present used as business premises.)

Other religious bodies were at work in Notting Dale. In the eighteen-fifties a Convent was placed

[8] William Taylor finally became the Navvy Preacher of the Evangelization Society ; their first working-man agent.

by the side of Pottery Lane and nuns were visiting the Irish Colony. At a later date they also cared for the group of Italians who came into the district when the slums of Drury Lane and St. Giles's were cleared away. On the Feast of the Purification, 1860, a church and a school for girls were opened. This one-sided church, dedicated to St. Francis of Assisi, with its beautiful Gothic interior, was connected with St. Mary and the Angels, Bayswater, and was an outcome of Cardinal Wiseman's Mission in London. It was built at the sole cost of the Reverend Father H. A. Rawes ; the architect was Mr. Clutten, but a much-admired Baptistery was added as a thankoffering, about 1862, by Mr. Bentley, afterwards architect of the new cathedral at Westminster.9

By 1859 Norland Chapel was built at the junction of Queen's, now Queensdale Road and Norland Road North, on part of the Latymer Estate, and the Baptist congregation under the Reverend John Stent came here from an old building facing Shepherd's Bush. Before 1879 this chapel passed into the hands of the " Christian Mission " of the Rev. W. Booth, better known as the " Salvation Army." It was renamed " Norland Castle," and a good work has been carried

9 This Baptistery has been enclosed by a grille in memory of the saintly and beloved Father White, who died in 1910. Silchester Hall in Silchester Road, a former Methodist Chapel, became St. Francis' School for Boys about 1870, and a school for 200 infants has been placed in Treadgold Street in recent times.

on there ever since.[10]   In 1864 T. Fowell, Esq., gave land for a Primitive Methodist Chapel, a yellow-brick building in Fowell Street, still in use ; Shaftesbury Hall, Portland Road was a City Mission Centre, and a party of Plymouth Brethren met in a room in Clarendon Place.

In the late fifties a project was started for connecting London and Hammersmith by a railway which should branch off from the Great Western Line at Green Lane Bridge (where Westbourne Park Station now stands), and cross Notting Hill in a south-westerly direction.   The construction of the Hammersmith and City Railway influenced the development of the whole district.   Hundreds of navvies were employed on the long series of high arches which were to carry the line over Latimer Road and the brick-fields then covering the site of the White City.   As it was expected that the work would be in hand for some years, about three hundred of these railway navvies settled in the neighbourhood, and the erection of houses was rapidly pushed forward.

Until 1860 Latimer Road had remained in a very countrified condition : " a kind of hamlet," cut off from the west by the embankment of the West London Junction Railway, and little accessible from

[10] *Broken Earthenware, the Wonderful Story of Twice-born Men*, by Harold Begbie, chronicles the efforts of the Army especially in the early years of the present century when Miss Kate Lee was in charge, and earned the name of the " Angel Adjutant."

other directions. But the chief drawback to locomo-
tion lay in the deplorable condition of the unmade
roads. In wet weather they were "a mere swamp,"
and in some places were entirely impassable. Many
persons can remember the time when a horse could
almost disappear in the ruts, and how, at the end of
Walmer Road, laundry carts would sink up to their
axles in the mud. On the morning of January 23,
1860, the body of a poor woman named Frances
Dowling was found lying in the middle of Latymer
Road. "In returning to her home about eleven
o'clock at night she had missed the crossing-place,
and stumbled into one of the miry pits." Cries for
help had been heard, but drunken brawls were so
frequent that no one troubled to get out of bed to
investigate the cause.[11]

In 1861 Mr. S. R. Brown was allocated by the
London City Mission "to visit in the new poor
houses north of the Potteries." A schoolroom,
used for church services, had been closed for the
building of the railway line, so that at that time neither
church, chapel nor school existed on the district.
A group of members of the "Workmen's Hall"
helped in organizing open-air services and house-to-
house visitation, and a Mothers' Meeting was started
in the drying-room of a laundry. A committee was
then formed of gentlemen living in the neighbourhood,

[11] This incident under the title of *Death in a London Bog* was used as an
appeal for a new Mission Hall.

with Dr. Gladstone as president, and George Maxwell, Esq., as hon. secretary ; land was obtained from Mr. Whitchurch, and the Latymer Road Mission Rooms were opened on February 23, 1863, as a Ragged Day and Sunday School and for devotional meetings of various kinds.[12]

The Mission Hall, with one small classroom attached, stood in the midst of a " primæval swamp, blossoming in broken bottles, pots and pans," the only means of approach being a narrow track bordered by white posts, a necessary precaution on winter evenings.   Two pathways were made by the mission helpers.   One started close to the " Lancaster Tavern," at the junction of Lancaster and Walmer Roads, and the other from Mr. Brown's house in Silchester Road at the corner of Lockton Street.   It is believed that the strange bend at the northern end of Blechynden Street is due to the course of these pathways.

Up to this time the Latimer Road district had been considered as an outlying portion belonging to St. Stephen's, Shepherd's Bush, in the parish of Hammersmith.   By 1864 it was evident that the northern part of St. James's Norland in Kensington parish must be made into a fresh ecclesiastical district. Bishop Tait came down and held a service in " Moore's

[12] This building was enlarged in 1866 and again in 1883, but was rebuilt in 1913, under the auspices of the Shaftesbury Society.

Field," behind No. 125, Latimer Road, speaking to the assembled throng from the wash-mill mound of the disused brickfield. After this visit, schools and then a church were commenced. St. Clement's schools were opened in 1866, and the adjoining church, designed by Mr. J. P. St. Aubyn, in 1867. The Rev. Arthur Dalgarno Robinson, curate of St. Stephen's, Shepherd's Bush, became incumbent, first of St. Andrews, an iron building at the junction of Lancaster and Walmer Roads, and afterwards of the new church : 1867 to 1881. St. Andrew's Church was unfortunately burnt down, through overheating, on the last Sunday before St. Clement's was opened. (In 1880 a handsome brick and stone Wesleyan Chapel was placed on this site.) Mr. Dalgarno Robinson collected large sums for St. Clement's, and he also built a vicarage, surrounded by a garden with fruit trees, in the northernmost part of his parish. (This house, now in Dalgarno Gardens, subsequently became St. Helen's vicarage.)

From 1881 to 1886 the Rev. Edwyn Hoskyns, who in time became Bishop of Southwell, took over the work at St. Clement's. Young and full of vigour, his influence soon made itself felt, and he gathered round him workers who came from the centre of Kensington. The parochial Relief Societies and the Mission Hall in Mary Place are due to his efforts. With the help of Miss Gore Browne the " Lily Mission " was started, chiefly as a centre for clubs

for girls and for men.   Miss Mason lived at the
Lily Mission.   Its name was changed to St. Agnes
Mission when the building came under the manage-
ment of the West London Deaconesses.

The influx of thousands of low-class inhabitants in
1862–1863, some attracted by the cheap rents charged
in Notting Hill, some coming as an overspill of
displaced populations from nearer the centre of London,
turned parts of Norland Town into a slum area, even
in those early days.   Whole streets were not inhabited
by the class of people for whom they were designed.
Nevertheless, the portion of the district remaining
within the parish of St. James's, that is south of
St. Katherine's Road, now Wilsham Street, never sank
so low as the St. Clement's district, for the simple
reason that St. James's is not entirely composed of
poor people.   Indeed one of the clergy who worked
there considers that it was an ideal parish between
the years 1875 and 1892 when the Rev. Arthur
Williamson was vicar.   The parish contained five
thousand poor, but in Mr. Williamson's time there
was a staff of ninety district visitors and a hundred
and twenty Sunday School teachers, besides a Sunday
congregation many of whom came from the large
houses in Holland Park.

Further light on the growth of the neighbourhood
is supplied by the dates at which various schools were
built.   In 1866, the year when St. Clement's National

School was opened, it had been found necessary to double the size of the Ragged School in Blechynden Street : " Brown's School " as it was familarly called. When in 1870 compulsory education became the law of the land, London was faced with an overwhelming problem. The fact that, by October 1873, a Board School for boys was opened in a hall in Crescent Street proves that, by that date, the population had far outgrown its school accommodation. A year later these boys moved with their headmaster, Mr. Williamson, to Saunders Road School, built on the Latymer Estate. In January 1875 the management of the school in Blechynden Street was handed over to the new Educational Authority ; four years later, on a rough winter's evening in 1879, the Latimer Road Board School was opened, and the children were transferred to the new building across the way.[13] This school was planned to hold twelve hundred scholars. Sixteen years earlier one hundred school places were deemed sufficient.

Crescent Street Hall was again in use from March 1877 to July 1880, during the building of a large school in St. Clement's Road. (Renamed Sirdar Road L.C.C. School, it has since that time been much enlarged by the addition of " Centres " and baths and a " Special School.") It is interesting to

[13] This school stands on ground that had been successively used by a wheelwright, for a laundry, and by a coalman before it was bought by the School Board.

note that in 1874 Crescent Street Hall provided boys
for a fairly high-class school, where a fee of twopence
per week was charged, whilst in 1880 the same
hall catered for children of a much lower type.
St. Clement's Road School was nicknamed "The
Penny Board," and it was said that children were
bribed there by the gift of sweets. Certainly they
were extraordinarily rough, ragged and undisciplined.
Whatever may be the verdict on the surrounding
district, the children at least, have improved in
tidiness and in their behaviour, especially during
school hours.

The maps of 1868 and about 1880, on pages 154
and 158, show how this part of North Kensington
was filling up. These pages are supposed only to
chronicle events before 1880. But it seems a pity
not to carry on the story of Notting Dale to the begining
of the present century. It was in 1882, a year after
the most northern portion of St. Clement's parish had
been handed over to St. Helen's, that the parochial
district now belonging to Holy Trinity was formed.
The large red-brick church in Latimer Road, which
serves as the centre of the Harrow School Mission,
was opened in 1884. It stands on land belonging to
Hammersmith, although reckoned among Kensington
churches. (St. Gabriel's, Clifton Street, a daughter
church of St. James's, was originally in the same
ecclesiastical position.) Most of the vicars of Holy

Trinity have been old Harrovians. The first priest-in-charge, the Rev. William Law, had formerly been a curate at St. Mary Abbots'. With the backing of the school interest, and the help of many friends in Kensington, the Harrow Mission has become a very important agency for good, but its work chiefly belongs to modern times. At the request of the Rev. Edwyn Hoskyns a Boys' Club was commenced by Mr. Arthur Walrond, an old Rugbeian, in a former woodyard in Walmer Road. In 1887 Rugby School made this club part of its Home Mission. The work has developed, and the Rugby Mission now owns good premises in Walmer Road. An earlier club, " the Boys' Evening Shelter," had been started at the Latymer Road Mission in 1880, when the rooms were no longer needed as school premises. The Latymer Crèche or Infant Day Nursery, which began at the same time, was a forerunner, a simple forerunner, of the great number of splendid agencies now connected with Infant Welfare.

Public bodies have not been behindhand in attempts to reclaim the neighbourhood. A plot of four and a half acres, at one time brick land, in the centre of Notting Dale, was bought by the Kensington Vestry. Part of the ground was laid out by private munificence. Avondale Park, or the " Rec " as it is called locally, was opened in 1892, and has proved an immense boon. It comprises a flower garden, a bandstand and playground for children. In one corner stands a beautiful

public Mortuary Chapel. Rent collecting by ladies
was organized by Miss Octavia Hill, and has grown
to large proportions since her death. For many
years a branch of Kensington Workhouse stood in
Mary Place behind the large police station. One of
the first acts of the Kensington Borough Council in
1900 was to purchase a large part of Kenley Street,
formerly William Street. During the mayoralty of
Sir Seymour King a row of dwellings was put up, and
other houses were adapted into workmen's flats. A
Home for District Nurses was placed in the same
street, a Home in which the nurses, in 1903, " were
valiantly holding their own in spite of the disturbance
caused by nightly brawls and the noisy and unsavoury
Sunday markets."

The Hon. Charles Booth [14] places the Kensington
Potteries among the criminal and irreclaimable areas,
largely on account of the overcrowded condition of
its unsuitable and derelict houses. This Housing
Problem has never been absent, though houses
constructed without through ventilation, in which
the toll of life was terrible in the cholera epidemic,
have now been abolished by law.[15] The advisability of
opening up the blind alleys, in that part where the
Hippodrome estate impinges upon Notting Dale,

[14] *Life and Labour of the People of London,* 1903.
[15] Mrs. Bayly wrote to *The Times* on the subject, and an article describing
the district appeared in the *Quiver* for 1882.

has been discussed again and again, but has not yet been accomplished.

Five short streets in the district are known as the " Special Area." These streets are Bangor Street, Crescent Street and three roads that have been renamed, St. Clement's, now called Sirdar Road, St. Katherine's Road, now Wilsham Street, and William, now Kenley Street. In 1899 an enquiry was undertaken at the instance of the London County Council, and it was found that the rate of mortality in these particular streets differed little from the figures given for the Pottery District in 1856, and that nearly half the babies born in this area died before they were a year old.[16] In 1904 there was a public-house to every twenty-five dwellings in these streets, and about twenty-three common lodging-houses provided accommodation for over seven hundred persons, at a nightly charge of fourpence or sixpence. Greater however than the evil of these licensed lodging-houses, was, and still is, that of the furnished rooms let from the evening until ten o'clock the next morning at tenpence or a shilling a night.[17] Such houses where " the street doors are open day and night . . . inevitably lead to moral shipwreck " (note 7).

In the early years of this century there was a large working-class population in Notting Dale " living

[16] The infant mortality rate has improved since 1899.
[17] Descriptions of these lodging-houses will be found in *Broken Earthenware*, by Harold Begbie, and in *Off the Track in London*, by G. R. Sims, 1904.

cleanly by honest industry," but, of a total of fifteen hundred families in the most congested portion, at least one thousand occupied one-roomed tenements furnished or unfurnished. Naturally overcrowding and pauperism go hand in hand ; to quote a recent publication on the subject, the " moral results of this herding together of human beings are deplorable, and it is little to be wondered at that such conditions breed discontent and worse in those who suffer from them."[18]

With the advance of years the means of livelihood in Notting Dale have changed. Pigmasters and brickmakers no longer exist, railway navvies are gone, even hand laundry-work has declined in importance, although great steam-laundries still employ a small army of women. Cabmen and horse-keepers have largely disappeared. The men now chiefly work in factories or as casual labourers in various trades, whilst many manage to earn a livelihood as costermongers, rag-and-bone men, street hawkers, flower-sellers and ice-cream men. To this list must be added professional cadgers, thieves, corner-men and other professions of a less reputable character.[19] The very nearness to a well-to-do neighbourhood is a source of

[18] Pamphlet by Kensington Representative Housing Committee, November 1923.

[19] See graphic descriptions in the *London City Mission Magazine* for March 1902, and October 1911. In 1902 the Missionary was stationed at the People's Hall, Latimer Road, now the centre of the Olaf Street Mission belonging to Kensington Congregational Church.

temptation, for precarious earnings can be supplemented by begging. So a wife may dress herself as a widow, and a short time ago children used to be hired out to add pathos to the appeal for charity. A story is told of a curate who, seeing an old acquaintance, accosted him with the words : " Why, Jones, you have got all your children of one size." To which the man replied, " Lor bless me, so I have, Sir. I must go back and change some of them ! " It has been said that " from the cradle to the grave the inhabitants rely first on the ever-ready gifts of the rich . . . ; and secondly, on the never-failing assistance of the Poor Law " (note 7).

Bad housing, and the inherited effects of alcoholism, improvidence and vice have tended to sap the vitality of the sons and daughters of the Dale. But other causes have contributed to its degradation. If the railway embankment of the West London Junction Railway had not cut off communication with the west, and if St. Clement's Road had been carried through St. James's Square, as was originally intended, instead of ending abruptly behind the houses, Notting Dale would not have been a backwater, and probably would never have become such a notorious " Guilt Garden," a sink for the dregs of other localities.

But, in all fairness, it must be remembered that the special group of bad streets only covers a small area, and that the bulk of the population are hardworking, respectable citizens, although belonging to a low stratum of society. And, bad as many of the conditions still are, there is a degree of comfort and of reasonable enjoyment in the lives of most of the inhabitants undreamed of two generations ago. The district is not so black as it has been painted, and those who know it most intimately feel that a locality, where there is so much patient continuance in well-doing, should never have been branded with the name of the Kensington Avernus.

CHAPTER VIII

THE BAYSWATER END, AND PORTO-BELLO ROAD

BAYSWATER owes its name to Baynard, companion in arms to William the Conqueror, to whom was granted land in Paddington, which he held from the Abbots of Westminster. Bays Water, a corruption of Baynard's Watering, is a name given to the upper reaches of the Westbourne. This stream began its course at Kilburn and was augmented by springs rising on Craven Hill. At the beginning of the nineteenth century a tiny hamlet stood " one mile from London on the road to Uxbridge," near the beehive-shaped conduit house known as the Bayswater or Roundhead Conduit. But, as building spread westwards along the high road, Bayswater was adopted as the name of the whole quarter between Craven Hill and the turnpike at Notting Hill Gate.[1] It is true that Mr. John Whyte advertised his race-course as the Hippodrome, Bayswater. This was incorrect,

---

[1] *Old Court Suburb,* by Leigh Hunt, 1856.

and was evidently done to minimize its distance from town.

The present chapter deals with the portion of Kensington parish lying east of Portobello Lane, from Uxbridge Road on the south to the line of the Hammersmith and City Railway on the north.   Much of this district is still described by its inhabitants as Bayswater, whilst, curiously enough, the name of Kensington Park was often used for the new quarter north of Westbourne Grove after it had ceased to be applied to the Hippodrome Estate.   " So eminently Bayswatery a neighbourhood as that of Pembridge Square and Chepstow Place is in Kensington parish," writes Mr. Lloyd Sanders.   But, although it has become the fashion to decry " the rigid and undeviating respectability of Bayswater . . . the horrors of its Mid-Victorian architecture . . . and the hardly less terrifying " interiors of its houses,[2] these houses are generally well planned according to the ideals of the fifties and sixties, and most of them are well built.

A drawing, dated 1842, made from the garden of one of Moscow Cottages, on the north side of Moscow Road, shows " mere country ; bright sweeping green expanses "[3] stretching away to the north.   Westbourne Grove crosses the drawing as a country lane with a few scattered houses.   The division between

[2] *Old Kew, Chiswick and Kensington*, by Lloyd Sanders, 1910.
[3] Description in a letter by Thomas Carlyle in 1855, quoted in *The History of the Squares of London*, by S. Beresford Chancellor, 1907.

the parishes of Kensington and Paddington was still an open ditch, running behind the houses of Victoria Grove, now Ossington Street, which forms the present boundary line. The ditch then skirted the garden wall of Grove House which stood at the west end of Moscow Road, just within the parish of Paddington. Some forty years ago a blocked-up drain was discovered in the garden of No. 17, now No. 20, Pembridge Square ; which certainly was part of this ditch. The further course of the ditch can be followed by blocks of granite, with incised dates, imbedded in the pavement at frequent intervals. Probably few passers-by are conscious of these boundary marks. (Grove House itself was not pulled down until 1900, though the beautiful garden, with its orchard and a stone-rimmed pool overhung by a fine mulberry tree, was parcelled out among the houses at the east end of Pembridge Square about the year 1869. There is a tradition that Captain Marryat, the novelist, once lived in this strangely planned house. See illustration page 166.) Westbourne Grove ended at Richmond Road, built 1848, where the omnibuses now cross. Here within living memory was a hedge broken by a stile. Slightly to the north of the Grove stood the " Princess Royal " tavern, now 47, Hereford Road. It was started in the early forties by Mr. James Bott, whose name is perpetuated in Bott's Mews off Richmond Road. The " Princess Royal " possessed a bowling green and tea-rooms, a fish-pond and archery

ground, where " any gentleman might practise archery
from 9 a.m. to 2 p.m. for ten shillings a year."
Another alluring attraction was that " the grounds
led by the nearest way to Kensal Green Cemetery." [4]
The public footpath crossing the tavern garden no
doubt connected Paddington with Portobello Lane
and Notting Barns Farm.   See page 76.

In the early forties the part of Mr. Ladbroke's
Notting Hill Estate between Notting Hill Toll Gate
and Westbourne Grove, was in the hands of a William
Howard.   In 1844 Mr. James Weller Ladbroke let
twenty-eight acres of this land, known as Longlands
and the Hooks, to Mr. William H. Jenkins, who
undertook to form roads, make sewers, and build
eighty or more houses.   Leases for ninety-nine years
were to be granted at a peppercorn rent, and it was
stipulated that no dwelling-house was to be of less
value than £300.   In 1847, Mr. Felix Ladbroke
came into the property and sold Longlands and the
Hooks " at or near Notting Hill," along with the
Westbourne Grove Estate and the Kensal Town
Estate, to William K. Jenkins, heir to William H.
Jenkins.   Pembridge Villas and Chepstow Villas were
already planned and named, and were crossed by
Denbigh Road, which included what is now Pembridge
Crescent, and Ledbury Road, with Ledbury and
Adelaide Terraces, now called Chepstow Crescent.

---

[4] *Cremorne and the later London Gardens,* by Warwick Wroth, 1907 ; also
Paddington Past and Present, by W. Robins, 1853.

But several years elapsed before these roads filled up with houses. Mr. W. K. Jenkins, a lawyer well-known in his day, lived in Westbourne Grove, the site of the house being now covered by Owen's Drapery Stores. He owned property in Hereford, and, as streets were laid out on the Westbourne Grove Estate and at this Bayswater end of Notting Hill, he gave them the names of places in Herefordshire and the neighbouring parts of Wales : Hereford, Monmouth, Newton, the River Garway, and Chepstow, Pembridge, Ledbury and Denbigh.5   Mr. W. K. Jenkins was succeeded by his son who became Canon Jenkins.

It has been suggested that " a lane or perhaps merely a track along one side of a hedge," crossed Portobello Lane by the line of Chepstow Villas and Kensington Park Gardens.6   If Chepstow Villas really followed the course of a field-path, Pembridge Villas connected the Westbourne Grove end of this path with Albert Place, and Notting Hill Gate. See page 121.   Houses at the north end of Pembridge Place and part of Chepstow Place belong to the late forties.   Other houses in Chepstow Place were built about 1855 by John Treadaway, a tailor of Old Paddington Green, who had made money through selling clothing to the navvies employed on the Great Western Railway line.   His object in 1855 was to provide work to

---

5 " Some Recollections of Bayswater Fifty Years Ago," by Sir W. Bull, in the *Bayswater Chronicle*, 1923.

6 In a series of articles on " Old Kensington," by Mrs. Henley Jervis, in the *Kensington News* for 1884.

meet the distress caused by the Crimean War. Both sides of Chepstow Place were then in Kensington parish. In 1852, the house now No. 23, Pembridge Villas, then No. 28, was included in the marriage portion of Mrs. Everard, formerly Arabella Matilda Amboise, and was called Amboise Mansion. No. 7, Pembridge Villas, then No. 10, was inhabited for a short time by a Greek family, before W. P. Frith, R.A., moved in with his wife and five children, towards the end of 1852. A charming picture painted by Frith, of himself and his wife in the studio of this house, may be seen in the National Portrait Gallery. " Pembridge Castle " was, and still is, the name of a public-house in Ledbury Road, and " Pembroke Hotel " was established in 1852 at the junction of Pembridge and Chepstow Villas. But about 1864 its license was stopped by means of a petition signed by neighbouring householders, and for many years the premises were used as a florist's shop.

A study of the map of 1850 on page 120, shows the amount of building that had taken place in the parallelogram or gridiron of streets, lying between Richmond Road and Ledbury Road, just beyond the limits of North Kensington. Artesian Road (see page 66), was then Westbourne Grove North, and the continuation of Westbourne Grove was for many years known as Norfolk Terrace and Archer Street. A brickfield owned by Mr. Bolton had covered the site of Archer Street and Bolton Road. The open ground between

the end of Westbourne Grove and this brickfield
seems to have been a recognized battle-ground.   Boys
from the village of Hammersmith and boys from the
village of Paddington would fight here for the honour
of their respective localities.   Parochial or district
fights between youths were of frequent occurrence
two generations ago, and encounters between the
boys of Kensal Road and Lisson Grove were organized
up to the end of the nineteenth century.   About 1850
a plank had to be placed across the open boundary
ditch when an inhabitant of Norfolk Terrace wished
to reach Norfolk Road Villas.   Since 1900 the
boundary has run along Ledbury Road.   Boundary
Mews has thus ceased to mark the division of the
parishes.   On the Paddington side of the boundary
line a quiet gentleman of literary tastes lived from
1854 to 1891 in a house on the site of No. 118–120
Westbourne Grove.   This was Prince Louis Lucien
Buonaparte.   Buonaparte Mansions perpetuate his
memory.   (His widow, Princess Clemence Buonaparte, was still in the neighbourhood at the time of
her death in November 1915.)

In 1850 there was open ground between Pembridge
Villas and the houses of Linden Grove and Campden
Place.   Several houses on the north side of Dawson
Place date from about 1852.   A tradition exists that
No. 28 covers the site of Dawson's Farm, but no such
farm appears on the maps.   It seems more probable
that the name is derived from Mr. John Silvester

Dawson who, perhaps, rented the fields which bordered
on the Gravel Pits Estate. See page 91. It was
well on in the eighteen-fifties before Messrs. John
and Joseph Radford bought Elm Lodge, and converted
its fine grounds into the double row of detached houses
known as Pembridge Gardens. They afterwards
acquired the remaining piece of land, and between
1862 and about 1866, mansions were gradually erected
round the garden of Pembridge Square, whilst others
on a similar plan were being built in Holland Park.
It is evident that the Radford brothers adopted the
name of Pembridge from Pembridge Place and
Pembridge Villas. The completion of Pembridge
Square was retarded until about 1870 by the construction of the Metropolitan Railway. This line
passed under three unfinished houses at the south-east
corner. These houses were supported by iron girders
inserted beneath their kitchen floors.

The Greek and the Jewish Communities have
always been well represented in the group of streets
bearing the name of Pembridge, and many interesting
persons have lived in this locality. Probably the
resident of Pembridge Square most worthy of note
is Field-Marshal Sir John Fox Burgoyne, Constable
of the Tower. "The great engineer, Commander in
the Peninsular, in France and in the Crimea," a fine
distinguished figure, was at No. 5 at the time of his
death, in 1871. Edward Middleton Barry, the
architect, lived for several years at No. 14, the house

afterwards used as St. Luke's Hospital for the Dying. (Other Institutions have occupied these solid houses. Many of them are now converted into flats or residential hotels.)

The scene of a somewhat sad story by Rita is laid in Pembridge Square, and shows an intimate acquaintance with the neighbourhood in the late sixties.7 Another interesting account of Mid-Victorian days in this locality is given in *Leaves from a Life* ; this book describes the simple lighthearted existence of the Frith family in Pembridge Villas from 1852 onwards.8 W. P. Frith's daughter tells of the alarm caused about 1857 by garotters : Notting Hill having an evil reputation for crimes of garotting. She mentions the dense black fogs of those days, and portrays many of their neighbours and the artistic and literary people with whom the family associated, including those, from royalty downwards, who visited her father's studio.

Guy Fawkes was much in fashion two generations ago, and guys are mentioned in the reminiscences of various inhabitants. Another old custom survived here until well on in the seventies. This was " Jack in the Green," attended by a group of sweeps dressed up as clowns or as girls, who danced and played and begged from the passer-by. Jack's extinguisher-shaped frame covered with leaves was probably a decadent form of the Maypole, and it is interesting to

7 *Saba MacDonald,* by Rita (Mrs. W. Desmond Humphreys).
8 *Leaves from a Life,* 1908, by Mrs. J. E. Panton.

find in Hone's *Every Day Book*, of 1827, that Bayswater was one of the suburbs " enlivened by the May Dance and the Jack o' the Green."

It is in this part of North Kensington that G. K. Chesterton centres his whimsical farce entitled " The Napoleon of Notting Hill." The story is of a tragic struggle between the armies of the various parishes or Free Cities of Western London. The " Holy Mountain " in this book was evidently Campden Hill. But the description of Pump Street, which Adam Wayne, the idealist and Lord High Provost of Notting Hill, refused to surrender in order that a road or " corridor for trade " might be run through from Hammersmith to Westbourne Grove, recalls the little old shops in Notting Hill Gate ; though Pump Street, itself, is an imaginary road connecting Clanricarde Gardens with Pembridge Square.

Before passing to Portobello Road and the north side of Archer Street the older places of worship in this district must be mentioned. These are Horbury Congregational Chapel, built in 1849, which was included in the chapter on Kensington Park, though just outside the Hippodrome enclosure, Westbourne Grove Baptist Chapel and the Wesleyan Methodist Church in Denbigh Road. Westbourne Grove Baptist Chapel dates from 1853, but it has a history going back for one hundred years. In 1823 a small Baptist Chapel had been erected in the village of

Kensington Gravel Pits. During the tenure of office of its fifth pastor, the Rev. W. G. Lewis, "Silver Street Chapel" became overcrowded ; so the congregation prepared for themselves the striking building with octagonal turrets at the corner of Norfolk Terrace and Ledbury Road. Under the direction of Mr. Lewis a large and powerful church grew up in the new premises. Additions to the building were made in 1859 and 1866, and again in 1880 shortly before Mr. Lewis's death. (Since 1890 this chapel has been just outside the parish boundary ; as is the neighbouring Roman Catholic Church in Westmoreland Road, which was also in course of construction in 1853. This church, St. Mary and the Angels, was served successively by Cardinal Wiseman and Cardinal Manning.) The third of the older churches, Denbigh Road Chapel with a classic façade dated 1856, was erected by a body of Wesleyans who previously had worshipped in Queen's Road, and they used the building whilst still in an unfinished state. In 1861 it became the centre of the Bayswater Circuit. A distinguished series of pastors have preached within its walls, including the Rev. William Archer and Dr. Morley Punshon. In the eighteen-sixties and seventies all these places of worship were filled to overflowing by congregations of thoughtful and influential people.

Portobello Lane has already been described as a

rustic footpath connecting the village of Kensington
Gravel Pits with the Harrow Road.   The south end,
near the Notting Hill Toll Gate, was considerably
altered during the period of the Hippodrome.   Then
came the building of Albert Place which was connected
with the new curved road called Pembridge Villas, so
that, since about the year 1845 " the Lane " has only
started from the sharp bend where it now abuts on
Pembridge Road.   Probably the " Sun in Splendour "
at this corner belongs to the early fifties.   This
public-house had on its cornice a massive rising sun
with golden rays, until this cornice was blown down
with fatal results some twenty years ago.   The " Earl
of Lonsdale," No. 16, Archer Street, was an earlier
building, and seems to have been in existence before
1850.   Small houses were growing up along the lane
between these taverns, houses which still have a
countrified appearance, but in 1850, with the exception
of Portobello Farm, there were no buildings north
of Archer Street.   Compare the map of 1850 on
page 120 with the larger scale map of about 1855 on
page 172.   This second map gives the original names
of many roads, and of terraces now merged in the
general numbering of the streets.

Before 1855 Bolton's brickfield had been built
over.   Bolton Road and Western and Buckingham
Terraces with Lonsdale Road formed communications
with Westbourne Grove and Ledbury Road.   Later
on Buckingham Terrace was largely swallowed up

by the elementary school of that name, opened in
1879. This group of streets included several cab
and omnibus Mews, and the inhabitants were chiefly
labourers, horse-keepers and horse-feeders, with a
shifting mass of those sorry folk who have come down
and down in the world " till their home is a loft in
some mews patronized by cabmen." All the elements
were present for the development of the degraded
conditions of to-day. In 1862 there was a Ragged
School in Lonsdale Mews, now called Colville
Mews, which was succeeded by All Saints parochial
schools.

The name of another church is here introduced,
but some earlier glimpses can be obtained of the land
subsequently included in this new parochial district.
It has been stated 9 that, about the year 1841, " pieces "
of the Hippodrome " were sliced off to form streets
and thoroughfares which lie to the north of Westbourne
Grove and south of the Great Western Railway," and
that St. Stephen's Church, Westbourne Park, covers
part of the site. It is needless to say that the race-
course never extended east of Portobello Lane. The
myth arose from combining the Hippodrome with one
of the later and smaller pleasure grounds. It appears
that a Mr. Jackson bought two fields in Westbourne
Green which were to be devoted to racing and open-
air amusements ; but the fields had to be relinquished
for the extension of the premises of the Great Western

9 See *Old and New London*, by E. Walford, 1897.

Railway Co.   The land to the immediate south, lying
between the chancel end of St. Stephen's and Portobello Road, was then obtained.   The whole of this
land belonged to the Talbot family (see page 58), and
Talbot Road is said to represent the central long axis
of the oval race-course.   Mr. George Hitchcock,
who lived when a boy in Norfolk Terrace, states that
in 1849 or 1850 fairs were held on this ground, and
a balloon was sent up from part of the field now covered
by the Church of St. Mary and the Angels.   This
open space was often called the Hippodrome, but
the proper name seems to have been Portobello
Gardens.   In the *Illustrated London News* of June 7,
1851, reference is made to the destruction of a balloon
after an ascent from the Portobello Gardens on
October 14, 1844.   Unfortunately neither the year,
nor any indication of the position of the ground is
given on a handbill announcing Mr. Gypson's " Third
and   Last   Balloon   Ascent "   for   the   season   from
Portobello Gardens ; to be held at 7 p.m. on Monday,
July 24th :   " On which occasion the whole process
of inflation may be witnessed by Visitors, as it will be
altogether Inflated in the Gardens with pure Hydrogen
Gas, having sufficient power for carrying up Two
persons."   This display was to be followed at half-
past nine o'clock by a " Grand Representation of the
Roman Festa, with Military Music, etc."   One
shilling was charged for admission.   As building
advanced the available open space was curtailed, and

by 1852 even the most northern part had to be given up.[10]

In 1852 the Rev. Dr. Walker (who was then building houses in Clarendon Road, see page 119) bought from the Misses Mary Anne and Georgina Charlotte Talbot fifty-one acres of Portobello farm-land. This covered the whole strip of North Kensington lying east of Portobello Lane from Portobello farm-house on the north to Lonsdale Road and Western Terrace on the south. On this land which joined the " Ladbrooke Estate," Dr. S. Edmund Walker commenced to build " a new town " and erect an elaborate church to the memory of his parents. The road on which the church was built was called St. Columb's Road, and the church was dedicated to St. Ann, but the name of " All Saints " was soon substituted.[11] See map of 1855 on page 172. This " very stately and abnormal stone church, built after the model of that at St. Columb's Major in Cornwall, from the design of William White, was structurally completed in 1855, but owing to pecuniary difficulties was left without glass or furniture till 1861." [12] Meanwhile it stood boarded up and weed-grown near

[10] This information has been pieced together from newspaper cuttings at the Public Library, a letter from Mr. C. S. Baldwin to Mr. F. L. Emanuel, 1911, and other sources.

[11] A daughter church, an iron building, was placed in Lancaster Road about 1877, and very rightly received the name of St. Columb's. About 1892 it was made a separate parish and the present fine Romanesque Basilica was built.

[12] *London Churches Ancient and Modern,* 2nd series, T. Francis Bumpus.

a pond, the open ground behind being sometimes
occupied by gipsies. A footpath which started beside
the church, for some years after this date, led over
fields all the way to Kensal Green. In 1861
Dr. Walker finished the church in a less costly
manner, and presented the living to the Rev. John
Light. But already it was known as Walker's
Folly, and was sometimes irreverently called " All
Sinners in the Mud."

The clustered columns of English marbles, the
great east window and other beautiful structural details
belong to the earlier period. Dr. Walker had intended
to crown the tower, one hundred feet high, by a spire
as lofty as that of Salisbury Cathedral. But " when
the tower itself had just been completed a settlement
made its appearance . . . and work had to be stopped
. . . on what would otherwise have been one of the
very finest towers and spires in the country." 13 " The
nobly proportioned tower, whose outline recalls that
of Ghent," when seen at sunset against the western
sky is, perhaps, the most beautiful object in the whole
of North Kensington. See illustration on page 166.

The land lying south and east of the new church
between Ledbury Road, Lonsdale Road and Portobello
Lane, was eventually bought by Mr. Tibbetts and
became Tibbetts' Brick Fields. A gate stood where
Talbot Road crosses Ledbury Road. Mr. Hitchcock,

---

13 *The Builder's Journal,* May 14, 1895. There have been many beautiful
additions to this church.

already referred to, was lost in this brickfield as a small child about the year 1856. And another friend can recall how, in 1860 or 1861, after watching her father who was laying the tiles in " All Saints," she was shut into the church, from which she was rescued by the night-watchman. The Messrs. Tibbetts are said to have built most of the Colville and Powis Square houses and the adjacent residential streets which were gradually covering the All Saints Fields. The names of Powis and Arundel are derived from the titles of the Earls of Shrewsbury and Talbot.

While this district east of Portobello Lane was in course of development, the lane itself had become what with little exaggeration has been described as " the Market Centre of Kensington." Until 1864 there were scarcely any buildings along the road. The first house, now No. 223a, Portobello Road, for several years stood alone and unfinished. It was known as " The Folly," and the name is perpetuated in Folly Mews. A shop has been built over the front garden. Formerly this house was a laundry with fields which stretched down to Ladbroke Grove. The " Warwick Castle " at the corner of Cornwall Road, is the successor of a small inn of the same name ; and opposite the inn, across Portobello Lane, was a cattle-pond at the edge of a field. In the early sixties there was also a two-storied country inn called the " Ben Jonson."

By 1872 houses and shops stood in an almost continuous line on each side of the road. It is in this part of the road that Portobello Market takes place : one of the distinctive characteristics of Notting Hill, and " of general London notoriety." (Even as late as 1919 the stalls hardly extended beyond the railway arch.) In a pamphlet, published in 1909, the statement is made that " the market was established some eighty or ninety years ago." [14] This is obviously incorrect. Two old ladies belonging to the coster fraternity, each about seventy years of age in 1916, had been amongst the earliest traders. Certainly this market did not exist before the early sixties, therefore some fifteen years after " the Market " commenced in Norland Road. Sir William Bull (see note 5), describes the scene from a boy's point of view. " Columbus discovered Porto Bello in 1502. We discovered Portobello Road about 370 years later. Carnival time was on Saturday nights in the winter, when it was thronged like a fair from Cornwall Road to Bolton Road. The people overflowed from the pavement so that the roadway was quite impassable for horse traffic which, to do it justice, never appeared. On the left-hand side (the east side) were costers' barrows, lighted by flaming naphtha lamps. In the side streets were side-shows," vendors of patent medicines, conjurors, itinerant vocalists, etc. Many

[14] *The Interesting History of Portobello Road, the Market Centre of Kensington*, by Ernest P. Woolf, 1909.

"THE BROOK."

"IN AND OUT."

From a set of four coloured prints of "The Last Grand Steeplechase" at the Hippodrome Race-
course, Kensington, 1841. By Henry Alken, Junr.

"AT MISS WILSON'S SEMENARY, KENSINGTON GRAVEL PITS," 1812.

NOTTING HILL GATE, FROM CHURCH STREET.
By W. Cleverley Alexander, 1912.

NOTTING HILL TOLL GATE, LOOKING EAST, ABOUT 1835.

Adapted by E. Woolmer, from a water-colour by H. Oakes Jones.

Kensington Public Library.

By Henry Alken, Junr., 1834.

St. James Norlands.

Cottages near the Potteries

1857

A Road through the Potteries

G.W.R. train crossing Wormwood Scrubs

1841

H. Alken Junr

In Norland Town.

F. Woolmer

Royal Crescent.
1857

VIEWS IN NORLAND TOWN.
Drawing by Miss Woolmer.

HIGH STREET, NOTTING HILL.

HIGH STREET, NOTTING HILL.
(Two pictures from a booklet containing six views, published by Churchill, 1857.)

PORTION OF MAP BY J. WYLD, 1850.

CHURCH OF ST. JOHN THE EVANGELIST, 1849.
Old drawing, copied by T. Butler Cato.

NOTTING HILL TOLL GATE, 1860.
Adapted by E. Woolmer, from picture in *Illustrated London News.*

KENSINGTON PARK ESTATE, NOTTING HILL.

Large lithographic view of Stanley Crescent and Kensington Park Gardens.

Drawn by Thomas Allom.

COTTAGES IN "KENSINGTON POTTERIES," 1855.
From "Ragged Homes and How to Mend Them," by Mrs. M. Bayly.

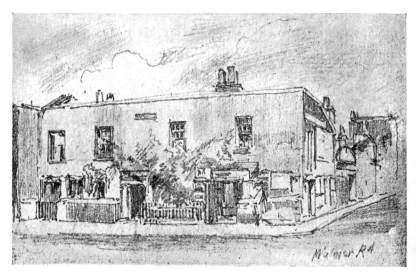

HOUSES IN WALMER ROAD.
Drawing by W. Cleverley Alexander.

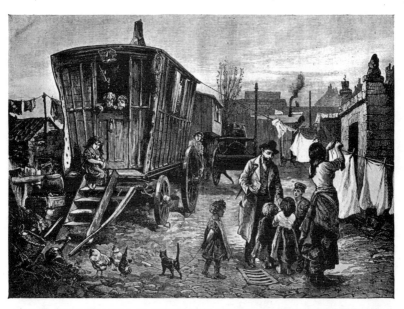

SKETCH OF GYPSY LIFE : AN ENCAMPMENT NEAR LATIMER ROAD, NOTTING HILL,
NOVEMBER, 1879.

" GYPSYS " : SKETCH NEAR LATIMER ROAD, NOTTING HILL, JANUARY, 1880.
(Both from the *Illustrated London News.*)

FROM POST OFFICE MAP, B. R. DAVIS, 1868.

PORTION OF SCHOOL BOARD MAP OF LONDON, E. STANFORD, 1880–1884.

All Saints Church

Boundary House

St Peter's Church

St John's Church

Grove House

Harbury Chapel and Kensington Park Road

E. Woolmer. del

GROUP OF BUILDINGS AT "BAYSWATER END."
Drawing by Miss Ethel Woolmer.

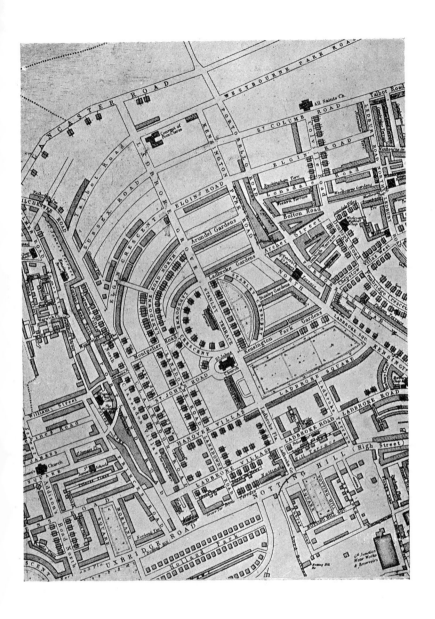

FROM SHEET I OF THE *WEEKLY DISPATCH* ATLAS, BY EDWARD WELLER, 1855–1860.

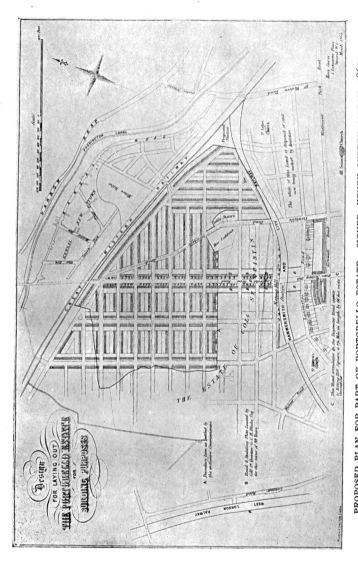

PROPOSED PLAN FOR PART OF PORTOBELLO ESTATE. SIGNED, HENRY CURREY, MARCH, 1865.

an older inhabitant of Notting Hill has come to shop
in " the Lane," not only for the sake of the excellent
quality of the food sold there, but also for sheer enjoyment of the cheery cries and the surging crowds and
heavily laden stalls, "where in the lamplight sepia
pavements shine, and the blue naphtha flames upon the
stall." [15] " Here one can see," writes Mr. Woolf, [14]
" mechanic and artisan life in its best and truest form
. . . the happy and sturdy husband with pipe in
mouth, looking after his children, perhaps with one
on his shoulder, whilst his better half is bargaining
for the Sunday joint or resolving on the most tooth-
some trimmings. Orderliness exists in the extreme,
and a police charge in Portobello Road on a Saturday
night is of the rarest occurrence." In 1909 Portobello Market was still chiefly in the hands of the old
breed of costermongers, and " the utmost good-fellow-
ship " existed between the shopkeepers and themselves. (Unfortunately the same cannot be said to-day,
when the street traders are largely recruited from the
neighbouring community of Jews, and the market
is held on every day in the week.)

The houses on the west side of this part of Portobello Road were originally built as private dwellings ;
but shops were soon placed over their front gardens.
The houses opposite from the beginning were built
as shops. Several old-established businesses still
exist, one of the earliest being the large drapery store

[15] From a poem *Celestial Beauty,* by Evelyn Underhill.

of Mr. William H. Gough, Nos. 146, 148 and 150,
which was founded in 1859. For many years the
timber-yard of Messrs. Horsman occupied the site
of No. 191, and during forty years a corn and forage
business, managed by Mr. John Green, stood at the
corner of Elgin Crescent. Mr. Green was on the
Kensington Vestry and was also known for a simplified
musical notation, used for teaching hymn-singing in
some of the neighbouring Ragged Schools. Another
trader, Mr. F. Charlton Frye, represented North
Kensington first on the London County Council, and
then in Parliament. In these pages, as far as possible,
the names of persons still living are avoided ; but no
account of Portobello Road as a trading centre would
be complete without some reference to the green-
grocery and florist's business of Mr. Jesse Smith,
which, from the humblest beginnings, has grown
within a lifetime to its present large proportions.
Much of the trading in this business and others takes
place from the pavement outside the shops.

A Ragged Day and Evening School was started
about 1870 on the site of the present Salvation Army
Hall ; but this came to an end when a Board School
was opened, in March 1876, on the long strip of vacant
ground beside the railway embankment. Portobello
Road School is only one story high. On account of
the convenience of the communicating class-rooms,
and also from its central position, this school has always
played an important rôle in the civic life of North

Kensington. Here also the July Exhibitions of the Notting Hill Flower Show and Home Improvement Society were held for several years.[16]

During the period in which Portobello Road was being developed as a centre for trade the Colville and Powis district was becoming consolidated. Among its earliest inhabitants was Mr. Walter Wren, the celebrated coach, who prepared hundreds of young men for the higher examinations, especially for the Indian Civil Service.[17] The coaching establishment of Messrs. Wren and Gurney, afterwards known as " Wren College," occupied a series of houses in Powis Square. Apartments and boarding-houses for students sprang up in the vicinity. So many of these were occupied by men of Oriental birth that the neighbourhood acquired the name of " Little India." Unfortunately this new quarter rapidly declined, and many of the houses were divided into flats or " maisonettes " at a comparatively early date. (Later on much of this property was included in the Strutt Estate.)

In 1869 an iron building, the forerunner of Talbot Tabernacle, was put up by Gordon Furlong, Esq., close to All Saints Church, as a " non-sectarian Church

---

[16] This Society will be referred to in Chapter X.

[17] Although a cripple Mr. Wren became a member of the London County Council and afterwards a member of Parliament. He died in 1898.

of Christ." For two years previously Mr. Gordon Furlong, formerly a barrister, had conducted services in Victoria Hall, Archer Street. From 1876 to 1906 Mr. Frank Henry White was the beloved pastor of this church ; a man whose character is said to have been described by his names of Frank and White. It was in 1888, during his ministry, that " the old tin Tabernacle " was replaced by the present chapel with its fine Romanesque façade in red brick.

In the remaining portion of Kensington parish, lying north of Talbot Road, the houses were built on a smaller scale, those nearest the line of the Hammersmith and City Railway being the poorest. Cornwall Road, within the northern edge of the Hippodrome Estate, was extended westward to join the course of the old " Green Lane," thus forming a connection with Paddington. This road, originally known as Westbourne Park Road West, may some day become part of the course of the Western Arterial Avenue. Probably Dr. Walker sold the northern part of his fifty-one acres to the railway company. By 1865 (see plan on page 178), the land north of Cornwall Road was " being worked by builders " all the way from Portobello Lane to the Great Western Road.

Here the south to north boundary line between the parishes runs along St. Luke's Road and crosses the railway at Acklam Footbridge. This bridge was opened about 1870. The streets bordering St. Luke's

Road were originally occupied by quite a good class of residents, including many literary, professional and military men, with their families and their servants. The children in these families usually attended one of the excellent private middle-class schools which then abounded in Bayswater. One such " Academy for Young Gentlemen " was started, about 1869, by Mr. Frederick Hopkins in St. Mary's Road, and a high-class " Boarding School for Young Ladies " was kept by the Misses Johnson at No. 12, The Terrace, Tavistock Road (see note 5).

The only other early building in this area which need be mentioned is the large Congregational Chapel, placed in Lancaster Road at a time when all this part was little more than open fields. The foundation stone was laid by Samuel Morley, M.P., in July 1865. For many years this place of worship was a power for good under the able and earnest ministry of the Rev. James Stuart Russell. The building remains, at the corner of Basing Road, though it is now used for trade purposes.[18]

[18] It is interesting to note that Notting Dale Chapel in Walmer Road was at one time in the hands of the same firm of Drapers' Stand manufacturers.

CHAPTER IX

PORTOBELLO ROAD AND KENSAL NEW TOWN

THERE seems to be a natural break where the railway embankment crosses Portobello Road. At this point the old lane was interrupted by low marshy ground, overgrown with rushes and water-cress, and it is said that snipe were shot here almost within living memory. The stream which commenced close to Portobello Farm was blotted out in the building of the railway, but it is quite understandable that the existence of water still makes itself manifest from time to time in the basements along Lancaster and Cornwall Roads. North of the hidden stream the ground rises sharply, and here, before the year 1864, stood Portobello Farm in the midst of widely extended cornfields and meadow-land, with scarcely a house to be seen all the way to Kensal Green. But a footpath leading to Notting Barns diverged on the left before the farm-house was reached (see page 76), and a "lodge" was situated by the gate where this footpath joined the lane. The elm trees bordering this path, and the lodge are shown in the drawing on page 188, see also the map of 1850. This lodge is still represented by a tiny house close to the railway.

In its later years Portobello Farm was known as Wise's Farm. The farm-house is said to have been built by Mr. A. Adams shortly before 1740, see Chapter III, although Abraham Adams does not seem to be mentioned in the Rate Books until 1795, when a man of that name leased nearly two-thirds of the pasture land belonging to the Manor of Knotting Barns. In 1816 William Wise appears on the scene. He took over the whole of Mr. Adams' farm, rated at £410, and, before the year 1829, had added to his possessions portions of Knotting Barns land which had already passed through other hands. " Portobella " was now rated at £700 or even more, and " Mr. Wise farmed all the land north of Cornwall Road." In 1854 the Misses Talbot (see page 59) offered " the substantial Farm Residence " with 12 acres of land for sale, and a further lot of 30 acres of freehold meadow land to the west of Portobello Lane. Probably this remained unsold.

The illustration on page 188, is from a drawing made in 1864, shortly before the farm-house was bought by the Institution of the " Little Sisters of the Poor " belonging to St. Servan, Brittany. St. Joseph's Home for the Aged was placed on the site, and was opened by this community about the year 1866. The last piece of old wall only disappeared in the year 1882 when a wing was added to the large building in Portobello Road. All that now remains of the farmstead is the memory of the orchard, which occupied the site of the charming walled garden presided over by the coloured figure of St. Joseph. Two hundred or more aged men and women, of various creeds, are tended by the Sisters, and, until war-time restrictions made it impossible, the inmates were largely supported by contributions of food and money collected daily by two Sisters, accompanied by a covered cart driven by an old man.[1]

In 1862, nearly four years before Portobello Farm disappeared, a large Franciscan Convent, with St. Elizabeth's Home for Children, was placed on the other side of the lane. (Since 1896 this convent has belonged to the Dominican Order, and the St. Elizabeth's Home has been turned into St. Anne's Home for Working Girls and a school for children suffering from diseases of the eye. Nuns in black and white habits may be seen sauntering among the beautiful trees in the garden behind the white brick building.) In the days of the Franciscan occupancy about a quarter of an acre of the grounds was reserved for the interment of the nuns. This cemetery, a triangular grass plot, edged with trees, was sanctioned by the Home Secretary in 1862. Eight nuns were buried there before the year 1895 ; then the coffins

---

[1] The account of this Charity is somewhat incorrectly given in *Kensington,* by G. E. Mitton, 1903.

were re-interred in St. Mary's Cemetery, Kensal Green. " Armed with the minute from the London County Council authorizing her to visit burial grounds " a sister of the writer, in 1893, applied at the gate for admission, and was courteously shown this hallowed spot by the Mother Superior herself.[2]

To return to about the year 1860. Just north of Portobello Farm was a gate where the lane split into two. The footpath to the right passed through " Meadowlands " to Kensal Road by a five-barred gate and a level crossing over the Great Western line. The other footpath, afterwards the continuation of Portobello Road, reached Kensal Green by foot-bridges over the Great Western Railway and the canal.

An interesting plan exists, dated March 1865, a " Design for Laying out the Portobello Estate for Building Purposes," signed Henry Currey, 5, Lancaster Place, Strand. The fields lying south of the Hammersmith and City Railway were then being built over (see page 178), and land had been taken already for the two convents ; but, in spite of this reduction in area, the remaining portion of the Portobello Estate was larger than the Hippodrome Estate. According to this plan it was proposed to build rectangular streets over the whole estate. The scheme was not carried out.

The triangle of North Kensington east of Portobello

[2] *The Burial Grounds of London,* by Mrs. Basil Holmes, 1896.

Road is now a distinct district, which, with Kensal
Town, forms the Golborne Ward.   It was late in the
sixties before any serious attempt was made to develop
this district ; but, when once set in hand, streets of
good-sized, middle-class houses soon covered the
meadows and the cornfield on the site of Warnington
or Wornington Road.   Portobello Bridge, a brick
bridge with a small signal-box beside it, replaced the
level crossing over the railway, and the path from
Portobello Farm to Kensal Road was planted with
trees, and was known as Britannia Road.   Later
on the trees were cut down and the name was changed
to Golbourne, and, still later, to Golborne Road.

Golborne Hall, " a plaster-fronted brick chapel,"
belongs to this early time.   It was erected by
Mr. Allen, a local builder and seems first to have been
used for Church of England services.   Then the hall
was bought by the Rev. Mr. Davies, a Congregational
minister. (It is now Golborne Road Protestant
Church.)   But the building of a large Gothic Church
was soon commenced in a field north of the Great
Western Railway, close to Golborne Road.   At this
spot the parishes of Paddington, Kensington and
Chelsea meet.   The Order in Council describes the
new parochial district as " certain extremities of the
parish of All Saints, Notting Hill, of the Consolidated
Chapelry of St. John's, Kensal Green, and of the new
parish of Holy Trinity, Paddington."   The church,
designed by E. B. Keeling, Esq., for a considerable

time was left unfinished, but was eventually consecrated during a furious gale on January 8, 1870. The Rev. Robert Towers had been appointed incumbent in 1869 ; he remained in charge of the parish until 1902. It had been arranged that the church should be dedicated to St. Andrew, but, at the suggestion of the Bishop of London, the name of St. Philip was added in order to distinguish it from St. Andrew's Lancaster Road, which had been destroyed by fire in 1867 (see page 153). Christ Church, Faraday Road, was not built until 1881. Christ Church is a simple Gothic church with the unusual feature of a narthex or vestibule. There is also a vicarage and parish-room and an enclosed garden containing tall plane-trees ; showing that there was land and to spare when the church buildings were planned. The Rev. Edward Wrangles Clarke was vicar from the commencement, and lived to see his parish entirely covered with houses. (The Christchurch Oxford Mission is now in charge.)

" Green Lane Park " was the name proposed for the new district. This was followed by " Portobello Park," and later by " Upper Westbourne Park," a name still occasionally used. Originally it had been intended that Golborne Road should cross Kensal Road and the canal, so as to connect North Kensington with Harrow Road. The Paddington Canal Company stopped this design by placing a footbridge over the canal where no thoroughfare existed. Wedlake Street

Bridge, built by the London County Council, afterwards took its place, and the halfpenny toll was
discontinued. Had the original plan been carried
out probably the whole district would have developed
in a more satisfactory manner. Between the Great
Western Railway and Portobello Road the growth
of population was so rapid that the school accommodation provided by churches and chapels was quite
inadequate, and Wornington Road School was
actually the first Board-school to be built in North
Kensington. It opened on March 2, 1874 ; and
has twice been enlarged. At that time the surrounding
streets were inhabited by superior mechanics and
railway employés. To a limited extent this character
has been maintained.

It is difficult to trace the origin of the names of the
streets in this quarter. Golbourne, now Golborne
Road may be derived from Dean Goulbourne, the
beloved vicar of St. John's, Paddington. Swinbrook
is probably the name of a person, not, as suggested,
the name of the brook which rose close to Portobello
Farm. St. Ervan's Road is named after a holy man
whom Prebendary Denison, formerly of St. Michael
and All Angels, sought for in vain in the Calendar of
Saints. (Could the name be derived from St. Servan,
Brittany, page 187 ?) But immediately surrounding
Christ Church is an interesting group of streets
representing leaders in the world of science and
engineering : Wheatstone, Faraday, Murchison,

Telford and Rendle or Rendel. The names of Hazelwood Crescent and Appleford Road do not refer to earlier conditions. In olden times there may have been nut-bushes in this part of Middlesex Forest, but no apple trees grew beside a ford, for there was no stream here until the canal was made along Harrow Road. Murchison Road was formerly known as Queen Anne's Terrace, probably because the houses were of red brick. There are few other signs of colour or variety.

The upper end of Portobello Road is peculiarly depressing. The long unbroken line of houses and shops on either side of the way look shabbier than the more uneven buildings in the older parts of " the Lane," and the shops have a dreary habit of keeping their blinds drawn half-way down. Naturally the street is the playground of children and dogs. Most of the houses are let out in floors, although built for a single family and quite unsuited to the needs of three or four. " I can imagine, if I try hard," writes Dr. Paget, " a world of dull tints and stupid outlines with no more claim to good looks than a house in Portobello Road might care to make." 3 It is only through an intimate knowledge of the heroic lives passed in these uninspiring surroundings that any enthusiasm can be aroused. The lowest depths of untidiness are reached in some of the mews ? Yet, just at the corner where Portobello and Wornington

3 *I Sometimes Think*, by Stephen Paget, 1916.

Roads meet, Lavie Mews carries the mind back to semi-rural days. Forty or more years ago a circus stood on this spot. Later on donkeys, used on Wormwood Scrubbs, were stabled here, and a half-penny was charged for a ride from one end of the mews to the other. This is the reason why " Donkey Mews " is its local name.

Immediately to the north of the Portobello Area is Kensal Town which covers the detached portion of Chelsea parish lying south of the Paddington branch of the Grand Junction Canal. Since the London Government Act of 1899 came into force, this " outland " of Chelsea has been reckoned as belonging for municipal purposes to the boroughs of Paddington and Kensington, though for parochial and parliamentary purposes it is still part of Chelsea. The portion belonging to Kensington now embraces Kensal Road between Bosworth Road and Ladbroke Grove, and, crossing the line of the Great Western Railway, includes some houses on the north side of Wornington Road. Blocks in the pavement indicate the boundaries of the parishes. The map of 1833 (see 40), shows the " outland " when it was divided by Harrow Road and the canal but was not yet hemmed in by the railway. It was still entirely rural. The larger portion lying north of Harrow Road remained as fields, chiefly used for the grazing of sheep, right up to about 1875 when the land was required for the building of Queen's Park Estate.

The early history of the Chelsea " Outland," first as part of Middlesex Forest, and then as four fields covering the whole 137¾ acres of the enclosure, has been told in Chapter I. Its temporary connection with Knotting Barns ceased in 1543, when Robert White was obliged to give up possession of all his lands in Kensington, Paddington and Chelsea, and these fields, as part of the Manor of Chelsea, were given by Henry VIII to Catherine Parr, as her marriage portion. As early as the middle of the fifteenth century part of this land was included in the " Manor of Malures " which Henry VI ceded to the Warden and Fellows of All Souls College, Oxford. That college still owns land in Kensal Green, and its name is perpetuated in All Souls Cemetery.[4] In 1557, during Queen Mary's reign, Thomas or Alexander Hues, Esq., one of the Queen's " phicisions," bought part of Chelsea and other lands from the Queen in order to found two or more scholarships at Merton College, Oxford. The names of the Chelsea fields in 1544 and 1557 are given in Chapter I. From the deed of 1557 it would seem that the wedge-shaped portion, now included in North Kensington, covered part of the field called Darking Busshes and part of the field of Baudelands. Two later surveys are recorded.

---

[4] *Memorials of Old Chelsea*, by A. Beaver, 1892 ; *History of Chelsea*, by T. Faulkner, 1810, and other works.

Early in the eighteenth century a List of the Chelsea
Fields was made by Dr. John King, rector of Chelsea.
By this time the quaint names given in Chapter I
had been replaced by the Mead, the Wood Ground
called Bushfield, the Barn Field. and the Four Hills.
These names suggest that groups of trees or thick
undergrowth still existed. The second survey was
made and a map drawn in 1767, by order of a later
rector, the Rev. Reginald Heber. This map was
preserved in St. Luke's vestry when Faulkner wrote his
History of Chelsea. The land was then divided into
eight or nine " pieces " distinguished chiefly by the
number of acres they contained.

At the end of the eighteenth century one building
stood perhaps on the south side of Harrow Road.
This was a mill for preparing from woollen rags a flock-
dust, which was sprinkled on paper hangings to give
them the appearance of cloth. This mill was said to
be in " Little Chelsea in Kensington parish." [5] Up to
the middle of the nineteenth century these pastures
were sometimes called " Chelsea Reach " ; [6] " Upper
Chelsea " is another and more suitable name. Little
change in the rural character of the district was
produced by the making of the Paddington Branch
of the Grand Junction Canal between the years 1795
and 1801. Some thirty years later the Flora Tea

[5] *Environs of London*, by the Rev. Dr. Lysons, 1790.
[6] Mr. W. Robins in his *History of Paddington*, 1853, refers to certain
fabulous tales, given as the reason for applying to this northern region the
name of the Thames opposite Chelsea.

Gardens and a few small houses appeared on Harrow Road at the point where the canal turns southwards. See pages 76 and 194. The back of these buildings overlooked " the canal with the rich pastures leading to the Uxbridge Road and the Surrey Hills." These words were written in 1838.

Already the Great Western Railway crossed the landscape. It was the building of this line, between the years 1832 and 1838, that effectually isolated the strip of land lying between the canal and the railway. From this time onwards a village, to which was given the name of Kensal New Town, began to develop on lines of its own. The map of 1841, on page 76, shows Kensal Road with some houses on the northern side. They had gardens opening on to the towing path, and a group of cottages stood by the ferry where the road emerged on Green Lane. East Row, Middle Row, West Row and South Row were built by 1850. It is evident, therefore, that Kensal New Town came into existence between 1835 and 1850 ; and this agrees with the date of St. John's, Kensal Green, a church which was commenced late in 1843. See illustration on page 214. For a good many years the village consisted only of the " Rows " and Albert, otherwise Kensall Road. The staple industry was laundry work, " in fact Kensal New Town was a laundry colony." In this trade men and women alike were engaged. But a good many pigs were kept,

and in the evenings the cottagers employed themselves
in their gardens, the produce from which proved a
further source of profit to the family exchequer. "Fifty
years ago there were more roses than houses in Kensal
New Town," and part of it remained very countrified,
although so near London, nearly up to the end of the
nineteenth century. A friend remembers how pleased
she was as a child to accompany her mother to the
cottage where their laundress lived, for she was always
given beautiful flowers from the garden which bordered
the canal.

The following particulars will become clearer by
consulting the *Weekly Dispatch* map of about 1855
on page 194. In 1845 a trotting match attracted
a great concourse of people to the village. A pony,
belonging to a Mr. French, harnessed to a light trap,
accomplished one hundred miles well under the
allotted sixteen hours. The race started from "The
Friend in Hand" in Middle Row, and must have
been run on ground known as "the Common,"
ground now occupied by the Omnibus Garage and
St. Mary's School. From the late fifties to "some
time in the seventies" a noted beer-house, known
as the "Beehive," stood where the pathway from
Portobello Lane, afterwards Golborne Road, joined
Kensal Road. A cheap-jack sold his wares outside
this tavern ; but further west, apparently on the
space now represented by Wedlake Street, a Saturday
night market was held : Edgware Road, the nearest

shopping centre, being difficult to reach across the fields. Frequent rowdy scenes took place in this open market, until at last the Rev. Bee Wright, well-known at the time for his opposition to Sunday trading, got permission to put up an iron chapel on the ground. But the first place of worship erected in the village was the tiny Primitive Methodist Chapel in Middle Row, now overshadowed by the lofty elementary school beside it. It has been claimed that this chapel has existed on this spot for more than one hundred years. This, however, is incorrect. Two Wesleyan Chapels are shown on the map on page 194, and the map also gives the names of six public-houses in the village.

Besides laundry-work there was another recognized local profession : that of dog-fancying and dog-stealing. The most noted character in the dog-fancying line was " Bill George," a famous " pug " or prize-fighter in earlier days, who lived first at the Paddington end of Kensal Road, but later on moved into the heart of the village. At " Canine Castle " he kept a remarkable collection of valuable dogs, and was often visited, so the story goes, by members of the aristocracy, as also by anyone who had lost a dog. For a consideration Mr. George could generally find the missing pet : in blunter language " money would get your dog back." [7]

[7] A visit to Mr. George's Home for Dogs is described in *Leaves from a Life*, by Mrs. Panton, 1908, and also in Sir William Bull's *Recollections*.

Many of the inhabitants were Irish, and racial
jealousy under the guise of religious feeling ran high,
just as it ran high in Notting Dale. " Who are you
for, the Pope or Garibaldi ? " was the favourite
challenge. Then the opposing camps would range
themselves for battle. There was a serious riot of
this kind in Middle Row about the year 1860 ; while
two or three hundred policemen were assembled
beside the canal to be called on if necessary. This
riot gave a bad name to Kensal Town. The organized
fights between Kensal Road and Lisson Grove boys
have been already referred to. See page 169.

The canal formed an integral part of the village.
Wharfs existed along Kensal Road, as they exist to
this day. Taft's Wharf was situated where Elcom
Street now stands. There was a good-sized stone
wharf which occupied the site of the Paddington
Baths and Wash-houses until 1866, and also the large
wharf at the western end of the road, from which
barges still carry bricks, sand, straw, hay, or rubbish
to be burnt in the brickfields beyond the limits of
London.[8] But bargees, who have always been an
hereditary and distinct race of people, unlettered,
hard-working and spotlessly clean, never seem to have
seriously influenced the inhabitants of Kensal Town.
Near the site of the Dust Wharf, opposite the gas-

[8] The Dust-Sorting Establishment at Kensal Wharf, whose quaint little
steeple forms such a pleasing object in the vista along Ladbroke Grove, is
of recent date.

works, stood two little cottages, in one of which a son of William Mulready lived for many years. He used to paint scenes visible from this high spot, and the drawing of Notting Hill Farm is probably from his brush. See page 62.

The canal was exposed all along this portion of the Harrow Road, and the tow-path always had, and still has, a great fascination for the boy population of the neighbourhood, although beyond Kensal Green, even in the seventies, it was very lonely and was infested with bad characters.9 In the present condition of the canal it is difficult to realize that pleasure trips were ever a favourite form of recreation. The accommodation barges of earlier days had disappeared (see page 73), but many drawings exist showing passenger steamboats laden with ladies and gentlemen in the costumes of 1840 to 1865, taking advantage of cheap trips arranged during the summer months. Almost to the end of the nineteenth century row-boats might be hired from Piner's Boat-yard, near the Great Western Road, or Sunday-school treat parties might be taken to Greenford by means of Brooks' barges.

As soon as Golborne Road connected Portobello Lane and Kensal Road the isolated character and village life of Kensal New Town began to disappear.

9 " Some Recollections of Bayswater Fifty Years Ago," by the Right Hon. Sir W. Bull, M.P., in the *Bayswater Chronicle*, 1923.

As already stated the new roads south of the railway line were inhabited by a respectable working-class population, largely recruited from railway men.   The roads planned north of the railway were intended for the same class of inhabitants.   Unfortunately most of the houses were at once claimed by a rougher set of people, and have since become more and more degraded.   Mr. Charles Booth [10] describes this as one of the worst districts in London, and social workers recognize that Southam Street (with its 140 nine-roomed houses in which 2,500 people were living in 1923, an average of two persons to every room in the street), and the equally crowded roads in the immediate vicinity, for bad housing accommodation surpass even the Special Area of Notting Dale.   It is the basements which are so appalling, those " slum basements, where rheumatism and consumption and drink scribble their names on the dirty wall-paper " (see note 3). Naturally this part of North Kensington figures week by week in the police news.

But from the earliest days of the colony the Powers of Light have contended against the Powers of Darkness.   Kensal New Town, being part of Chelsea, belonged to the parish of St. John's, Kensal Green, but after 1870 the church of St. Andrew and St. Philip also served the growing population.   Bosworth Hall

[10] In *Life and Labour of the People of London,* by the Hon. Charles Booth, 1903.

was opened for worship in the same year. From 1870 to 1878 this was a branch of Westbourne Grove Chapel, and was ministered to by the Rev. H. W. Meadows. Bosworth Hall was then acquired by Mr. Hammond of Edgware Road, and continued to be used for Divine Service until Mr. Hammond handed it over to the Rev. Dr. John Clifford, in 1884, for a Mission Centre connected with Westbourne Park Chapel. (Clifford's Inn, a public-house without drink, was added in 1901, and Bosworth Hall was rebuilt in 1903.) In 1872 a Roman Catholic Mission was established in Absolom Road, now part of Golborne Gardens. It is represented by the fine, lofty, brick church of " Our Lady of the Holy Souls " in Bosworth Road opened in 1882, by the " Convent of Mercy " in Hazlewood Crescent, and by St. Mary's Schools in East Row, accommodating nearly seven hundred scholars. For many years St. Andrew's Parochial Schools have stood in Bosworth Road facing Southam Street. But the Mission day school held at Bosworth Hall was of still earlier date. This little school, twenty-one feet long, twelve feet wide, and nine feet high, with one small window to the outer light,[11] became woefully inefficient for the teeming multitude of children for whom little other school accommodation was available. But it was not until August 1878 that a Board-school was opened in Middle Row.

[11] These figures are from a letter written by the Hon. E. Lyulph Stanley (Lord Sheffield) to Dr. Gladstone in October 1877.

(Middle Row School has been twice enlarged and now accommodates 1,600 scholars.)

Many social and philanthropic agencies have been situated at the Paddington end of Kensal Road, and their number has been added to in recent times. The Cobden Club, affiliated with the Club and Institute Union, was largely helped in early days by Mr. Passmore Edwards, and the foundation stone of the present tall building was laid by Lord Lyttelton in November 1880. Before 1899 the Cobden Club had a membership of nearly 1,000. The part played by this Club in social welfare is differently estimated by different persons. There was also the little Mission Room where Jim Salmon, a painter, and Owen Murphy, the evangelist, from their own experience of slum life and its temptations, were able to influence for good many of their former companions; and the " Railway Mission " (now known as the West London Open-Air Mission), largely supported by Mr. C. J. D. Derry, the founder of the drapery business in Kensington High Street.

The first Mission building to be placed in Kensal Town itself seems to have been the Gospel Mission Hall, built by Miss Thompson about 1882, between Middle Row and West Row, where a number of small houses had formerly stood. Here Miss Thompson has lived for over forty years, and no account of Kensal Town could be written without mention of her self-sacrificing labours for the good of the people. She came to the district in 1873 when it was still a village, with flower-bedecked cottages, in order to help Miss Merrington with her Infant Day Nursery in Edenham Street. This was one of the very earliest Crèches to be opened in England, and, as pioneer work, is worthy of special notice. (A Crèche is locally known as " the Screech.") In 1877 Miss White of Porchester Gate, with the aid of Miss Thompson, opened a Coffee Room and Centre for Mission work in Golborne Gardens, which was shifted at a later date to 21, Appleford Road. About the year 1890, a Free Medical Mission was added to the other forms of charitable relief. " Nurse Thompson's," as the Medical Mission is generally called, is popular in the neighbourhood, and is interesting as being a unique effort of its kind.

By 1885 the whole of Upper Chelsea, both north and south of Harrow Road, was covered with houses, and the parish of St. John's, Kensal Green, contained some 20,000 souls. At this juncture the Rev. G. W. Lawson was induced to take up work in Kensal Town. In a letter to the present writer Mr. Lawson tells how at first services were held over a butcher's shop. The room soon filled in spite of odours which were anything but pleasant. An iron building belonging to the London City Mission was then used. " It soon became evident that a church was required. . . . And, as St. Thomas in the Liberty of the Rolls was being pulled down, the proceeds in part were devoted

to the new St. Thomas's Church . . . the rest was
raised by subscriptions and donations." The foundation stone was laid by H.R.H. Princess Christian
in May 1889. With its steeple and the large Parochial
Hall this church forms an effective group at the corner
of Kensal Road and East Row.[12] Mr. Lawson was
inducted to the living, and was faced with a flock of
over 3,000 souls, closely packed and somewhat
uncivilized. But he reckons that between Mr. Towers,
at St. Andrews, North Kensington and himself
" there must have been some 14,000 people." It is
a significant fact that, for health reasons, the vicarages
of both these churches are outside their respective
districts. (The fourth vicar is now in possession.)

Very little has been put into print about this corner
of London, and, in gathering together the story of
Bygone Days, it has been necessary almost entirely to
rely on the reminiscences of persons still living. Few
distinctive features remain and " Kensal," as it is
familiarly called, is fast becoming much like other
suburban slums. But in South Row and at the west
end of Kensal Road some vestiges of village life may
still be found, and certain corners and courtyards lower
down the road retain a strangely old-world appearance. Most of the cottages in the centre of " the
Town " have disappeared, for houses, left empty,
become derelict in an incredibly short space of time.

---

[12] Both Bosworth Hall and this hall have been used as centres for the
feeding of necessitous school children.

(The story is told of two or three dwellings in Middle Row from which all the available woodwork was stolen within two days.) Cottages have been replaced by poor shops or by rows of uninteresting houses, and factories and other trade premises now cover what used to be gardens and drying grounds for linen. But typical one-storied houses stood on the east side of East Row until they made way for the dainty Japanese water garden and Children's Recreation Ground known as Elmslie Horniman Park or The Pleasance. The illustrations on page 202 are of these houses shortly before they were pulled down in 1911. It was on open ground between these houses and Bosworth Road that a group of gipsy families used to establish themselves during the winter. A fair was held in the encampment, and other members of the group helped at the annual entertainment in the Agricultural Hall. This was at the beginning of the present century, but may be regarded as a survival of a former age.

Besides distinctive features, the special characteristics of the inhabitants are being lost. On good authority it is stated that before the War nearly two-thirds of the women supported their husbands. Steam laundries have replaced hand laundries. But far less laundry work is done, and many of the women of Kensal, like their sisters of Notting Dale, have had to take to other employments. It may be that moral conditions are not so bad as has sometimes been asserted ; but they are bad enough, and the enormous rateable value attached to some of the public-houses tells its own tale. A dweller of long standing in Kensal Road confessed that, though he had carried on business with these people for many years, he could not fathom their ways, for people who live in degraded conditions become very deceptive and refuse to be interfered with. And in graphic language he added : "As long as four or five families inhabit one house so long there will be awfulness ! "

CHAPTER X

ST. CHARLES'S WARD.

THE Borough of Kensington is divided into nine Wards, five of which are on the south of Uxbridge Road, and four on the north of that road. Of the four northern wards Norland Ward and Pembridge Ward lie between Uxbridge Road and the curved line of Lancaster Road ; they are divided by Ladbroke Grove. Golborne Ward, a comparatively small area to the east of Portobello Road, includes Kensal Town, and was dealt with in the preceding chapter. St. Charles's Ward, the remaining tract of land, is much larger than any of the others. It is bounded on the east by Portobello Road, on the north by Harrow Road from Ladbroke Grove to the western limit of Kensal Green Cemetery, and on the west by the parish boundary as far south as Lancaster Road.

When Mr. Loftie wrote of Kensington in 1888 " a new quarter " was " rapidly springing up on the slope towards Kensal Green," and " New Found Out " was a local name given to the district. But, although this " quarter " is of recent growth, some of the earliest

associations of Notting Hill fall within St. Charles's
Ward.   The Manor House and farmstead of Notting
Barns, surrounded by wide-spreading pastures, was
in the valley to the north of Notting Wood, and
on " the way from London to Harrow " a few small
houses, some in Kensington, some in Willesden
parish, formed the picturesque hamlet of Kensal or
Kellsall Greene.   Up to quite recent times this part
of Harrow Road was little more than a country lane.
It is reported to have been the scene of some of Dick
Turpin's exploits.[1]   In Cary's Plan of London,
1810, it is only marked by a dotted line, but from the
sixteenth century onwards the " Plough " with its
oak timbers and joists had stood beside this track.
According to Faulkner " Morland the celebrated
painter was much pleased with this sequestered place,
and spent much of his time in this house towards the
close of his life ; surrounded by those rustic scenes
which his pencil has so faithfully and ably delineated."

George Morland was born in 1763 and died in
1804.   In the year 1786 he married Nancy Ward ;
her brother William Ward, the engraver, marrying
Morland's sister.   The Morlands lived in Kensal
Green until after the death of their little son.   The
well-known picture of " Children Nutting " was
engraved in 1788, two years after this marriage.
It seems quite possible that the subject was suggested

---

[1] *Rookwood*, by Harrison Ainsworth, 1834.   Mr. Ainsworth had a house
on the road just beyond Kensal Green.

by the nut-bushes which, according to tradition, were plentiful all over the neighbourhood.

The " Plough " at an earlier period has already figured in Chapters I and II, and pictures of the inn with sign-board and trough appear on pages 14 and 22. It was still very countrified even in 1868, as is seen from the drawing on page 210. No signs of rustic beauty remain in the present large brick building at the corner of Ladbroke Grove and Harrow Road, but it must be remembered that this is the only house in North Kensington that has a name dating back four hundred years.

A description of the district written by Mrs. Henley Jervis in 1884 is of special value. She states that before the nineteenth century this part of Kensington was " an extent of woodlands, cornfields and heath, the heavy clay ground often becoming well-nigh impassable in rainy weather, as even the present generation can understand if they recollect Lancaster Road and Elgin Road in 1862. Tradition tells us that Prince George of Denmark (Queen Anne's Consort) well-nigh came to grief by his horse becoming completely bemired somewhere near the present St. Charles's Square. The old ' Plough ' was the most distant dwelling in the north-west of Kensington parish ; upon the borders of the debatable land to which we (Kensington) Chelsea and Paddington have rights of so ill-defined a nature, that within the last three years the highway near the Canal Bridge was a grievance to man and beast, and it was no person's business to mend it."[2]

Chapter I of these Chronicles shows how difficult it is to determine the limits of Kensington and Paddington in early days, so this reference to the continued vagueness of the boundary line is most interesting. Dr. Stukeley, the Antiquarian, in Notes written about 1760, speaks of Kelsing or Cansholt Green as belonging to the parishes of Paddington, Kensington, Chelsea and Willesden, and says that at Canshold Green on the road to Harrow " the parish of Chelsea have erected two posts in this road showing how far they are to mend thereof "[3]. After the Perambulation of Kensington Parish in 1799 boundary posts were placed on the south side of Harrow Road.[4]   The " Beating of the Bounds " seems to have been carried out for the last time on Ascension Day 1884, but disputes about the division of the parishes continued until Kensal Town was definitely handed over to the care of the Borough of Kensington.

The first encroachment on this stretch of open land was the cutting of the Paddington Branch of the Grand Junction Canal, which was opened for water transport in 1801.   Some thirty years later land lying between the canal and Harrow Road was converted into a burial ground.   Kensal Green Cemetery occupies

[2] Notes in *Kensington Parish Magazine* for 1884, by Mrs. Henley Jervis.

[3] This valuable MS. was kindly lent to the writer by its owner, the late Mrs. St. John, of Dinmore.

[4] *History of Kensington,* by T. Faulkner, 1820.

the highest ground in North Kensington and reaches
150 feet above sea-level. The view from the terrace
in front of the Cemetery church is still beautiful, and
must have been far more beautiful in bygone
days. The 56 acres of 1832, see page 77, have been
increased to 77 acres, and many of the most con-
spicuous personages of the Victorian Era rest in
Kensal Green. Modern writers on the subject are
apt to decry this " forlorn necropolis," " the bleakest,
dampest and most melancholy of all the burial grounds
of London," and to deplore the waste involved in
its huge mausoleums and oceans of tombstones.5
But the walks are lined with beautiful trees, and, as
with other cemeteries near London, children haunt
the place and get a grim satisfaction out of watching
the interments. Besides this, on a summer Sunday
afternoon, Kensal Green is largely visited by mourners
and their friends ; thus to some extent taking the
place of a Public Garden or Park.

The track of the Great Western Railway, running
south of the canal, and opened for traffic in 1838,
further curtailed the fields, and this curtailment
increased with the widening of the line. Before
1850 (see map on page 120), the ground between the
canal and the railway was taken over by the Western
Gas Company, and certain buildings were put up.
A countrified house still stands within the boundary

5 See *History of London*, by W. J. Loftie, 1881 ; *Burial Grounds of London*,
by Mrs. Basil Holmes, 1896 ; *London Revisited*, by E. V. Lucas, 1916, etc.

walls. In the early eighties the premises were acquired
by the Gas Light and Coke Company. The whole
intervening space is now covered by their works, and
the Sunday storage gasometer is one of the largest
in London.

Until the eighteen-seventies the canal and railway
line were reached only by footpaths and were crossed
by ferry or footbridge. All funerals approached the
Cemetery along Harrow Road, the northern half of
Ladbroke Grove being then unmade. In the original
copy of the photograph, dated 1866 (see page 184),
hay-fields are seen beyond the railway arch, and,
for several years after its construction, the embankment of the Hammersmith and City Railway was the
limit of building in this direction. The first bridge
at Notting Hill Station, now Ladbroke Grove Station,
collapsed and had to be rebuilt. Gradually the road
was pushed further and further north until it joined
Portobello Lane and Wornington Road close to the
bridge over the Great Western Railway, and thence
proceeded along the old track to Harrow Road. This
extension beyond the Hammersmith and City line
was called Ladbroke Grove Road, and it is only in
recent years that " one of the finest streets in London "
has become known as Ladbroke Grove throughout
its whole length. Formerly a country inn occupied
the position of the large corner house, the " Admiral
Blake," close to the bridge over the Great Western
Railway. Locally the "Admiral Blake " is known as

" The Cowshed," a reminiscence of the time when Admiral Mews was occupied by a series of sheds for cows. Drovers bringing their cattle to the London markets would house them in these sheds for the night, whilst they themselves found shelter and refreshment in the neighbouring tavern.

As stated in previous chapters, the building of the Hammersmith and City Railway forms a very important landmark in the development of North Kensington. Between Notting Hill Station and Latimer Road the line crossed the fan-shaped group of streets, bounded by Walmer Road, which Mr. James Whitchurch had planned in the middle forties. The land immediately to the north from Walmer Road to St. Quintin Avenue had been the extension of the Hippodrome grounds. For some years after 1842, when the race-course came to an end, these fields were, apparently, still used for the training of horses, and were known as Notting Hill Hunting Grounds. It is said that, had the Chartist Rising of April 1848 been successful, the party leaders intended to encamp on these fields.[6] No doubt the enclosure of this ground was the reason why building for many years did not extend beyond Walmer Road. See the map of 1850, on page 120. But in the sixties this land was laid out in market gardens, and terraces of small houses were built along the north end of Latymer Road. The three

[6] *Recollections of a Royal Academician*, J. C. Horsley, 1903.

brothers Keen, John the dairyman, Joseph the market
gardener, and Thomas the coal-merchant, had three
houses on the site occupied since 1885 by Jubilee
Hall. Opposite these houses, on the Hammersmith
side of the road, stood the row of little dwellings
forming Windsor Terrace, known locally as " The
Sixteens." Each house had its pigsty and vegetable
plot. Latymer Road ended with the " North Pole,"
at this period a one-storied country inn. But the
" North Pole," was preceded by the " Globe,"
which probably dated from about 1839, when
the Hippodrome grounds reached to this point.
Globe Terrace recalls the name of this earlier inn,
and the North Pole Road contains the modern
tavern of that name. In later days this part of the
Latimer Road district gained the name of Soapsuds
Island.

The history of Notting Barns has been told up to
the earlier years of the nineteenth century, when
the larger portion of the old Manor was known as the
Portobello Estate. But until 1860 the Notting Barn
fields extended from Lancaster Road to the Great
Western Railway, and probably covered 150 acres, the
size of the estate in 1828. Before 1865 Colonel St.
Quintin had bought the farm-house and the remaining
portion of the Notting Barns land.7 For many years it

7 The name of St. Quentin occurs in the locality in 1839 in connection
with the Hippodrome, when the " Notting Barns Stakes " were augmented
by the generosity of " W. St Quentin, Esq." The family still own the
St. Quintin Park Estate.

had been known as Salter's Farm, and the farm land had been Salter's Fields. Mr. Baldwin, who built houses on part of this land, employed an old carter who worked as a boy on Mr. Salter's farm " about Waterloo year." [8] If this statement is correct Salter must have rented the place while the name of William Smith, Esq., was still on the Rate Books. A Mr. Salter occupied the farm in 1873 ; he died shortly afterwards as a very old man at a house in Lancaster Road. The drawing made in 1873, on page 222, more closely represents Faulkner's description of an " ancient brick building surrounded by spacious barns and out-houses " than does Henry Alken's view of the house in 1841. See page 88. Compare also the illustration on page 14. By 1873 the large barn was let to Mr. Leddiard, cowkeeper and dairyman of Ledbury Road. The man who attended to Mr. Leddiard's cows lived in the cottage beside the barn. But Salter's cows fed on fields further to the north, and were milked under a group of elms on land now covered by the Clement Talbot Motor Works in Barlby Road.

The Salters must have been kindly folk, for Mr. Herbert Friend remembers having his head bound up at the farm after an accident with a toy cannon, and children were often allowed to clamber through the fence, and swing on a branch of the tree overhanging the pond. In winter this pond became quite a lake, and more than one child was nearly drowned

[8] From a letter to Mr. F. W. Emanuel dated 1911.

in it. Between 1870 and 1873, on a Sunday afternoon, the late Lord Cozens Hardy and Mr. W. H. Gurney Salter used to enter the farm-yard by a five-barred gate, and emerge by another gate for a country walk. So rural were the surroundings that boughs of hawthorn in blossom might be carried home from the site of Oxford Gardens, and violets are said to have grown where the " Earl Percy " tavern now stands. To go to Notting Barn Farm for a glass of milk became a recognized excursion; but about 1880 the dilapidated remains of the Manor House were pulled down. A French laundry, named Adelaide House, occupied the spot until about 1886, when it also had to make way for the encroaching building operations of St. Quintin's Park. The farm-house stood where Bramley Road, if continued north, would have crossed Bassett and Chesterton Roads. For awhile the name was retained in Notting Barns Road. But, since that road became St. Helen's Gardens, the old Manor which covered the whole district is only commemorated in the " Notting Barn Tavern," at the corner of Bramley and Silchester Roads.

For some years after the construction of the Hammersmith and City Railway, cricket fields lay to the north of the embankment. Here on one occasion the Notting Hill Flower Show and Home Improvement Society held its Exhibition, and the Duke and Duchess of Teck, accompanied by their young daughter,

distributed the prizes.[9]   But in the middle seventies
a series of good residential roads were planned running
parallel with the railway, and as these roads were continued east across Ladbroke Grove Road, they linked
up this district with the smaller houses of the Portobello Road area.   Naturally there is little of notoriety
or public interest to record in connection with these
somewhat " featureless streets," but pleasant vistas
may be obtained along Cambridge and Oxford Gardens.
and Bassett Road, with its avenue of plane trees, is
often beautiful in the glow of sunset.

The building of these streets commenced at Ladbroke Grove Road ; many years elapsed before their
western ends were completed.   (Most of these good
detached houses are now divided into maisonettes
or adapted into small flats.)

The plan of 1865 shows that building plots along
the south end of Ladbroke Grove Road had been
leased by Colonel St. Quintin to Charles H. Blake,
Esq., who already owned much property on the top of
St. John's Hill.   Mr. Blake must have acquired
further plots along the road within the Portobello

9 During the seventies and eighties this Society was worked in connection
with most of the North Kensington parishes and Mission districts, and did
much to encourage the tending of home-grown plants and of such cottage
gardens as remained in Notting Dale and Kensal Town.   Prizes were also
given for handicraft and for well-kept homes.   After awhile the annual
Show and Entertainment was always held in Portobello Road School.
See page 183.   The hon. secretaries were successively Miss Sophia Gill,
Mrs. Bassett and Mrs. Meade.

Estate, for, about the year 1870, Messrs. Blake and
Parsons gave the site for St. Michael and All Angels.
This church was built by Mr. Cowland (see pages
117 and 125), in terra cotta and ornamental brick
in a style called " Romanesque of the Rhine." It
was consecrated for worship in May 1871, and is,
therefore, ten years older than Christ Church, Faraday
Road.   The first vicar was the Rev. Edward Ker
Gray, formerly curate at St. Peter's, Bayswater.   Mr.
Gray lived with his parents in Linden Gardens (see
page 92).   In 1871 his ministry was described as
" Evangelical in its character, and his services lively
and devotional without ritualistic features."   But for
many years the services at St. Michael's have been
adapted rather " to those souls for whom an ornate
worship is a necessity."   Rackham Street Hall, built by
Mr. Allen (see page 190), later known as St. Martin's
Mission, was long used as the Mission Church of
St. Michael's.   Here the Rev. Henry Stapleton carried
on good work from 1882 to 1889.   (Since 1916, St.
Martin's has become a separate parish with a district
stretching from Ladbroke Grove to St. Quintin's
Park Station.)

Shortly after St. Michael and All Angels was opened
the freehold of eleven acres of Portobello Estate was
obtained for St. Charles's College, and by 1874 a
handsome range of buildings in red brick and stone,
with a central tower, 140 feet high, stood surrounded

by a garden and recreation grounds. This college, dedicated to St. Charles of Borromeo, was founded by Cardinal Manning in order to provide education at a moderate cost for Catholic youths. It began in 1863 in a room near St. Mary and the Angels, Bayswater. By 1890 twelve hundred students had been prepared for various professions.[10] (Within the last few years the building has been sold to the Community of the Sacred Heart as a Training College for Women Teachers, and a small Practising School has been added.) The enclosure is faced on three sides by the houses of St. Charles's Square. These houses at first were " inhabited by quite aristocratic people." A convent belonging to the close order of the Carmelites lies between the grounds of St. Charles's College and the imposing red-brick pile of the Marylebone Infirmary. Miss Vincent, matron of the Infirmary from 1881 to 1900, tells how the parents of one of the nuns on a certain day for three successive years begged permission to gaze from one of her upper windows into the convent garden.

Marylebone Infirmary was one of the earliest experiments both in taking the sick poor outside the boundaries of their parish and in arranging an Infirmary on purely hospital lines. Only a few wards

---

[10] See "Kensington," by G. E. Mitton, 1903, in the *Fascination of London* Series, and *History of the Squares of London*, by E. Beresford Chancellor, 1907.

were occupied when the hospital was opened by the
Prince and Princess of Wales in 1881. The excitement of this Royal visit is still remembered. In 1884
Marylebone Infirmary became also a Training School
for Nightingale Nurses, financed from the Nightingale
Fund. Part of the magnificent building which now
covers several acres is on the site of an old pond, a
pond shown on the Ordnance Survey Map for 1862-
1869. Some years after construction the whole block
sank and had to be underpinned.

Besides the large area of the Portobello Estate
occupied by these extensive institutions, many
builders in a small way of business bought land and
put up houses for working-class tenants. One of the
present dwellers in Rackham Street came there with
her parents for the sake of their health about the year
1877. Building plots were then being taken up, but
the north side of Rackham Street was open ground.
The inhabitants were largely laundry-workers and
casual labourers, an overflow from Kensal New Town.
Edinburgh Road Board-school, now known as Barlby
Road School, was placed in 1880 among the half-made
streets near the Great Western Railway line ; and
children from temporary schools in Kensal Town and
at Rackham Street Hall were transferred to the new
building. When the school was first opened pigs
were slaughtered in a shed close by, and for many
years carpets were beaten on the adjoining open space.
On a summer day the noise made by the beaters, and

the dust from the dirty carpets, floated in at the open windows of the school. Carpet beating as a recognized industry has practically disappeared, though the cleaning of carpets by steam power is still carried on in Kensal Town. (Since those days factories of various kinds have been built, and the character of local occupations has considerably changed, but this corner has always remained rough and rowdy. Certain common lodging-house keepers, driven out by improvements in Notting Dale, have migrated to this district, and the Treverton Street area here and the Lockton Street area near Latimer Road Station, are reckoned among the black spots of the Borough of Kensington.)

Gradually during the eighteen-eighties the old track from Wormwood Scrubbs to Notting Barns was transformed into St. Quintin Avenue. At first there were heaps of refuse along the road, suggesting that it had served as a common dumping ground for rubbish. The earliest houses were built at the Triangle and in Highlever Road. It was by this road that troops on horseback would often make their way to their exercising ground on Wormwood Scrubbs. Sometimes these troops were accompanied by the Duke of Cambridge, and the loud voice in which he gave words of command is still remembered by one who lived as a child in Chesterton Road. It was in 1881 that the parish of St. Clements was divided (see page 153), and that the Rev. Dalgarno Robinson

built the church of St. Helen's on St. Quintin Avenue
close to the site of Notting Barns Farm-house. This
church, which resembles St. Clements in architectural
features, now stands in a commanding position at the
junction of several roads, and is a stately edifice,
even though the tower is unbuilt. Mr. Robinson
remained as vicar till his death in 1899.

Until the beginning of the present century there
was "a great stretch of Common "[11] between St.
Helen's Gardens and Latimer Road. Here cattle
and horses grazed. This space had been curtailed in
1884 by the opening of Oxford Gardens School.
This school originated in some of the leading tradesmen
in the neighbourhood petitioning the School-board
to provide State-aided education for their children,
but at the highest possible fee. And Oxford Gardens
was a 6d. school until fees were abolished in 1891.
North of St. Quintin Avenue was "another great
stretch of Common" divided into three parts by
Barlby Road and Dalgarno Gardens. (A little open
ground still remains devoted to playing fields, but it
is being encroached on from all sides.)

By 1840 the eastern edge of Wormwood Scrubbs
had been cut across by the Birmingham, Bristol
and Thames Junction Railway, now the West London
Junction Railway. See the map dated 1850, on page
120. In 1852 it was proposed to use this detached
piece of the Scrubbs, belonging to the parish of

[11] *Kensington,* by G. E. Mitton, 1903.

Hammersmith, as a Cemetery for Kensington people. The project was successfully petitioned against, and it has been made into a public Recreation Ground called Little Wormwood Scrubbs with an ornamental water-course along the upper reaches of the Rivulet.

Strange tales are told of what has happened even within living memory in this distant portion of Kensington hemmed in by two railway lines. Here a man hanged himself. The question at once arose on which side of the ditch the man's death had occurred, as that point determined which parochial authority should follow up the case. An important tributary of the boundary stream rose near the Gas Works. See page 74. This brook ran as a drain across the fields of St. Quintin's Park, and was enclosed in " a neatly bricked half-barrelled culvert with a perpetual flow of clean water with a curious acrid but not unpleasant smell. . . . At the elbow where the culvert turned, the brickwork rose to the height of six or seven feet." This tower with two adjacent tunnels proved a tempting point for school-boy fights.[12] The drain has disappeared, but the ground near by is still " very mashy " in wet weather.

In this distant corner a gunmaker of Bond Street owned a shooting range provided with an iron stag which ran backwards and forwards on rails. Purchasers would test their guns on this stag, and at other

[12] " Some Recollections of Bayswater Fifty Years Ago, by Sir W. Bull, M.P., in the *Bayswater Chronicle*, 1923.

times children rode on its back. By the eighteen-seventies it was derelict, "a rusty fixed stag," but "being in a secluded spot, partly railed off by a high fence . . . it was used on Sunday mornings as a rendez-vous for prize-fights—prizes of from £10 to £15 being won by contest with the bare fists." A hefty gipsy, who lived in the Potteries, unfortunately killed a man in an encounter behind the Stuck Stag. He was arrested, and got off with some difficulty (see note 12). Drinking booths and roundabouts were erected on Little Wormwood Scrubbs when Bank Holiday Fairs were being held on the larger space beyond the railway embankment, and in summer-time the proceedings every Sunday evening were so disorderly that respectable people could not walk in that direction. It was only after the Wormwood Scrubbs Regulation Bill was passed, in 1879, that this corner settled down to an orderly existence.

North Kensington has now been traversed. Mere fragments of its story have been told, but these Chronicles will have fulfilled their purpose if they remind some readers of their own early days, or provide an explanation of certain characteristic features. Notting Hill, its former name, does not mean "Nutting Hill" in allusion to the rich woods which "no longer cover it," and assuredly is not "a corruption of Nothing-ill." But those who inhabit the neighbourhood may well echo the brave words of Adam Wayne,

in G. K. Chesterton's inspiring story. When asked
if he did not consider the Cause of Notting Hill
somewhat absurd, " Why should I ? " he said,
" Notting Hill is a rise or high ground of the common
earth, on which men have built houses to live in, in
which they are born, fall in love, pray, marry and die.
. . . These little gardens where we told our loves.
These streets where we brought out our dead. Why
should they be commonplace ? Why should they
be absurd ? There has never been anything in the
world absolutely like Notting Hill. There will
never be anything quite like it to the crack of doom.
. . . And God loved it as He must surely love anything which is itself and unreplaceable."[13]

[13] *The Napoleon of Notting Hill*, by G. K. Chesterton, 1904.

A RE-ASSESSMENT OF NOTTING HILL

by ASHLEY BARKER

IT is a matter for reflection that Florence Gladstone was writing in the early 1920's about a district built almost entirely between 1825 and 1870. That is to say she was writing about a Victorian suburb at a time when Victorian architecture had reached the very nadir of fashion. The aesthetics of Victorian house-building and estate-development were certainly not considered to be subjects for serious study and there is little of specifically architectural comment in her book. When dealing with Pembridge Square she tells us how it had become fashionable to decry the horrors of mid-Victorian architecture in Bayswater. On the other hand, her love for the unfashionable houses, the streets and the gardens of Notting Hill is clear on every page. Perhaps this is not really so strange, because the distinctive structure of Notting Hill, seen in the relationship of terraces and gardens and in those concentric crescents and associated squares, forming the patterns which stand out so clearly on the Ordnance map, gives the place a character so marked and so different from other parts of London that it can

inspire affection even in those who find themselves
unable to admire the taste of its Victorian builders.
To plead the architectural interest of the houses
would probably have seemed unprofitable to Miss
Gladstone, but the time which has since passed may
have brought us to a point from which we are able to
search more seriously for their merits.

We have seen in the book how the rural landscape
which Faulkner described as late as 1820 became
rapidly transformed into the brick and stucco suburb,
with its orderly ranges of substantial houses, its
semi-detached villas, its churches and its newly
planted gardens.   " As buildings increase " says Miss
Gladstone in Chapter VI " the story necessarily
becomes more local " and she puts Kensington Park
under her magnifying glass.   We may find it helpful,
if we are to place Notting Hill in the context of
London's growth, to stand back for a moment and
review the situation at the end of the Napoleonic Wars
just before London engulfed the hamlet of Kensington
Gravel Pits.   If we were to retrace her story from this
point we should witness the building of everything
which is left to us in the second half of the twentieth
century.

During the Wars the western edge of London had
been clearly marked along the line of the Edgware
Road, Park Lane and St. James's.   To the north and
south of Hyde Park still lay country; the rich market
gardens of Brompton, the more open farmlands beyond

Paddington and at Notting Barns and the villages and hamlets each with its own separate identity still detached from the City.   Buckingham House to the west of St. James's had not yet been transformed into Buckingham Palace and the undeveloped site which was to become Belgravia was still known as the " Five Fields."   Low lying, ill-drained and of somewhat sinister repute, this remnant of countryside had already been hemmed in by Henry Holland's Hans Town Development stretching along the line of Sloane Street.   It was rather as if London had jumped the Five Fields having rejected them as unpromising.

It was in this landscape at the time of Waterloo that the hamlet of Kensington Gravel Pits stood with its toll-gate " enlivened every hour by the passage of mail coaches, stages and wagons passing to and fro on the road to Uxbridge."

By the mid 1820's, with peace returned and building booming again, Nash's work for the Crown had realised not only the new Regent Street and the spectacular terraces around Regent's Park but also the transformation of old Buckingham House into the principal Royal Palace.   This had assured the fashionable future of the adjoining " Five Fields " as the new Belgravia.   The great speculation on the Duke's land, with Thomas Cubitt at its centre, taking place from 1825 onwards firmly established the new aristocratic quarter of London, and in so doing it not only set the direction for London's new growth around Hyde Park but also largely determined the kind of architecture it was to have.   If Nash's terraces in Regent's Park could be criticised for their shortcomings in detail, their success in scenic effect was outstanding.   The repetition of narrow house fronts which made up the undeniable boredom of Gower Street and so much of the Georgian West End had been transformed into a succession of apparent palaces and the influence must have been felt in Belgravia.   In Belgrave Square the façades designed by George Basevi, Disraeli's nephew, brought the new neo-classical stucco architecture into the London tradition of square and terrace building. Intended to be frescoed in imitation of Bath stone these distinguished façades with their enriched centres and outer pavilions set around a garden square created a new architectural ideal.

These were buildings to set a fashion which the great and growing body of wealthy middle-class citizens might follow.   The westward growth of London was re-established and the perimeter of Hyde Park was the obvious place to live.   The result in the later 1820's and 1830's was that the owners of land all round the Park, realising their good fortune, turned to thoughts of laying out their estates for new high class speculative housing.   The land was owned in fairly large parcels, particularly to the north the Park where it was farmland, as against the smaller market-garden holdings of Brompton to the south.   Any study of Victorian development in west London depends on an understanding of the estate pattern over which the building occurred.

But before Metropolitan London engulfed the countryside of Kensington in this way, at the time when Cubitt's work in Belgravia had hardly begun, each of the villages on London's western fringe was adding to itself a new suburban growth; terraces and squares which we can still recognise as springing from the villages themselves, rather than the growth of the main body of London. They were neat ranges of brick boxes with a little stucco dressing, essentially the same as the houses of the Georgian West End although more modest in size. The excesses of ribbon development which occurred to the north and south along the roads out of London were less noticeable through Kensington where the additions were generally closely attached to the parent village or hamlet. These houses presumably satisfied the needs of those who wished to enjoy the benefits of fresh air, open scene and cheaper land whilst remaining within daily reach of the City. The 1820's were the age of the pre-railway commuter. By 1822 William Cobbett contemplating the growth of houses along the roads out of London could write in anger, " What an at once horrible and ridiculous thing this country would become if this thing should go on for a few years ". It was already possible to travel from Brighton to London by coach and return the same day having transacted business in the City! It must have seemed

attractive to live in the cleaner air by Kensington
Gravel Pits and to make the short journey into London
every day.

During the period before 1830 Alexander Square
and Brompton Square had gone up beyond Knightsbridge, and Edwardes Square and Pembroke Square
were added to Kensington.   In the same way Hanson's
or Notting Hill Square (now Campden Hill Square)
was added to the western end of Kensington Gravel
Pits.   Whether we should regard this town square
set down in the countryside as the arrival of London
on Notting Hill or as part of the old village is something we could argue either way.   On contemporary
maps it seems to belong to the village, filling in the
space between the end of the old village street and
Holland Park.   Compared with the big estates which
were to follow it seems essentially pre-metropolitan.
On the other hand, it took an urban form and owed
its existence to the Great Wen itself.

As against contemporary squares in Kensington and
Brompton, Notting Hill Square was noticeably less
formal.   The very sharp northern fall of the land on
the long dimension of the square may have had a great
deal to do with this; it ruled out the long symmetrical
terrace forms.   Nevertheless, it may not be entirely
fanciful to see the more polished work in Brompton as
appropriate to the village closest to the West End, and
Notting Hill Square as belonging to a more rural, less
sophisticated situation.

Behind their generous front gardens the Notting
Hill Square houses were more varied in size and detail
than the strictly regimented rows which lined the back
edges of London pavements, but we still recognise
them as stemming from the old London square–
building tradition of Bloomsbury and the West End,
with its roots in the previous century.   The typical
house with its stock brick face rising plain above a
stuccoed ground storey was the result of a tradition
which by the end of the eighteenth century had produced and refined an answer to the urban domestic
problems of the day so satisfactory that it could hardly
be improved upon—so uniform and restrained that
many who saw it repeated by the thousand were beginning to revolt against it.   The house plan with two
rooms to a floor, probably 18 or 19 feet wide and some
30 feet deep, was as predictable as its external architectural expression.   It scarcely enters the mind to
ask who the designer was, or to consider whether any
one could have been said to have designed them at all.
The houses would hardly seem to require more than a
selection of iron-work from a catalogue, but the difference between success and failure could be a subtle
matter of detail and dimension.   Yet these were
matters in which most builders could succeed because
previous generations had faced and solved the problems and tradition had all the answers.

Towards the bottom of Notting Hill Square on
either side, we find house fronts which show a little

more originality. They have flat brick bays set out from the main face with wide windows, as if determined to break away from repetition and to stamp some special character on the square. But the real departure was to be seen on the other side of the Uxbridge Road where the vista down the eastern side of the square was closed by a very much more up-to-date range. These are houses which Miss Gladstone notes as being built on Mr. Turley's land before 1827, and our view from the square is of a trio of houses the centre of which is formed by a giant Tuscan Order, tetrastyle in antis, surmounted by a full Attic Order and pediment. This sort of architectural display clearly belongs to the forward-looking 1820's. The age of Metropolitan Improvements had come to Notting Hill and London itself could not be far away.

Development was not so much like a wave sweeping from the east as a series of explosions all the way from Marble Arch to Shepherd's Bush. In the late 1820's and early 1830's the Bishop of London's estate in Tyburnia next to Marble Arch set out to out-rival Belgravia itself and the excitement amongst all land owners in the district must have been intense. One frequently finds that the development of an estate had been under consideration some years before building commenced, but it is something of a shock to learn that as early as June 1821, in the same year that Buckingham Palace became a Royal residence and four or five years before Cubitt's work in Belgravia, a private Act of Parliament was passed " to enable James Weller Ladbroke, Esq., and others to grant building leases of land in Kensington, Notting Barns and Westbourne in the County of Middlesex and for other purposes relating thereto." Although no building followed immediately, two years later in 1823 a drawing of particular interest was presented to the Commissioners of Sewers for Westminster in which we shall find the key to much that was to happen later.

With the title " A Plan of Notting Hill Estate (as arranged for building thereon) the Property of James Weller Ladbroke, Esq.," this remarkable drawing shows Ladbroke's land to the north of the Uxbridge Road intersected by a broad avenue marked " Ladbroke Place " along the present line of Ladbroke Grove and at right angles to it " Weller Street " (East and West) along the line of the present Ladbroke Road. To the north of the intersection of these two roads however there is shown one vast complete circus 560 yards in diameter; that is to say just about one mile in circumference. To appreciate this in terms of what happened later, we must imagine the intersection of Kensington Park Gardens and Ladbroke Grove in front of St. John's Church to be the centre of the great circle which would be set out to a radius bringing the outer edge almost as far as Clarendon Road in the west, to within a short distance of Arundel Gardens to the north and to Kensington Park Road to the east. Areas of building land are shown lining the road and enclosing

garden areas marked " paddock " but no indication of
the houses themselves is given.   The drawing is not
signed, but along the western boundary a drainage
proposal has been added later in pencil together with
the note " I approve this line of open sewer on the part
of James Weller Ladbroke."   This is signed T.
Allason and dated 22 November 1831.   Whether or
not Allason was the original author of the layout, there
is little doubt that by 1831 he was Ladbroke's official
surveyor.   This is the same Thomas Allason referred
to by Miss Gladstone as living at Linden Grove
House.   His signature appears on plans given in the
leases to Edward Orme of some of Ladbroke's property
further east along the Bayswater Road and the initial
inspiration for the Kensington Park estate may well
have been his.

Allason was born in London in 1790.   He became
a pupil of William Atkinson, winning the silver medal
of the Royal Academy School in 1809 and taking an
early interest in topographical drawing.   In 1817 after
a tour of the Continent he published his " Picturesque
Views of the Antiquities of Pola in Istria ".   His most
important public building in London was the Alliance
Fire Office in Bartholomew Lane.   He carried out
repairs and redecoration at Blenheim Palace under an
Act of Parliament passed for that purpose and he built
a number of country houses.   He held the post of
surveyor to the Stock Exchange, the Pollen Estate and
the Pitt Estate, Kensington.   The biographical entry

on Allason in The Architectural Publication Societies
Dictionary published during the 1870's notes that he
was surveyor to the Ladbroke Estate, Notting Hill,
and significantly draws attention to his work for the
Earl of Shrewsbury at Alton Towers where " He was
engaged in laying out the gardens and from this period
he was very much employed as a landscape gardener."

We have then, as Ladbroke's surveyor at this critical
time, an architect with a taste for the Picturesque and
for gardening.   If the circus layout was his, how did
he visualise its completion?   Smaller circuses than
this—one thinks of the circus at Bath with a diameter
of 318 feet or less than one-fifth of the Ladbroke
proposal—may be treated in a strictly classical manner,
but the prospect of a circus a mile round to be surrounded by houses of less than palatial dimensions is a
little daunting, particularly when they are to be laid
out over hilly ground.   Circuses in London have been
more frequently projected than they were built.
There was, of course, a double circus in Nash's
original layout for Regent's Park but a closer parallel
with the Ladbroke Estate occurs in an abandoned
scheme of uncertain authorship for the Eyre Estate in
St. John's Wood.   Dated 1794 this proposed circus
(The British Circus) was, like Ladbroke's, to have
been just one mile in diameter.   An engraved plan
shows the development carried out entirely in semi-
detached houses and Sir John Summerson has drawn
attention to it as probably the first indication of semi-

detached housing used in this way.   Had the Ladbroke
intention been to develop the east and the west circus
roads with semi-detached villas in a picturesque garden-
city?   The fact that when building did take place,
some years later on a different ground plan, the
buildings were at first mainly semi-detached villas,
lends support to this view.   It would have been
unlike anything attempted in the London of those
days but, together with the Eyre Estate's British
Circus, the 1823 Ladbroke sewer plan is an indication
of the way ideas were changing.   If Regent's Park
and Belgravia had established the big stucco palace
façade as the prototype for the major terraces in
Kensington and Bayswater, Nash's Regent's Park
scheme had also proposed some 50 detached villas in
the Park.

The great circus was never laid out and progress at
first was slow, although along the southern fringe of
the estate around Weller Street houses were going up
with Allason himself making applications to the Commissioners for Sewers.   Some existing houses around
the southern end of Ladbroke Grove appear to date
from this period.

Miss Gladstone has described in detail the whole
history of the race-course.   Fascinating as this story
is, I doubt whether its existence has made any noticeable contribution to the Ladbroke Estate as we see it
today, and since the thread of estate development is
broken until the early 1840's, we might leave the

Ladbroke lands and cross The Potteries to look at the
next important estate to the west which although
starting later made rapid strides, to be completed
before the building work on the crown of the hill to
which we must return later.

In January 1839 Norlands Farm and Norlands
House standing just to the north of Uxbridge Road
were sold with 50 acres of land to be re-developed.
The sale took place between Benjamin Lewis Vulliamy,
the clockmaker and Charles Richardson, a solicitor.
The registration of the sale does not give enough
detail for us to be precise as to its significance, but
reference to certain trusts rather suggests that Vulliamy
may not have been giving up his interest in the estate
so much as adopting a legal device to make development easier, with Richardson acting as his agent. In
1843 a private Act of Parliament entitled " An act for
the improvement of the Norlands Estate in the parish
of St. Mary Abbot's, Kensington in the County of
Middlesex " provided for the appointment of commissioners with powers to levy a rate for the better
paving and lighting of the estate. A sewer plan dated
1841 shows the beginning of the layout. A very wide
road running north and south off the Uxbridge Road
(" Addison Road North " now Addison Avenue) is
crossed by the main east/west thoroughfare (" Queen's
Road " now Queensdale Road). Within the angles
of the cross thus formed, a fine crescent is shown in
the south-west quarter and a square to the south-east,

both of these layouts giving onto Uxbridge Road at
their open southern ends.   There is as yet no indication of St. James's Square (later St. James's Gardens)
although the outline of a church is indicated in pencil
on the axis of Addison Road North.   The presence of
a good church was essential to the success of any of
these estates and an inducement to the intending
purchasers of property.   The architect of St. James's
Church, which was consecrated in 1845, was the very
successful architect, Lewis Vulliamy, the son of
Benjamin.   He built a number of churches in London
but his most celebrated metropolitan work was
Dorchester House in Park Lane.   It is difficult to
ignore the idea that he may have had some connection
with the design of the estate layout, but there seems to
be no direct evidence.   Charles Richardson is referred
to in the 1843 Improvement Act as having made
contracts with the Gas and Water Companies, and he
also signed sewer plans together with Joseph Dunning,
a surveyor whose name does not appear in any other
connection with the estate.   A sale plan of 1848 shows
the layout virtually as it was to become on completion
although with many of the sites not yet built on,
particularly around St. James's Square where work on
the houses started only in 1847.

The layout is at once less remarkable and in some
ways more practical than the Ladbroke giant circus
design.   It incorporates however some of the new
ideas of the time.   The central avenue is again lined

with two-storeyed houses in pairs; semi-detached in the southern half, linked pairs to the north. This reaction against the plain terrace and the search for diversity in architectural form is in one way or another the keynote of the whole estate. Royal Crescent and Norland Square remain perhaps the closest to traditional urban ideals but even there we sense the search for novelty. Throughout Norland Square the segmental bays in the ground floor add the flavour of a seaside town or a spa, but in the northern terrace the channelling of the stucco to the height of the main cornice and the curious relationship of the brackets in the cornice itself to the windows below is mannerism of a more pronounced form. The architecture of the great sweep of Royal Crescent lacks the bland restraint of Nash's Park Crescent or Basevi's Pelham Crescent. The added emphasis at the angles with the turretted houses may owe something to Victoria Square in Westminster designed just two or three years earlier, but the assertiveness of the Roman Doric Order with full entablature and fluted shafts begins to take us out of the Regency and into Victorian Kensington.

St. James's Gardens is one of that fascinating sequence of London designs, which may have begun with the Paragon at Blackheath, in which a terrace is articulated not into one palace façade but into a series of paired blocks with some sort of linking device; in this case with the entrances in recessed bays still holding the terrace together. The rhythm can be made

more or less complicated by varying the groupings, as
in the 1:3:1 ranges on the short side of the square
where an orthodox three-bay house is placed between
two outward turned pairs. It is worth noting that
the early sewer plan shows the abandoned " Otway
Crescent " as one of these paired ranges.

The two northern quarters of the cross on the
Norland Estate produce further surprises. On the
western side the central axis of Royal Crescent leads
into St. Ann's Villas where we find, not the expected
continuation of stuccoed architecture, but pairs of
handsome red brick villas with diaper ornament and
detail in the Jacobean manner of the kind which had
been popularised by such architects as C. J. Richardson.
Apparently at variance with everything else on the
estate, they are nevertheless all part of the search for
variety and the Picturesque.

In the remaining quarter where " Otway Crescent "
failed to materialise, the developers had to contend
with the immediate proximity of The Potteries. This
fact may well have accounted for the abandoning of
intended grandeur and the fact that the somewhat
inaccessible Prince's Place came to be built as a double
row of humble artisan cottages without any architectural ambition whatsoever.

This exception may serve to underline the one-class
nature of the Notting Hill estates and to emphasise
the cut-throat competition for purchasers of the
necessary financial standing. From Belgravia to

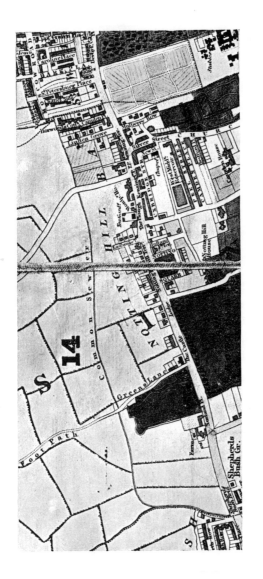

FROM A "NEW PLAN OF LONDON," BY CRUCHLEY. "IMPROVED TO 1831."

THE HIPPODROME, NOTTING HILL, ABOUT 1839.

NOTTING BARNS FARM IN 1873.
Water-colour drawing by W. E. Wellings.

"KENSALL GREEN CEMETRY," ABOUT 1845.

KENSAL GREEN CEMETERY.
By J. Harwood.

THE ENTRANCE, KENSAL GREEN CEMETERY, ABOUT 1845.
Showing St. John's, Kensal.

THE PLOUGH INN, KENSAL GREEN, 1868.
From water-colour drawing by J. T. Wilson.

BACKS OF HOUSES IN EAST ROW, KENSAL TOWN.
Drawing by W. Cleverley Alexander, 1911.

THE COTTAGES, EAST ROW.
Water-colour drawing by W. E. Kell, 1911.
(At Queen's Park Public Library.)

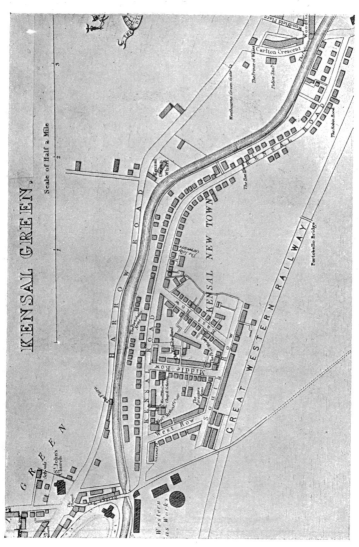

KENSAL GREEN.

Scale of Half a Mile

FROM SHEET I OF THE *WEEKLY DISPATCH ATLAS*, 1855–1860.
By Edward Weller, F.R.G.S.

PORTOBELLO FARMHOUSE.

From a sepia drawing by W. E. Wellings, developed from a sketch made in 1864.

LADBROKE GROVE ROAD, 1866.
From photograph at Kensington Public Library.

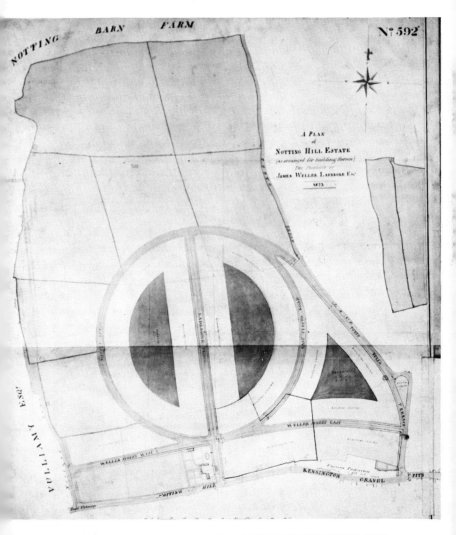

A PROPOSAL (1823) FOR THE LAYING OUT OF THE LADBROKE ESTATE WITH
A CIRCUS ROAD ONE MILE IN CIRCUMFERENCE. THE LINES OF LADBROKE
ROAD AND LADBROKE GROVE ARE ALREADY ESTABLISHED.
By courtesy of Hubert Bennett, F.R.I.B.A., Architect to the Greater London Council.

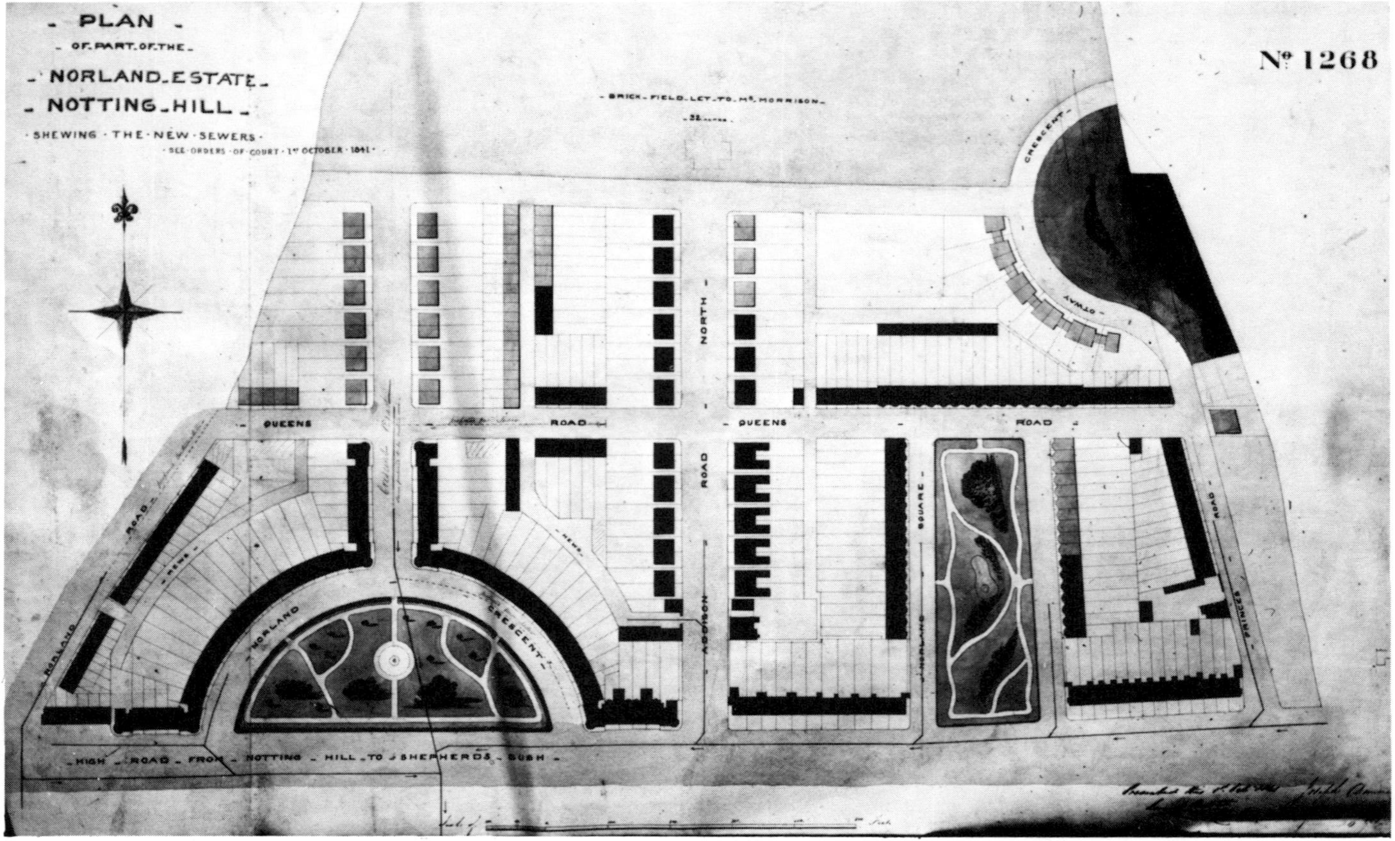

- PLAN -
- OF PART OF THE -
- NORLAND ESTATE -
- NOTTING HILL -
SHEWING THE NEW SEWERS
SEE ORDERS OF COURT 1st OCTOBER 1841
No. 1268
BRICK FIELD LET TO Mr. MORRISON
CRESCENT
OTWAY
NORTH
QUEENS
ROAD
QUEENS
ROAD
ROAD
SQUARE
NORLAND
ROAD
PRINCES
ADDISON
NORLAND
CRESCENT
MEWS
MEWS
NORLAND
ROAD
HIGH ROAD FROM NOTTING HILL TO SHEPHERDS BUSH

… FOR THE NORLAND ESTATE AND (BELOW) A SALE PLAN (1848) SHOWING ACTUAL PROGRESS OF

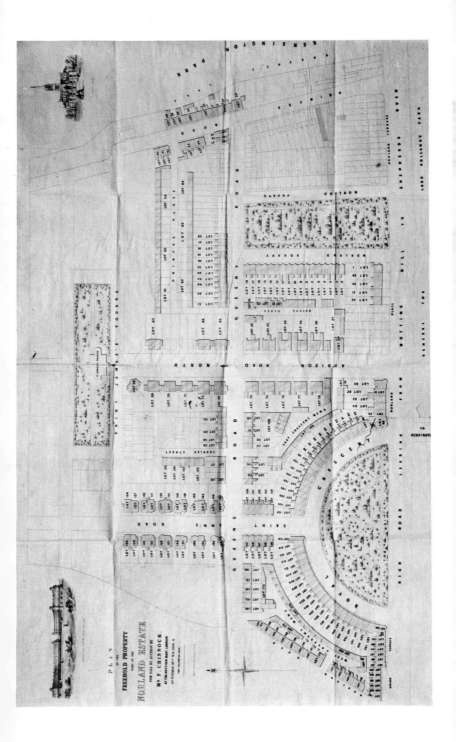

PLAN
OF THE
FREEHOLD PROPERTY
PART OF THE
NORLAND ESTATE
FOR SALE BY AUCTION BY
Mr. T. CHINNOCK
AT THE AUCTION MART, LONDON

A PLAN (1842) FOR THE WESTERN HALF OF THE LADBROKE ESTATE. THE ROAD PATTERN IS APPROACHING THAT FINALLY [...] ONLY IN THE SOUTHERN PARTS.

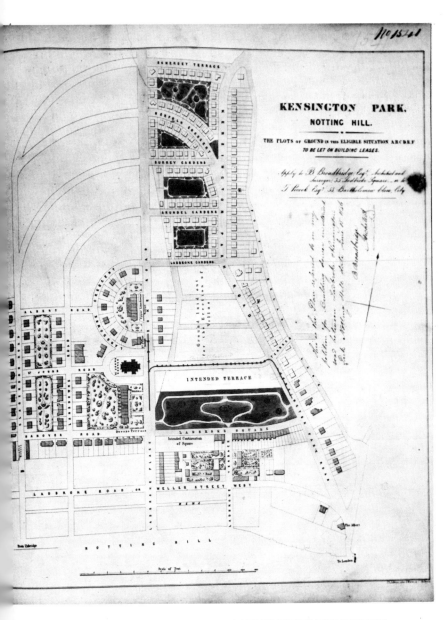

A PLAN FOR PROSPECTIVE BUYERS (1846) SHOWING HOUSES ALREADY BUILT
AROUND ST. JOHN'S CHURCH, TOGETHER WITH PROPOSALS FOR THE AREA
TO THE NORTH OF LADBROKE GARDENS.
By courtesy of Hubert Bennett, F.R.I.B.A., Architect to the Greater London Council.

DAW'S MAP OF KENSINGTON 1852.
By courtesy of Hubert Bennett, F.R.I.B.A., Architect to the Greater London Council.

Notting Hill and from The Boltons to Maida Vale the
second and third quarters of the nineteenth century
saw a gross over-provision of houses for the substantial
middle classes, and the constant references to bank-
ruptcies and houses standing for years in carcass bear
witness to this fact. Developments on the best sites
around the Park and near the West End could be sure
of takers, but those in more distant situations to the
far west and away from the Park could be very
uncertain indeed. The history of St. James's Gardens
itself bears eloquent witness to this fact. These outstandingly pleasant and not overlarge houses were
building from 1847 to 1868, interrupted by bank-
ruptcies and with the scheme finally abandoned in the
north-eastern corner. The houses of alien design in
this corner were erected as late as 1878–9 when, being
built across the end of Sirdar Road, they effectively
sealed off the further access to the north which had at
one time been intended.

Whilst this work was going on construction had
been occurring concurrently on Ladbroke's land to the
east. Miss Gladstone tells us at the beginning of
Chapter VI how John Whyte, the lessee of the Race-
course had renounced his interest in the western half
of the course in October 1840 and the remainder of
his interest the following year. We have seen how
between 1840 and 1844 five building contracts were
drawn up with William Chadwick, Jacob Connop,
John Duncan, Richard Roy and William Jenkins all

of whom were to erect a minimum number of houses
within periods of up to 19 years in accordance with the
requirements of Ladbroke's surveyor. An Act of
Parliament was passed in 1844 to confirm these contracts. Building was going on in Kensington Park
Road and the eastern part of Ladbroke Square but by
the following year, Connop and Duncan were bankrupt. It was at this juncture that Miss Gladstone
suggests that Thomas Allom was entrusted with the
carrying out of the whole estate, but I am not so far
aware of any documentary evidence to this effect.
Neither, on the other hand, does Allason's signature
appear on any of the sewer plans after 1840.

The earliest surviving proposal for the layout of the
western half of the estate seems to be that presented
to the Commissioners for Sewers by Richard Roy in
1843. The previous year he had made an application
to the Commissioners for drainage to Lansdowne
Terrace (now 37–49 Ladbroke Grove), which was
then half built, and the plans had been signed by
James Thomson as architect. Among the list of
works given in Thomson's obituary in *The Builder* in
May 1883, was " the laying out of Mr. Roy's estate
at Notting Hill west of Ladbroke Road ". For
Ladbroke Road we must of course read Ladbroke Grove.
It is of interest to note that amongst Thomson's other
works the obituary mentions his assistance on Cumber-
land Terrace and Place, Regent's Park in 1827.

It is hardly profitable to speculate what relationship

there might have been between the scheme shown on Thomson's sewer application and any layout which Allason may have devised as estate surveyor since his great circus arrangement of 1823. At all events Allason's original proposal for a great circus must have been the starting point influencing all that subsequently happened. Thomson's 1823 drawing shows an extravagantly low density layout based on detached and semi-detached villas set in private gardens. The houses would be set out in crescent formation concentric with Lansdowne Mount in a layout approaching the scheme finally built. The ideal was that of a Garden City. The terraces and the traditional forms of urban building had been finally dispensed with. But not only were the paired villas set in gardens, they were in addition given large communal gardens with access through the private ones. This was quite unlike any previous London layout. The areas marked " paddock " on Allason's plan may have been the beginning of the idea. The benefit to the City dweller in these park-like grounds accessible from his back door and garden gate was enormous, but the low density of the development was perhaps uneconomic, particularly where the houses themselves were not so very grand. By the end of the 1840's the paired villas had reached just north of the present Lansdowne Rise and after that the Garden City ideal seems to have died. One can only assume that it had proved unprofitable.

The architecture of the villas which had been built was varied in nature and it is difficult to see much sign of a single personality behind the designs, although we may detect several well defined groups. Amongst the more successful are the three pairs of brick faced houses at Nos. 2–12 (even) Lansdowne Road, somewhat countrified with giant stucco pilasters surmounted by paired consoles supporting the wide eaves—a pleasantly wayward device. Then come more serious and dignified stucco pairs higher up on the other side of the road at Nos. 29–47 (odd). These generous houses are rather more substantial than the usual paired villas. Showing a combined front six windows wide and three storeys high with a full aedicular treatment to all the first floor windows, a broad bracketed cornice and the other parts of architecture appropriately matched, one can imagine that they approach closely to the developer's dreams for the area. We may imagine too that we detect a little of the influence of Barry, the Pall Mall Clubs and the great houses which were going up on the Crown land of Kensington Palace Gardens at the same time. One wishes that there were more of them.

On the inside of Lansdowne Crescent and at the beginning of the curve of Lansdowne Road we find more characteristically picturesque villas with sharp gables and a rather Northern look, although most of them retained classical detailing and only very occasionally is there a pointed light or a drip mould to be found. These are reminiscent of the Eyre Estate buildings at St. John's Wood and one is once again reminded of the parallel history of these two areas. Elsewhere are brick and stucco treatments of less pronounced character but with certain details and forms recurring from time to time, such as a stucco shell within the tympanum of the arched first floor windows and similar personal foibles showing a hand of one or another builder involved.

It is noticeable that as we get to the less accessible and less desirable parts of the estate the development becomes looser and less distinguished. On the other hand, one may suppose that the most desirable and therefore valuable land would be that at the top of the hill around Ladbroke Square and to the east of St. John's Church, which had been left open since the earlier failure of Connop and Duncan. It was the easiest of access from London, well away from the unsavoury influence of the piggeries, enjoying the summit of the hill and the amenity of the church itself. In 1846 when a plan of the whole estate signed by Benjamin Broadbridge was presented to the Commissioners for Sewers, we see that although the villas of Clarendon and Lansdowne Roads south of Lansdowne Rise were completed and the eastern half of Ladbroke Square was built up, the land to the north of the great square garden was still advertised for letting on building leases. Applications were to be made to B. Broadbridge, Esq., Architect and Surveyor of 35 Ladbroke Square. Detached villas were still suggested for each plot, although along the northern boundary of the Ladbroke Square Garden was inscribed " intended terrace " and the area now occupied by Stanley Crescent and Gardens was marked " ground laid out for the erection of villas ".

In the following year, 1847, James Weller Ladbroke died, and in 1850 we find his cousin Felix leasing the whole of the north-west corner of the estate bounded by Lansdowne Rise and Crescent and Ladbroke Grove to Charles Henry Blake, who also seemed to have taken over most of the north-east corner at about the same time. It is at this point that Thomas Allom's name does occur in the estate records. In his obituary entitled " The Builder " in October 1872 one of his principal works is listed as " The covering of the Kensington Park Estate with mansions for Mr. C. H. Blake at a cost of nearly £200,000 ". In 1853 Allom exhibited at the Royal Academy a drawing entitled " Stanley Crescent Ladbroke Gardens ". A grand lithographic view taken at the junction of Kensington Park Gardens and Stanley Crescent was dedicated by him to C. H. Blake. Allom was also the architect of St. Peter's Church, an integral part of the estate which closes the vista eastwards of Stanley Gardens. *The Builder* noted in November 1855 that " the first stone of a church to be called St. Peter's has been made on the Kensington Park Estate. We are informed that it is to be in the Italian style of architecture and

Mr. Allom is the architect." (The confusion with Hallam noted by Miss Gladstone is easily explained!) With the exception of churches built for the Roman Catholic communion, it is probably true to say that St. Peter's was the last classical church to be built in London during the nineteenth century.

Once again, as with Allason and James Thomson, the precise extent of Allom's responsibility for the layout of part of the estate is difficult to determine, particularly when he seems to have become involved in the development some time after the characteristic street pattern had been laid down. As we have seen, the earlier versions of the estate layout show a self-contained pattern on the eastern side of the estate which was subsequently straightened out to make through connections with the Paddington developments to the east. The site of Stanley Crescent and Gardens had earlier been marked out as "Beaufort Square". The balance of probability seems to be that Allom was responsible for the final formation of at least the part of the estate around Stanley Crescent and Gardens, and that the distinctive and ambitious character of the architecture on this part of the estate was entirely due to him. A plan of Kensington Park Gardens and Stanley Gardens appears in the miscellaneous papers of the Metropolitan Sewer Commissioners but it is undated and unsigned. Its position in the sequence of papers suggests that it was submitted about 1853. Stanley Crescent was completed and partially occupied by 1856 and Stanley Gardens by 1858. With Kensington Park Gardens and Stanley Gardens, the architectural forms changed completely from those previously employed. This part of the estate already had several terraces to show from the 1840's in Lansdowne and Upper Lansdowne Terraces, in Ladbroke Square and in Kensington Park Road. They were dignified and handsome enough ranges, still showing their Georgian ancestry with the stucco kept to the ground floor, window architraves and cornices. For Mr. Blake's estate in the 1850's however, Allom seems to have spared no effort to make the grandest display in the latest taste. It is a freely treated neo-classical or Italianate with the pictorial possibilities of the style exploited to the full. Along the northern side of the great seven acre garden of Ladbroke Square were ranged very large houses of four main storeys above a basement, completely stuccoed back and front with great segmental bows to the south facing garden side. Their situation and size must have marked them as outstandingly desirable. In the principal range (which began only after three very odd and rather earlier trios at the eastern end) we find in the façades that all-over richness which the Victorians admired so much. The design is really a study in terrace articulation of the same kind as that which we observed in St. James's Gardens on the Norland estate, but far more complicated and now, thanks to later additions and mutilations, extremely

difficult to analyse. On careful inspection, however,
it resolves iself into the formula:

$$AB^1A - AA - AB^2A - AA - AB^1A.$$

The B type house in the centre of each block has a
colonnade with paired columns and pilaster responds
in the ground storey. The order is Tuscan in the
wings and Corinthian in the middle.

It says much for Allom's brilliant scenic display
that his strange sort of grandeur is still evident in
spite of all the damage that the twentieth century has
done. Allom adopted a more flexible, more romantic
approach than the architects of South Kensington or
Bayswater. His skill was to make use of the terrace
ends, the junctions and the curves in the streets, to
introduce special emphasis with great bowed pro-
jections, turrets, columnar screens and houses of
curious plan forms. His predilection for paired
houses placed side by side on the terrace ends thrusting
out bows on all sides is apparent over and over again.
The detail is not outstandingly distinguished, but it is
adequate and displayed with professional assurance to
gain the maximum scenic effect. To the northern
side of Kensington Park Gardens, he placed two
palace façades of more restrained form flanking an
arched entry to the communal garden. This entry
was set on an axis with the northern gate to Ladbroke
Square so that the two gardens were closely related
since many owners had rights of use over those gardens.
Every terrace was in this way related to a garden at the

rear, and this was to apply throughout the whole of
the remainder of the estate. Sometimes the houses
were given private gardens interposed between their
back doors and the communal garden but sometimes
they stood directly on the edge of the large garden itself. In either case where the back of the terraces
were exposed in this way they were treated with as
much care as the front. In some cases they were
even more ambitious. Allom's lithographic view
gives us a glimpse of the rear elevation of Stanley
Gardens (South) where the garden is lined by south
facing bows of varying heights ornamented with
superimposed orders of architecture.

This union of scenic architecture in orderly but
varied compositions with its complementary landscape
gardening creates the variety of views which gives the
area its undoubted special character.

The concentric crescents and the streets down the
hill which were also part of Mr. Blake's speculation
are yet another study on their own. The influence of
Ladbroke Square and Kensington Park Gardens can
be said to extend as far north as Ladbroke Gardens and
Lansdowne Crescent, the latter presenting to the
street a fine succession of flat segmental bow fronts of
a pattern almost identical with contemporary houses
of Prince's Square and in other parts of Paddington.
Further down the hill, however, the treatment became
freer and looser with a sort of seaside holiday abandon.
The curved part of Lansdowne Road is remarkable

for some sequences of three-storeyed stucco houses in which Dutch gables alternating with pierced parapets were employed over groups of round headed windows set in complicated rhythms. Together with the three-sided bay windows in the ground storey and strangely detailed doorways with shallow hoods on consoles over half round arches, these elements form an amalgam which it is hard to take seriously and which is unlike anything else in Kensington. In Elgin Crescent we return to something more obviously akin to a standard classical stucco treatment of the 1850's, but increasingly loose in the detail and the handling. These again are ranges which must have suffered from the proximity of the piggeries and the potteries and from all the uncertainties of speculative estate development of the time.

When Kensington Park was all completed, the geometrical patterns of the streets and the great gardens stood out prominently from the general texture of London even on the smallest scale street plan, and still do so today. To the east of Portobello Road, however, James Weller Ladbroke owned further parcels of land which never formed a part of the great scheme, and it can be seen again by the contrasting street pattern to have been developed as a separate entity. As Miss Gladstone tells us, 28 acres of this land in two meadow plots known as Longlands (four acres) and The Hooks (23 acres) were leased to William H. Jenkins in 1844 for development, and subsequently the freehold was

sold by Felix Ladbroke to William K. Jenkins, a
lawyer, in 1847. The Jenkins layout was altogether
less remarkable than the ones we have seen. There
does not appear to have been a surveyor of any standing
connected with the works—applications were signed
by Jenkins himself. Neither are there any communal
gardens or grand architectural compositions. On the
other hand, it cannot be said that one is conscious of
any dramatic change of character on crossing Kensington Park Road into Chepstow Villas, which Jenkins
laid out with detached stuccoed villas, commodious
rather than architecturally ambitious, but of notably
pleasant character. The other streets were lined
variously with villas or fairly loosely designed stucco
terraces. The feeling is rather akin to the outer parts
of the Ladbroke scheme and the Jenkins' estate may
be seen as a pleasant pendant to it.

Crossing Pembridge Villas into Pembridge Square,
however, we come to something quite different; one
of two remarkable Notting Hill developments which
have claim to be regarded as having special architectural
character of another sort. The house types in Pembridge Square and those in the streets collectively
known as Holland Park to the south of Holland Park
Avenue are so similar that they clearly have a common
parentage. The first of the two to be developed that
centred on the present Pembridge Square, was closely
linked with both the Ladbroke and Jenkins developments. The Hall family who owned the land in the

early nineteenth century at one time leased some 211
acres from Ladbroke in addition to their own freehold
of 15 acres. The main development of the Hall
property did not begin until the end of the 1840's,
although by 1847 Robert Hall had built houses at the
northern end of Pembridge Villas and in Chepstow
Place on the leasehold Ladbroke land. By 1849 Hall
had died and the property was in the hands of Trustees.
The Trustees granted the first important lease on the
estate to William Radford, a builder, in May 1849 and
building commenced on the northern side of Dawson
Place. The Radfords in due course obtained leases
on most of the Hall land with the exception only
of some of the present Pembridge Road frontage
although even here they built Devonshire Terrace (the
present numbers 2–28 Pembridge Road) which they
completed in 1854.

In Dawson Place the Radfords built stuccoed villas,
some paired and some detached—whatever was hap-
pening in Kensington Park Gardens the day of the
stuccoed terrace was clearly nearing its end. A substantial house three windows wide and of two storeys
above a basement with only shallow excavation was
the characteristic pattern. The dressings to these
earlier houses were pleasant and restrained, of a con-
servative post-Regency form. Jenkins had built
very similar ones in Chepstow Villas. Daw's map
of 1852 clearly shows the ' L ' shaped site of the old
Hall freehold land which was to become Pembridge

Gardens and Pembridge Square, still undeveloped. Pembridge Gardens came first, being laid out in about 1854 and representing a clear transition between the villas of Dawson Place and the mansions of Pembridge Square. The Radfords' speculation appears to have been prospering and they were working their way towards something more ambitious. They clearly skimped nothing and their standard detached mansion, which they repeated over 30 times in Pembridge Square between 1857 and 1864 and about 90 times more in Holland Park within the same period, was quite a triumph of its kind. At a point in the 1860's when one might have supposed that the market for large houses in Kensington and Bayswater was completely saturated they could produce and sell this surprising number of houses yet larger than any of those we have so far seen. It can only be assumed that they offered something special in solid value.

The solemn repetition of these great blocks lacks the variety and panache of Allom's layouts. It may be a little dull from over repetition but the house type itself is worthy of careful consideration. It has a symmetrical fully stuccoed front, three windows wide. The width is in fact something over 45 feet, an extraordinary dimension for a London house. There are three main floors above a basement and a further storey in the roof. The central doorway is flanked by two projecting bays which rise into the first floor and these are the fully-fledged three-sided mid-Victorian bay which channelled piers in the ground storey and Corinthian or sometimes Ionic pilasters to the angles in the upper parts. These would presumably have looked more up-to-date in the 1860's than Allom's semi-circular bays of 10 years earlier. The doorways have a Doric Order with a triglyph frieze breaking forward over the columns and surmounted by a pedestal course with pierced panels. The pedestal is repeated across the bays to support the Order. The treatment of the detail was uncommonly rich. The façades were furnished with urns carried above the crowning balustrade to the bays, with quoins plain and rusticated, with balconettes and with a fine modillioned cornice, but the most remarkable display was above the cornice where the balustrades were interrupted by a very full aedicular treatment to the windows of the roof storey; one hesitates to call them dormers. The outer ones have round headed openings with moulded architraves and surmounted by dentil cornices and segmental pediments, whilst the central ones carry groupings of flues into a trabeated structure with an Attic Order and bracketed cornice. All these structures are linked to the balustrades by consoles, as are the tall main chimney stacks on the outer walls where great swept brackets with urns at their feet rise to support the console against the stacks.

The standard of execution of the Radfords' work makes the rest of Notting Hill look a little sketchy. Many of their houses have been mutilated by addi-

tions above the main cornice, but few, if any, seem to
have suffered from structural failure or decay of the
stucco detail.   If only Allom's work in Kensington
Park had been as finely executed and well maintained
it would have possessed all the virtues.   On the other
hand if the Radfords produced the best value for
money, their schemes certainly lacked Kensington
Park's scenic display and one is glad of the enlivening
effect of the iron and glass entrance canopies before
the front doors in Holland Park and for the street
planting throwing a tracery of branches across the
repetitive stucco.   But one can understand the Victorian enthusiasm.   They were fine generous houses.

We have now looked again at the best of Notting
Hill.   To the south beyond Peel Street and the water
tower is really Camden Hill.   The more northerly
parts seemed to have been condemned to failure from
the very beginning.   In spite of the Radfords' late
success there must always have been a strict limit to the
number of substantial middle class houses which could
be successfully built and let.   The best situations
around Hyde Park and Kensington Gardens were
clearly at a premium and Notting Hill itself was perched
precariously enough on the corner of this desirable
territory.   The Forsytes were, it is true, represented
on Notting Hill, but only by the Nicholases " . . .
in Ladbroke Grove, a spacious abode and a great
bargain . . .".   This is probably a very acute social
comment on the whole area.

Private estates by their very nature tended to be self-contained developments which blocked the way to land beyond, so that with the Norland and Ladbroke lands built over there was little communication to the north. St. James's Square blocked Sirdar Road, the crescents of the Ladbroke land turned their backs on Lancaster Road, Kensington Park Road stopped at Westbourne Park Road and Ladbroke Grove itself once stopped short at Lancaster Road. It is interesting to see how Allason's original great circus scheme, which would have been completely self-contained, had had to adjust itself to communication from the south east where it had to connect with developing London, but retained its barrier crescents to the north west where communication was undesirable. Those areas which were not only remote but sealed off from the centres of fashion in this way were doomed. Where ambitious developments were attempted, the houses became tenements from the start. Colville and Powis Squares were amongst these. Too remote and with no special compensating advantages, they could not compete with Ladbroke Square or Pembridge Square. The houses were large but Miss Gladstone notes their early decline. Beyond this, architectural ambition hardly ventured.

The conflicts between well-being and poverty which had existed between Kensington Park and the Potteries were to persist between the estates which we have examined and the areas to the north of them, until by the end of the 1960's great tracts of this part of Kensington had been redeveloped, including virtually the whole of Kensal New Town where little more than Bentley's Church of Our Lady of Holy Souls in Bosworth Road remains of the nineteenth century settlement. The social malaise which Miss Gladstone traces through this hinterland remained so acute in some parts of Westbourne and Golborne Wards that these parts of Notting Hill had in the 1960's become journalists' symbolism for every kind of social distress. If none of the houses in these parts of North Kensington could be said to possess any architectural merits of any kind, nevertheless, the disaster which overtook them was mainly one of occupancy rather than of structural inadequacy.

It is a characteristic in the operations of fashion that after the age of denigration has passed, the qualities with which were once admired, become appreciated again. The pattern of appreciation and the degree of esteem may not be exactly as it was at first but it has a way of being at least very similar. Since architecture must serve a practical function and since societies change their way of life, the desirability of old houses for living in is not so easily re-assessed as the merits of other works of art. However, in 1969 whilst the depressed areas to the north of the Hill became confirmed in their depression or rebuilt, and after the old village street had disappeared under new offices and shops, virtually the whole of the earlier estates, that is to say the Norland, Ladbroke, Hall and Radford lands were designated by the Royal Borough of Kensington and Chelsea as Conservation Areas under the Civic Amenities Act of 1967. And so the seal of twentieth century approval was set upon nineteenth century achievement. Ladbroke with its fifteen communal gardens and scenic architecture, the sequence of garden squares and crescents of Norland and the mansions of Pembridge Square and Holland Park, all of these were judged worthy of " preservation and enhancement " under that Act. The passage of over 100 years which had brought the trees and landscape to maturity had been less than kind to much of the architecture. The first part of the twentieth century saw the large houses divided into flats as families became smaller, domestic assistance became unobtainable and owners migrated into the outer suburbs and beyond. Additional storeys were added to form further flats and the unfashionable detail reduced and mutilated. The Hitler war saw paint and stucco neglected, and the neglect was followed by outbreaks of dry rot as the weather penetrated the ill-maintained fabrics. The iron railings were removed from most of the squares, although by good fortune, since many of the houses have areas at the back edge of pavements, the street railings were left to guard them.

In 1950, Michael Sadleir writing about the Ladbroke estate could say " ... the contribution of the blitz has keen so forceful that, when money and materials are available, the whole area must surely rise anew ".

The contribution of the war—decay rather than destruction—had probably been less damaging than the mutilation and modernisation of the preceding years, but the powers of recovery of a district so interestingly conceived as the better part of Notting Hill should not be too easily discounted. Nothing is so depressing as neglected stucco and the long neglected façades of 1950 were certainly a dreary sight, as they were throughout West London. Stucco is always a maintenance problem and we tend to regard buildings covered in it as less worthy of serious respect than buildings faced in stone. Through the 1950's and 1960's there were signs of improving maintenance and improving occupancy. The failure is those years as far as external improvement were concerned was one of control and co-ordination. In Victorian London estate leases stipulated the redecoration of house fronts at a specified time and in a specified colour; or in the earlier part of the period " to be frescoed in imitation of Bath stone ". The Estate Offices ensured that decoration was carried out and architectural detail maintained. The success of the more ambitious terraces depends on unity of colour and detail and without guidance and control of these factors it is difficult to maintain unity once freeholds are sold. It is a matter for speculation in 1969 how far a planning authority designating a conservation area may be able in future to do what the estates could do in the past, and in some other parts of London still do today; or indeed how far it may subsequently be found possible or reasonable to set right the mutilations and restore the cornices.

In spite of all of the errors of decoration, the erosion of detail and the inappropriate development of individual sites, Notting Hill has within its Conservation Areas at the end of the 1960's a Victorian heritage of a notable and distinct kind. At a time when every town is fast growing to be identical with every other and all sense of place is disappearing, the affection which Notting Hill seems to inspire may yet win back more of the order and the dignity which its builders intended it to have and which even through hard times it has never entirely lost.

LIST OF CHIEF BOOKS OF
REFERENCE

ALEXANDER, AGNES MARY. *Some Kensington Problems* (printed for private circulation, 1904). 146, 159, 161.

ANONYMOUS. Diagram of the Parish of St. Mary's, Kensington, 1846 (at the Public Library, Kensington). 96, 132.

BAYLY, Mrs. MARY. *Ragged Homes and How to Mend Them* (Nisbet, 1859). 68, 138.

BAYLY, Mrs. and Miss. *Home Weal and Home Woe* (Nisbet, 1892). 138, 147.

BEAVER, A. *Memorials of Old Chelsea* (1892). 195,

BEGBIE, HAROLD. *Broken Earthenware ; The Wonderful Story of Twice-Born Men.* 109, 150, 159.

BOOTH, Hon. C. *Life and Labour of the People of London* (1889–1902). 158, 202

BOWACK, JOHN. *Antiquities of Middlesex* (1705). xv, 29, 38, 43.

BOYNE, WILLIAM. *Tokens Issued in the Seventeenth Century in England, Wales and Ireland, by Corporations, Merchants, Tradesmen, etc.* (1858). 30–32.

BROWN, R. WEIR. *Kenna's Kingdom* (D. Bogue, 1881). 5, 108.

BRYCE, G. R. *History of Trinity Presbyterian Church* (published by Tamblyn, 1913). 124.

BULL, Sir WILLIAM, M.P. "Some Recollections of Bayswater Fifty Years Ago" (articles in *The Bayswater Chronicle*, July to December 1923). 95, 167, 180, 199, 201, 225-226.

BUMPUS, T. FRANCIS. *London Churches, Ancient and Modern.* 177.

BURT, Miss ISABELLA. *Historical Notes of Chelsea, Kensington, Fulham and Hammersmith* (1871). 24.

CATO, T. BUTLER. "The Hippodrome," in *Home Counties Magazine* for March 1912. 81.

CATO, T. BUTLER. "Notes on Notting Hill," in *St. Peter's Year Book*, 1913. 96.

CHANCELLOR, E. BERESFORD. *History of the Squares of London* (1907). 56, 164, 221.

CHESTERTON, GILBERT K. *The Napoleon of Notting Hill* (1904). 172, 227.

CLIPPINGDALE, Dr. S. D. Articles in *The Kensington News*. 32, 41–42.

CODRINGTON, THOMAS. *Roman Roads in Britain* (S.P.C.K., 1905). 2.

FAULKNER, THOMAS. *History and Antiquities of Kensington* (1820). XV, 14, 22, 31, 36, 45–48, 57, 62, 65, 76, 210, 212, 217.

FAULKNER, THOMAS. *History of Chelsea* (1810). 195, 196,

FAULKNER, THOMAS. *History of Hammersmith* (1839). 141.

FERET, CHARLES JAMES. *Fulham Old and New* (3 vols., Leadenhall Press, 1900). 29.

FOORD, ALFRED STANLEY. *Springs, Streams and Spas of London* (T. F. Unwin, 1910). 43, 65.

FRITH, W. P., R.A. *My Autobiography and Reminiscences* (1887). 93.

FRITH, Miss. *See* PANTON.

GOVER, J. E. B., B.A. *The Place Names of Middlesex* (Longmans, 1922). 10, 15, 21

HASSELL, JOHN. *Single Day Excursions from the Metropolis* (1817). 72.

HASSELL, JOHN. *Picturesque Rides and Walks Thirty Miles Round London* (1818). 72.

HOLMES, Mrs. BASIL. *The London Burial Grounds* (T. F. Unwin, 1896). 189 213.

HOME, Hon. J. A. *Letters and Journals of Lady Mary Coke* (1889-1896). 49.

HORSLEY, J. C. *Recollections of a Royal Academician* (1903). 28, 93, 101, 215

HUNT, LEIGH. *The Old Court Suburb* (1855). 41, 163.

JERVIS, Mrs. HENLEY. "Notes on Parish Church Registers," in *Kensington Parish Magazine*, 1881–1884. 11, 18, 36, 167, 212.

JERVIS, Mrs. HENLEY. Papers in *The Kensington News*, 1884. 211.

LEIGH, HENRY S. *Carols of Cockayne* (1869). 130.

LOFTIE, W. J. *A History of London* (1884). 213.

LOFTIE, W. J. *Kensington Picturesque and Historical* (Leadenhall Press, 1888). xv. 3, 5, 8, 14, 21, 27, 44, 62, 81, 114, 209.

LUCAS, E. V. *London Revisited* (1916). 213.

LYSONS, DANIEL. *Environs of London* (1792). xv. 14, 196.

MACKY, or MACKAY, JOHN. *A Journey Through England in Familiar Letters from a Gentleman Here to his Friend Abroad* (published Anonymously, 1714). 42.

MACNAMARA, Dr. F. N. and MASKELYNE, A. STORY. "Notes on the Parish Church Registers, 1539–1675," in *Kensington Parish Magazine* (subsequently published by the Harleian Society, 1890). *See* JERVIS, Mrs. HENLEY.

MARRIOTT, CHARLES. *Now* (1910). 129.

MITTON, G. E. "Kensington" in *Fascination of London* Series (1903). (Edited by Sir Walter Besant). xv. 3, 14, 188, 221, 224.

OGILBY, JOHN. *Britannia, a Survey of all the Direct and Principal Cross Roads in England and Wales* (1675). (Parts of *Britannia* were published as *Roads out of London*, by the London Topographical Society, Edited by Fairman Ordish, Esq., F.S.A.). 30, 35, 38.

OLD INHABITANT, AN. *Kensington, Notting Hill and Paddington* (1882). 46–47, 88, 96, 98, 119–120, 140.

PAGET, STEPHEN. *I Sometimes Think, Essays for the Young People* (1916). 193, 202.

PANTON, Mrs. JANE ELLEN. *Leaves from a Life* (1908). 93, 168, 171, 199.

PEPPERELL, Rev. WILLIAM. *The Church Index* (1872). 114, 220.

PHILLIMORE, W. P. W. *In the London and Middlesex Note-Book* (Elliott Stock, 1892). 31.

"RITA" (Mrs. DESMOND HUMPHREYS).   *Saba Macdonald.*   171.

ROBINS, W.   *Paddington Past and Present* (1853).   8–9, 68, 166, 196.

SANDERS, LLOYD.   *Old Kew, Chiswick and Kensington* (1910).   17, 19, 29, 164.

SIMS, GEORGE R.   *Off the Track in London* (Jarrold & Sons, 1911).   133, 145, 159.

SKEAT, Dr. WALTER W.   *Notes and Queries* (June 4, 1910).   3, 4.

STOUGHTON, JOHN, D.D.   *Congregationalism in the Court Suburb* (1883).   123.

UNDERHILL, EVELVN.   *Immanence, A Book of Verse.*   131, 181.

WALFORD, EDWARD.   In *Old and New London* Series (Cassell, 1897).   xv. 39, 46, 54, 68, 74, 78, 81, 88.

WHYTE, JAMES CHRISTIE.   *History of the British Turf* (1840).   81.

WOOLF, ERNEST P.   *Interesting History of Portobello Road, the Market Centre of Kensington* (price 1d., Tamblyn, 1909).   47, 180–181.

WROTH, WARWICK.   *Cremorne and the Later London Gardens* (1907).   85, 104, 166.

INDEX

compiled by BRIAN CURLE

To avoid excessive referencing, the following entries have been arranged alphabetically under the following subject heads, Churches and Chapels, Inns and Taverns, Schools and Colleges. In the case of former and present street names, page references have been given under both, the present name being given in brackets after the old name(s) to facilitate identification.